Imagination, Music, and the Emotions

Imagination, Music, and the Emotions
A Philosophical Study

SAAM TRIVEDI

Cover art courtesy of fotolia.

Published by State University of New York Press, Albany

© 2017 State University of New York

All rights reserved

Printed in the United States of America

No part of this book may be used or reproduced in any manner whatsoever without written permission. No part of this book may be stored in a retrieval system or transmitted in any form or by any means including electronic, electrostatic, magnetic tape, mechanical, photocopying, recording, or otherwise without the prior permission in writing of the publisher.

For information, contact State University of New York Press, Albany, NY
www.sunypress.edu

Production, Diane Ganeles
Marketing, Anne M. Valentine

Library of Congress Cataloging-in-Publication Data

Names: Trivedi, Saam, 1968– author.
Title: Imagination, music, and the emotions : a philosophical study / by Saam Trivedi, State University of New York.
Description: Albany, NY : State University of New York, 2017. | Includes bibliographical references and index.
Identifiers: LCCN 2016054531 (print) | LCCN 2017032652 (ebook) | ISBN 9781438467184 (ebook) | ISBN 9781438467177 (hardcover : alk. paper) ISBN 9781438467160 (pbk. : alk. paper)
Subjects: LCSH: Music—Philosophy and aesthetics. | Emotions in music.
Classification: LCC ML3800 (ebook) | LCC ML3800 .T75 2017 (print) | DDC 781.1/1—dc23
LC record available at https://lccn.loc.gov/2016054531

10 9 8 7 6 5 4 3 2 1

For Malcolm, Jerry, Tara, and Sarah

Contents

Introduction		1
Chapter I: Emotions, Moods, and Feelings		9
I.1.	Introduction	9
I.2.	What are Emotions?	9
I.3.	Emotions, Beliefs, and Moods	15
I.4.	Other Views: Martha Nussbaum's Neo-Stoic Cognitivism	17
I.5.	Paul Griffiths's Theory	21
I.6.	Jesse Prinz's Somatic View	24
I.7.	A Concluding Concession	29
Chapter II: Expression Theories and Arousalism		31
II.1.	Introduction	31
II.2.	Bruce Vermazen's Expression Theory	31
II.3.	Jerrold Levinson's Persona Theory	35
II.4.	Jenefer Robinson's Theory	38
II.5.	Contra Simple Arousalism	39
II.6.	Aaron Ridley's Moderate Arousalism	41
II.7.	Derek Matravers's Moderate Arousalism	44
II.8.	Charles Nussbaum's View	46
II.9.	Conclusion	48

Chapter III: Metaphors and Metaphorism — 51

- III.1. Introduction — 51
- III.2. Against Metaphorism (Part 1) — 53
- III.3. Metaphorical Meaning and Paraphraseability — 55
- III.4. Against Metaphorism (Part 2) — 59
- III.5. Metaphors, Resemblance, and Imagination — 61
- III.6. Against Metaphorism (Part 3) — 67
- III.7. Conclusion — 72

Chapter IV: Resemblance-Based Theories — 75

- IV.1. Introduction — 75
- IV.2. Resemblance-Based Views — 76
- IV.3. Criticisms — 79
- IV.4. Objections and Replies — 89
- IV.5. Conclusion — 94

Chapter V: Imagination — 97

- V.1. Introduction: Different Kinds of Imaginings — 97
- V.2. Imaginative Perceptions and Perceptual Imaginings — 100
- V.3. Children's Imaginings — 104
- V.4. Gregory Currie's View — 109
- V.5. Imagination, Music Perception, and Musical Culture — 115
- V.6. Conclusion — 120

Chapter VI: Imaginationism — 123

- VI.1. Introduction — 123
- VI.2. Against Formalism about Music — 124
- VI.3. How We Imagine in Relation to Music — 133
- VI.4. Why We Imagine in Relation to Music — 145

VI.5. Musical Arousal	148
VI.6. Objections and Replies	151
VI.7. Conclusion	162
Summary and Conclusion	165
Notes	171
References	179
Index	189

Introduction

This book has been a long time in gestation. I first started thinking philosophically about music while studying musical composition in my late teens on a small Inlaks Foundation grant that took me to the Guildhall School of Music and Drama, London, and Dartington College of Arts, Devon, in 1985, exactly 300 years after the birth of J. S. Bach, G. F. Handel, and Domenico Scarlatti. On encountering ultraserialized avant-garde musical works by composers of the Darmstadt school such as Karlheinz Stockhausen and others, at some level I wondered if that was music; and if so, what made it music; what music is in the first place; what is its purpose; what makes a work of music good; and so on. These kinds of questions were all playing around at the back of my mind, even if they were not well-formulated, and I had no idea back then (and perhaps even today!) how to even begin to answer them.

However, it was not until a few years after these sorts of worries led me to philosophy (as they did also in the case of the Harvard philosopher Stanley Cavell) that I started thinking about musical expressiveness per se, when I wrote a short philosophy thesis on musical aesthetics at Oxford, and first came across the expression theory associated with Benedetto Croce and R. G. Collingwood. But I was still more interested in musical meaning than in musical expressiveness. That changed as I went on to study, first for a year as a graduate student with Malcolm Budd at University College London, and then right after that with Jerrold Levinson, my doctoral adviser at the University of Maryland. Both of these philosophers made me realize the significance of the problem of musical expressiveness, an issue that has gripped me since then and happily taken up a lot of my time (despite some sleepless nights).

So, what *is* the philosophical problem of musical expressiveness, you might ask? I favor the formulation of this problem given by Peter Kivy and Stephen Davies. According to this formulation, it is the problem of explaining how something inanimate and insentient such as music can be sad or happy or some such mental state. Put differently, it is the problem of explaining how something *without* life and mental states such as music (an abstract art-form[1] consisting of sets or sequences of sounds) can be heard readily, immediately, and willy-nilly by many people—both musicians and laypersons—as sad or happy, etc. Note here that this problem, as stated, is more acute for pure or absolute or instrumental music without words than it is for music with words, or for music with a story or a program such as Beethoven's "Pastoral" Symphony, No. 6 in F Major, Op. 68. For in the case of vocal and program music, it might be thought that the music derives its expressiveness *at least partly* from the accompanying words, or from the story or program associated with it. Accordingly, most of my examples in this book will be about both Western and non-Western *pure* music, which is the primary focus of the philosophical problem of musical expressiveness. The reader should bear in mind that this is the reason why many of my examples do not feature much vocal music and songs from more popular Western musical styles and traditions such as jazz, the blues, rock, rap, hip-hop, and the like, which I might add are all musical styles and traditions that I respect and enjoy greatly.

An alternative formulation of the problem of musical expressiveness comes from Derek Matravers. According to this formulation, the problem of musical expressiveness consists of finding a link between using emotion-terms to describe people, and using emotion-terms for artworks, including musical works.

As I hope will emerge, my solution to the problem of musical expressiveness answers to both formulations of the problem of the musical expressiveness, even though I favor Kivy and Davies's formulation, as stated above. Here, very roughly and in a nutshell, is my resemblance-plus-imagination or imaginationist (a term I will use for brevity) solution: sad (or happy) music is only *imagined* in various, not always highly conscious, ways to be sad (or happy), in virtue of various heard *resemblances* to sad (or happy) people, their vocal and behavioral expression, and the affective feel of emotions and other mental states. This solution is spelled out and defended in the six chapters that follow.[2]

Before I set out briefly what the various chapters of this work try to do and then express my acknowledgments, a word about the very diverse influences that helped shape my solution. For some years, I was tempted by a kind of arousalist-projectivist solution, not too dissimilar from a view that might combine the varying arousalisms of Aaron Ridley, Derek Matravers, and Charles Nussbaum with the projectivism associated with Richard Wollheim. I was also briefly attracted to metaphorism, a view associated with Nelson Goodman and Roger Scruton. But I came to see arousalism and metaphorism as flawed, for reasons I set out in chapters II and III. I next came to see the merits of various resemblance-based theories, associated with Peter Kivy, Stephen Davies, and Malcolm Budd, even as I also saw the merits of Jerrold Levinson's persona-based theory. That led to an attempt to reconcile the insights in resemblance-based and persona-based theories, as found respectively in the work of Budd and Levinson, while trying to avoid what I took to be their respective drawbacks (Trivedi 2001a). Around this time, I also came across Kendall Walton's influential work on imagination, which made me wonder if imagination, resemblance, and personae could somehow be combined in one solution. And it so happened, when I was about a year from finishing my doctorate, that one day in January 1998 while improvising (very badly and therefore privately!) on my Kashmiri hammer-dulcimer (the *santoor*, also found in parts of Central Asia, Iran, and Greece, where it is known as the *santuri*, an instrument also played by Zorba the Greek in the "splendiferous" novel and film of that name), I had this very strong and unshakable feeling that the music *itself* was sad, that somehow it *itself* was alive and possessive of mental states such as sadness. That made me reflect on this experience and think about it in terms of animation, akin to what happens when we read comics or see animation films or what our pagan ancestors did with regard to nature and the elements in it such as the sun, the wind, the ocean, and so on. When Jerrold Levinson then directed me to Peter Kivy's very brief but insightful remarks about animation, which I had read many years back but mistakenly neglected, animation became a central element of my imaginationism, though I understand animation to involve *much* more than what Kivy suggests, as should be clear from chapters IV and especially VI.

Now on to what I set out to do in the six chapters of this book. Chapter I briefly explores the nature of emotions, moods, and feelings, and rejects alternative views about these mental states that music might be thought to be expressive of. I argue for a cognitive-affective view of the emotions, to wit, that emotions involve and are caused by a cognitive element such as evaluative judgments or beliefs or thoughts or imaginings or seeings-as, and that they also involve affects or feelings; and that sometimes (e.g., in love or anger) they may involve desires as well. I also distinguish emotions from moods and feelings; a distinction that I use later in chapter

VI against the formalism about music associated with Eduard Hanslick. I then briefly discuss some recent views of the emotions, as put forth variously by Martha Nussbaum, Paul Griffiths, and Jesse Prinz so as to situate my view in context. I conclude by conceding that it may be possible to reconcile a cognitive-affective view of the emotions with a somatic theory of the emotions, as Ronald de Sousa and Jesse Prinz have recently suggested.

In chapter II, I reject expression theories. These theories claim that to say the music is sad is to say only that it expresses the sadness of the composer or performer. Amongst other things, a basic problem for these theories is that it is just false that the composer or performer must necessarily be sad to create or perform sad music. I also discuss more recent expression theories, as advanced by Bruce Vermazen, Jerrold Levinson, and Jenefer Robinson, ones that do not tie musical expressiveness to particular historical acts of expression but instead posit an indeterminate, imagined musical persona, an agent in the music, expressing mental states through musical gestures, development, and such. Recently advanced versions of arousalism are also the target of this chapter. These theories claim, very roughly, that to say the music is sad is only to say that the music arouses or evokes or causes sadness in listeners; that the music makes us sad when we hear it. As opposed to strong or extreme arousalism, which faces many problems, various philosophers such as Aaron Ridley and Derek Matravers have advocated various versions of "weak" or moderate arousalism. These moderate arousalists rightly grant that one need not be aroused to sadness every time one hears music as being sad or as being expressive of sadness. However, these arousalists still face various problems, most notably that they conflate expressiveness with arousal, and that their view does not address the basic problem of how something *inanimate* and insentient such as music can be sad when they claim that to say music is sad is to say it is appropriate to be aroused to sadness when hearing sad music. I conclude the chapter by discussing the arousalist view of Charles Nussbaum.

Chapter III rejects metaphorism, the view expressed by Nelson Goodman and Roger Scruton that to say that music is sad is only to use a metaphor, for sad music can only be sad metaphorically, not literally, given that it is inanimate. Amongst other things, I argue that such a view cannot give an adequate paraphrase of the emotion-terms involved in the alleged metaphor "The music is sad." In the process, I reject Donald Davidson's view that metaphors only have a literal meaning, one that is false, and do not have a metaphorical meaning that is paraphraseable. I also survey some writing on metaphor by Max Black, Monroe Beardsley, and Josef Stern, among others, and express my hunch that metaphors involve resemblance plus imagination, at the very least. I then proceed to raise a new objection against metaphorism, to wit, that if metaphors themselves involve resemblance and imagination, at least, then a metaphorist view of musical expressiveness might collapse or otherwise lead on to an imaginationist view of musical expressiveness, such as mine, as being more fundamental.

Chapter IV discusses various versions of resemblance-based theories, for which I have some sympathies, and which form the causal foundation of my own imaginationist view. Resemblance-based theories have been put forth by Peter Kivy (who claims music resembles human vocal expression), Stephen Davies (who claims musical movement resembles human bodily or behavioral expression), and Malcolm Budd (who claims the sound of music resembles the affective feel of emotions). But while these views give us the causal story about how various resemblances allow us to hear music as expressive, they do not explain how something *inanimate* and insentient such as music can be sad. In contrast, my imaginationist view, which is built on resemblance, does so when it claims that in virtue of its resembling various things to do with sad people and their sadness, sad music is only *imagined* to be sad in various but not always highly conscious ways, one of which involves animating the music, and imagining that it is the very thing that is sad.

The nature of imagination is briefly explored in chapter V. I draw upon work on imagination by Gregory Currie, Paul Harris, Brian O'Shaughnessy, and others, and argue that there are many notions of imagination: imaging, pretending to oneself, fancying, entertaining a proposition without actually believing it, and so on. Moreover, imagination need not be very highly foregrounded and we can be engaged in various imaginings (e.g., dreaming and daydreaming) without being aware that this is what we are doing. Imaginings can also be intermittent; voluntary or otherwise; short or long; and so on. The chapter concludes by discussing the recent debate about basic music perception between Roger Scruton and Malcolm Budd, and with some reference to Nicholas Cook's claims about music, imagination, and culture.

Finally, chapter VI advances and defends my imaginationist solution to the problem of musical expressiveness, after I offer a rebuttal of the sort of musical formalism associated with Eduard Hanslick, Nick Zangwill, and Robert Kraut. Drawing upon the various notions of imagination canvassed in chapter V, I argue that we imagine in various not always highly conscious ways that sad music is sad. Sometimes we may imagine there is an indefinite musical persona in the music expressing its sadness musically; sometimes we may identify with the music and imagine it is expressing our sadness; and sometimes we may animate the music, *imaginatively projecting life and life-like qualities including mental states onto it* and imagining that it is the very thing that is sad. I also defend my imaginationist view against various objections, and conclude by sketching the various rewards of hearing musical expressiveness with imagination; imaginationism about musical expressiveness may well give us insights into human nature, our powers of imagination, and why we imagine various things.

It remains for me to acknowledge my various intellectual and personal debts. My greatest intellectual debts are to Malcolm Budd and Jerrold Levinson, and I dedicate this (my first) book to both of them and to my daughters. Though I do not agree entirely with Budd's and Levinson's views nor will they agree fully with my position, they are not responsible for my mistakes and my position should in part—and only in part—be seen as reconciling and building on their views, somewhat in the manner in which Newton claimed to have seen further only by standing on the shoulders of giants such as Kepler and Galileo (though I do not claim to be like Newton in any other significant respect!), and in the manner in which functionalism (which incidentally does not attract me) builds on earlier theories of the mind such as behaviorism and the identity theory. There are many others across four continents I am indebted to and who have, for better or worse, variously influenced the gestation of this book over several years, even though sadly my middle-aged memory cannot recall everyone. In addition to thanking anonymously those who I should thank but have forgotten to mention below, those who come readily to mind and who I thank (in alphabetical order) are: the late Jonathan Adler, Philip Alperson, Hanne Appelqvist, Andrew Arlig, Jeanette Bicknell, Emily Brady, John Brown, Daniel Campos, Arindam Chakrabarti, David Cummiskey, Stephen Davies, Jeffrey Dean, Ronald de Sousa, Fabian Dorsch, Richard Eldridge, Stephen Everson, John Fisher, Saul Fisher, Berys Gaut, Lydia Goehr, Theodore Gracyk, Patricia Greenspan, Robert Hopkins, John Hyman, Andrew Kania, Samuel Kerstein, Matthew Kieran, Peter Kivy, David Kolb, Amresh Kumar, Tom Leddy, Dominic Lopes, Robert Lurz, Derek Matravers, Patrick Maynard, Andrew McGonigal, Joseph Moore, Margaret Moore, Michael Morreau, Nirmalangshu Mukherji, Cathleen Muller, Daniel Nathan, Jonathan Neufeld, Henry Pratt, Jesse Prinz, Diane Raymond, Aaron Ridley, Peter Rinderle, Tiger Roholt, William Seeley, K. P. Shankaran, Nancy Sherman, Michael Slote, Brian Soucek, Allen Stairs, Susan Stark, Robert Stecker, Kathleen Stock, Frederick Suppe, Katherine

Thomson-Jones, Kendall Walton, and Nick Zangwill. Thanks also to the Mrs. Giles Whiting Foundation for generous leave allowing me to work on this book; to the PSC-CUNY Research Foundation for research grants; to the University of Fribourg in Switzerland for inviting me to participate in a workshop on imagination, expression, and depiction; and to Brooklyn College for granting me a sabbatical which released me from chairing my department and teaching and so allowed me to bring this project to fruition at last. Humongous thanks to Andrew Kenyon and SUNY Press for taking a chance on me in our fast-paced branding culture where books are sadly often judged only by their cover and who published them, and a big thanks to Chelsea Miller for the cover design and for editorial help. A very special thanks for useful comments and suggestions to three referees for SUNY Press, including Tobyn De Marco whose identity has been revealed with his consent. Finally, I thank my wife, Isabelle, and our daughters, Tara and Sarah, who greatly slowed down the writing of this book, while I tried to console myself that the writing of Darwin's *On the Origin of Species* was greatly slowed down by concerns about his children's health, even though a draft of the entire work had been lying in his desk drawers apparently for quite some time.

Revised material from the following previously published essays appears in this book, and I thank Wiley, Routledge, Cairn, Palgrave Macmillan, and Oxford University Press for permission to use this material:

(1) "Expressiveness as a Property of the Music Itself," *Journal of Aesthetics and Art Criticism*, 59 (2001): 411–20;

(2) "The Funerary Sadness of Mahler's Music," in Matthew Kieran and Dominic Lopes (eds.), *Imagination, Philosophy, and the Arts* (Routledge, 2003), 259–71;

(3) "Imagination, Music, and the Emotions," *Revue Internationale de Philosophie*, 60 (2006): 415–35;

(4) "Metaphors and Musical Expressiveness," in Kathleen Stock and Katherine Thomson-Jones (eds.), *New Waves in Aesthetics* (Palgrave Macmillan, 2008), 41–57;

(5) "Music and Imagination," in Theodore Gracyk and Andrew Kania (eds.), *The Routledge Companion to Philosophy and Music* (Routledge, 2011), 113–22;

(6) "Resemblance Theories," in Theodore Gracyk and Andrew Kania (eds.), *The Routledge Companion to Philosophy and Music* (Routledge, 2011), 223–32; and

(7) Review of Aaron Ridley, *Music, Value and the Passions* (Cornell, 1995), in *Mind*, 109 (2000): 387–90.

I

Emotions, Moods, and Feelings

I.1. Introduction

In this opening chapter, I begin by sketching a positive account of emotions, moods, and feelings. I then briefly discuss some (of the many) recent views advanced by philosophers (rather than psychologists) about these mental phenomena, arguing against accounts of these that I take to be mistaken and thus trying to show that my view has certain advantages over these current theories. Note that I cannot comprehensively discuss here all recent theories of emotions; nor do I claim to give an exhaustive theory of the emotions beyond a preliminary sketch, which should suffice for the purposes of a study focused primarily on musical expressiveness, after all.

More specifically, here is what I do in the different sections of this chapter. In section I.2, I sketch a cognitive-affective view of the emotions, as you will see shortly. Section I.3 distinguishes emotions from beliefs and also from moods; note that this latter distinction will in fact be used in section VI.2 against the musical formalism of Eduard Hanslick. The next three sections of this chapter critically discuss, respectively, Martha Nussbaum's neo-Stoic cognitivist view, Paul Griffiths's position, and Jesse Prinz's somatic theory. The chapter concludes by conceding that it may be possible to reconcile a cognitive-affective view of the emotions with a somatic theory.

I.2. What are Emotions?

So, let us begin with the emotions and the question "What are emotions?"

In a nutshell, the cognitive-affective view of emotions that I favor claims that emotions, standardly, are dynamic complexes consisting of two components: (1) an affective element, consisting of affects or feelings; as well as (2) a cognitive element, consisting of (evaluative) beliefs, thoughts, judgments, imaginings, seeings-as and the like.¹ In virtue of the cognitive element, emotions have intentionality, i.e., they are directed upon or about things such as states of affairs, actions, events, people, physical objects, and so on. Furthermore, it is claimed that desires, which are distinct from emotions, may often accompany or even constitute emotions, though this need not be the case for all instances of every emotion.² Also, underlying bodily processes are the neurophysiological *bases* or causes of emotions that allow emotions and may be necessary for emotions, but are not themselves parts of emotions. And as for behavior, while emotions often have (typical) behavioral expressions, these latter are neither necessary for emotions as some people may feel emotions (e.g., sadness) without expressing or manifesting them outwardly, nor is behavior sufficient to actually have an emotion as an occurrent state of one's psychology as shown amply by the case of very good actors; here I borrow Hilary Putnam's decisive super-Spartan and super-actor objections against Behaviorism. Moreover, against Agnes Moors, Phoebe Ellsworth et al. (2013a, 119-20), emotions need not have an action tendency or action readiness or some sort of motivational component associated with them; think of couch potatoes wallowing in boredom in front of the television. It is granted, however, that emotions are often *shaped* by social and cultural influences, though I will not dwell on the point as this concession is not itself a part of the cognitive-affective view of the emotions. Note in passing that the cognitive-affective view I favor combines earlier judgmentalist or cognitivist views of the emotions with feeling views of the emotions, a claim made by Paul Griffiths on behalf of perceptual theories of emotions (Griffiths 2013, 220). Note also that while the claim that emotions are perceptions of evaluative properties suggests that emotions may give evaluative knowledge, the cognitive-affective view can also grant that emotions may give us evaluative knowledge *both* about what is of value in the world as well as about what we value (compare de Sousa 2011).

At this stage, let us specify what the elements of the above account of the emotions amount to. It is difficult to give a very precise account of affects, but I will make a start here and claim that very roughly one may say that affects are the non-cognitive, non-intentional part of emotions. They involve (a) "raw feels," or inner "psychological" affects, of pleasure or pain, and they may also involve (b) physical or bodily affects (compare Oakley 1992, 9-14).³

It is easier to give an account of physical than psychological affects, though an adequate theory of the emotions must account for both—instead of denying the latter, or else reducing them to the former. Physical affects involve bodily reactions like hearts pounding faster, pulse rates quickening, hair standing on ends, breathing getting faster, etc. Such affects may be found when we have feelings of excitement or fear, though one general worry may be that these "physical affects" are just *external*, behavioral manifestations of inner, psychological affects, not affects themselves. To dispose of this worry, consider the case of being extremely drowsy. Now, being drowsy need not involve *any* inner, psychological affects of pleasure or pain, even as accompaniments, but may *only* involve physical affects like yawning and a general lethargy. This drowsiness may be so strong that it may induce us to go to sleep before we realize that we are drowsy, or else it may take a little while before we realize that we are drowsy. Thus, this state of drowsiness is non-cognitive insofar as, at least for a little while, it does not involve a belief or a thought or a judgment, and it is also non-intentional insofar as it is not about, or directed toward, anything. Moreover, we have here a feeling or affect of drowsiness, but not an emotion. All of this goes to illustrate my claim above that feelings or affects are non-cognitive, non-intentional parts of emotions. And it also serves to illuminate the distinction between emotions and feelings or affects. Note also that one can have emotions that involve physical or bodily changes (in terms of neuron firings and other changes in one's neurophysiology) without having physical affects or feelings, and without being aware of the underlying physical changes.

Psychological affects, on the other hand, are best seen in cases of intense emotions. Suppose X's mother, who X is very attached to, dies, and X feels an emotion of intense grief. Such grief involves not only assent to beliefs about her mother's death, but also an inner, psychological feeling or affect of pain (or distress) that may (or may not) be behaviorally or physically manifested through crying, dejection, and the like. Psychological affects of pleasure, as opposed to pain, can be seen in aesthetic experiences of great works of art, or of beauty in nature, as the inner psychological affect of intense pleasure (or joy) that I feel when I admire Michelangelo's *David*, for instance,[4] or when I admire the beauty of a stunning landscape in the Himalayas.

Here are some more differences between physical and psychological affects. Affects of pain can be both physical as well as psychological, but while physical pain is *usually* localized to some part of the body that is in pain, psychological pain is not so localized. For example, the physical pain of being pinched or hit is restricted to, and felt in, the concerned part of the body, whereas the psychological pain felt upon the death of one's mother is not localized to any particular part of the body (although one may have a heavy heart, metaphorically speaking), though it is not located outside the body either. Similarly, affects of pleasure can be both physical as well as psychological, but while physical pleasure is *usually* localized to some part of the body, the same need not be true of psychological pleasure. For example, the physical pleasure of being tickled is localized to the body part being tickled, whereas the psychological pleasure of aesthetic experience is not so localized; I do not feel the pleasure of seeing a beautiful Himalayan landscape (just) in my eyes, even if that sight is soothing to my eyes in some sense. Note that I said that unlike psychological affects or feelings, which are usually *not* localized, physical affects are *usually* only localized. But physical affects need not always be localized, as shown by the physical affect of being drowsy which is spread all over the body and not localized to, say, the eyes or the mouth.

Psychological affects of pleasure (or comfort) are, roughly, the "feel good" aspects common to all positive emotions (joy, elation, contentment, etc.), while psychological affects of pain (or discomfort) are, roughly, the "feel bad" aspects common to all negative emotions (anger, hatred, sorrow, despair, anguish, etc.). Perhaps there is a third genus of "neutral" psychological affects or feelings that involve neither pleasure nor pain. For example, there might be a neither pleasurable nor painful psychological affect associated with the physical affect or feeling of drowsiness. It is a further, open, question whether there are distinct psychological feelings involved in many emotions, psychological feelings that are unique to the emotion in question. For example, it might be thought that anger involves not just painful psychological feelings but "burning" ones; similarly, sorrow may involve a "sinking" feeling and not just painful psychological affects. If this is right, then the distinct psychological feelings involved in some emotions would all be species of one of the three genera of psychological feelings. At any rate, it needs to be clarified further what exactly psychological affects are and what they involve; what I have said so far is only a preliminary, rough sketch, one that suffices for my purposes.

Let us turn now to the cognitive element of emotions. As seen in the above example of intense grief felt by X upon her mother's death, the cognitive element of emotions involves a belief that a certain judgment is true, or at least justified by the present evidence—X believes that it is true that her mother is dead.[5] Sometimes, though, the cognitive element involved in emotions is *weaker* than strict beliefs and may involve thoughts or imaginings, as, for example, is the case when I fear small, 3-inch lizards, knowing fully well that they are harmless. At any rate, the cognitive element is also often evaluative. In the case of the example above of X's grief, X not only judges that it is true her mother has died but also believes that this is somehow bad, which in turn causes feelings of loss and sadness.

As indicated earlier, in virtue of their cognitive elements, emotions have intentionality, i.e., they are about something, or are directed or focused upon some object. Thus, X's grief is about her mother's death, and my fear above is directed upon lizards; it is a fear *of* something, vis-à-vis lizards in this case. Emotions acquire intentionality because their constitutive cognitive elements (whether beliefs, judgments, thoughts or imaginings) have intentionality—a thought, for instance, must be a thought *about* something; it must be directed upon an object, including not just physical objects, but also states of affairs, actions, events, persons, and the like.

It is sometimes held that emotions also involve a desiderative element consisting of desires for action, or strivings, in addition to the affective and cognitive elements specified above.[6] I believe that such accounts of emotions are mistaken in making desires *constitutive* elements of *all* emotions, though desires may partly constitute some emotions such as love (which typically involves a desire or yearning to be with the objects of one's love) or anger (which typically involves a desire for revenge).

To begin with, I think we must distinguish clearly between the concepts of emotions, desires, and beliefs. The idea of a unidirectional fit (or agreement, if you like) with the world, with different directions of fit, *applies* standardly to beliefs and desires, but need not apply in the same way (if it applies at all) to emotions, where the fit with the world is bidirectional. In contrast, when emotions involve the idea of a fit with the world, this is true in a *bidirectional* way.[7]

To illustrate, my desire to listen to, say, Beethoven's Seventh Symphony involves the striving that the world should change to match my desire so that somewhere in my vicinity there is a recorded or a live performance of this musical work; though this is *not* to say that we should *always* try to change the world to fit our desires, even if we want this typically, all else being equal. In contrast, we typically want our beliefs to be true, i.e., we want that our beliefs should match the world, not vice versa, and that we give up false beliefs, which do not match the world. So, for instance, when we realize that the belief that the earth is flat is false, we want to give it up and hold instead the true belief that the earth is round.

Emotions which do involve the idea of a fit with the world typically involve the direction of fit going from the world to the emotion, and also sometimes the other way around. Thus, the fit between emotions and the world may be *bidirectional*. Many emotions involve the idea that the world should come to fit the *desire* that is involved in, or constitutes, that emotion. There is, however, a sense in which the direction of fit may go from emotions to the world. The idea here is *not* that some emotions are true, as beliefs that fit the world are, but that some emotions may be *appropriate* given the way the world is, e.g., moderate fear of a deadly snake may be an appropriate emotion that fits the world. Such fitting emotions would involve assent to the true beliefs that constitute them. Thus, when emotions fit the world in the same direction in which beliefs do, the senses of fit involved are different. While true beliefs fit the world in a representationally faithful sense—they "mirror" or "picture" the world, if you like—appropriate emotions fit the world in the nonrepresentational sense of being befitting or suitable. It is also possible that one and the same emotion can fit the world bidirectionally, for so far what I have said is that some emotions may fit the world, whereas the world may fit some other emotions. For example, my moderate fear of the deadly snake may be appropriate, and moreover that emotion may involve the desire to flee so that the world comes to fit that desire when I do run away from the scene.

Now, emotions are often constituted by desires. For instance, the emotion of love for someone is standardly constituted by, or involves, a desire to be with the object of one's love (be it a person, pet, place, book, musical work, film, or something else), and in this sense involves the idea that the world should come to fit this desire. Similarly, the emotion of being angry with someone may involve a desire for revenge,[8] and in this sense may involve the idea that the world should fit this desire.

But there are other emotions where it is not clear that they are *constituted* by desires. For instance, suppose a student gets an "A" grade on a philosophy paper. The ensuing emotion of happiness is certainly *caused* by the *satisfaction* of the desire to fare well,[9] and certainly the emotion involves, as its constituents, affects of pleasure as well as the student's assent to the true, evaluative belief that she has obtained an "A" and that is a good thing. But it is not clear that this emotion itself is constituted by the satisfied desire to fare well, nor is it clear that this emotion is constituted by, or necessarily involves, a desire for action of the sort often found in anger or love. Of course, she may have a desire, *later* in time, to continue to fare well, but it is not clear that this later desire constitutes the very emotion of happiness that she feels when she is happy at her grade upon *first* coming to know of it. And she may also have a desire, later in time, to tell friends and loved ones about her grade, but again it is not clear that this later desire *constitutes* the very emotion of happiness that she feels when she is happy at her grade upon *first* coming to know of it. In this example, the first rushes of happiness, I contend, consist *only* of affects and belief, yet there *is* a full-fledged emotion of happiness. Moreover, I claim that even if the student is very modest and never has a desire to tell anyone about her grade, she can still have the emotion of happiness so long as there occur (a) the appropriate evaluative belief, and (b) the relevant pleasurable psychological affect.

Justin Oakley claims that one problem for accounts of emotions which do not include desires as constituents of emotions is that they may fail to distinguish between some emotions, like my fear (involving the desire to flee) felt upon seeing a snake, and interest (involving the desire to stay and examine) felt by a naturalist upon seeing the same snake (Oakley 1992, 22-28). Oakley thinks that only desires can distinguish fear from interest in this case. However, it seems that Oakley is mistaken here, for clearly there are different affects involved in this example given by Oakley, an affect of pain (or distress, more properly) in the case of fear, and an affect of pleasure (or excitement, more properly) in the case of interest; one may also question whether interest is an emotion or a mode of belief, though for argument's sake let us grant Oakley that it is an emotion. Moreover, there are also different cognitions involved in the two cases: I cognize that the snake is deadly, while the naturalist cognizes that the same snake is harmless but rare. Alternatively, if the snake is indeed deadly, then the naturalist may indeed cognize that it is deadly but rare, and his affects may be both of pleasure (or excitement, more properly, given his interest in the snake) and pain (or distress, more properly, given his fear of the deadly snake). Even so, the cognitions and affects involved in the naturalist's emotion, which is a mix of interest and fear, will be different from the cognitions and affects involved in my emotion of fear. These differences in affects as well as cognitions may serve to distinguish fear and interest, without having to bring in desires, contrary to what Oakley thinks. Oakley is, however, right to say that acting out of emotion involves being motivated by desires; and acting out of emotion is not requisite for *having* emotion. For example, acting out of compassion involves being motivated by the desire to help the needy. In such cases, desires explain the motivational power of emotions.

I.3. Emotions, Beliefs, and Moods

But enough of desires and their distinction from emotions. The distinction between emotions and affects or feelings should be clear from what has gone before; affects are necessary but not sufficient for emotions since they lack the cognitiveness and intentionality involved in emotions. I believe it is important to briefly make clearer two further distinctions: (a) that between emotions and beliefs or judgments, and (b) that between emotions and moods.

We have already seen part of the distinction between emotions and beliefs in terms of the idea of a fit with the world. We want our beliefs to fit the world, but this idea of a fit with the world, when it does apply to emotions, can do so in both directions: typically, with the world fitting the emotions, and also sometimes with emotions fitting the world.

But there is more to the distinction between emotions and beliefs. Beliefs, like emotions and desires, are cognitive and intentional. Beliefs may also sometimes be necessary for some emotions like grief, though some emotions may instead involve thoughts or imaginings, as seen earlier. Beliefs may, thus, at best be necessary components for some, but not all, emotions. The important point I wish to make here (contra cognitivists such as Nussbaum who I discuss later) is that beliefs alone cannot, in general, be sufficient for emotions, for beliefs themselves usually lack the affective component of emotions, a component which is so essential and distinctive to emotions.[10] For example, my belief that "Schnee ist Weiss" is true if and only if snow is white does not involve an affective component, nor need it be accompanied by any affects, even if there is something it is *like* to have such a belief. Of course, it may be true that some beliefs may be *accompanied* by affects, or else may *cause* affects, or else may be *necessary* for affects, but none of these shows that beliefs are *constituted* by affects; just as the fact that some desires may cause some emotions, or may be necessary for some emotions, does not show that desires are constituents of even these emotions, leave alone all emotions, as argued before. For instance, my assent to the belief that the snake I see is harmful may cause, or be necessary for, or be accompanied by, an affect of distress that is part of the emotion of fear that I feel. But in no way is the belief, which is cognitive and intentional, constituted by the affect of distress, which is non-cognitive and non-intentional. Similarly, evaluative beliefs such as that women should be given equal pay as men may cause or be necessary for or be accompanied by affects, perhaps as part of an emotion, but it is not clear that such a belief itself includes affects as components. Note that I grant that there may be something it is like to have conscious beliefs, and that what it is like to have conscious evaluative beliefs may be different from what it is like to have conscious factual beliefs. But this phenomenological aspect of beliefs is different from affects or feelings of pain or pleasure that are part of emotions.

Very briefly, let us now turn to the distinction between emotions and moods.[11] We have seen already what emotions are. Now first, moods, unlike emotions, are non-intentional, i.e., they are not directed upon any particular object, though they may be set off or caused by particular events or things. For example, someone's depression may be triggered or *caused* by her mother's death; and thus she may be depressed "about" her mother's death, in a non-intentional sense of aboutness, so to speak. But when she is depressed, her mind need not always be *directed* or focused upon her mother's death (unlike say an emotion of grief about the same event); though, from time to time, her thoughts may wander back to her mother's death, thus being directed upon that event. Nor is her depression directed or focused upon anything else in particular, unlike her emotions, beliefs, and desires. Second, moods are pervasive, affecting or coloring all other conscious mental events (like thoughts, desires, etc.) in their wake, whereas this need not be true of emotions. Thus, for example, our agent's depression may "negatively" affect her thoughts, her disposition toward the world, her desires, and so on, while this need not be true of an emotion of grief, unless of course it turns into depression. We find thus that moods are non-intentional, and involve pervasive affects, and very roughly one may thus say that moods are objectless "emotions" (compare Sherman 1994, 9–11).

Note now that this distinction between emotions and moods is important, as is the one made earlier between emotions and feelings or affects. In fact, I will use it later in chapter VI.2 to argue against the formalism about music associated with Eduard Hanslick.

I.4. Other Views: Martha Nussbaum's Neo-Stoic Cognitivism

So much by way of clarifying the philosophical ground underlying the emotions. Having stated my positive view about the emotions, I now turn to assessing some other views about the emotions, though I cannot survey them all here. My own view of the emotions will, I hope, become clearer in relation to others' views, and the survey that follows will situate my view. I hope it will emerge that my view has advantages over several theories of the emotions.

Consider first the neo-Stoic cognitivist view of the emotions held by Martha Nussbaum (Nussbaum 2001). I first summarize Nussbaum's cognitivist view before offering my criticisms of it. Nussbaum holds that emotions are, centrally, cognitive (where by "cognitive" she merely means "concerned with receiving and processing information") and evaluative appraisals or beliefs or judgments or thoughts. There are type-identities between emotions and judgments (or value-laden cognitive states, more broadly), on her view. These cognitive-evaluative beliefs or judgments need not, she claims, be linguistic or propositional or verbal and can be seeings-as. Thus, she claims that animals and very young children can have emotions, as the cognitions that form (and in her view are) emotions need not be inherently human or verbal. She also claims that emotions are intentional and beliefs are essential to their identity, and thus emotions cannot be mere thoughtless natural energies.

Nussbaum claims that objectless feelings of pain or pleasure are not absolutely necessary definitional elements of emotions, even though they may often accompany emotions. She claims that judgments of the right sort are both necessary and sufficient for emotions, and constitute emotions.

Now on to my criticisms. Nussbaum is right to say, I think, that very little children and perhaps some animals too can have emotions. If so, then I grant her that the cognitive component of emotions need not be strict propositional beliefs or judgments, but can be seeings-as or imaginings (or perhaps even visualizings), as I claimed above in my brief mention of the example of fear of lizards. Note this is not to say that beliefs can be non-propositional. However, once we have clearly distinguished, as above, between emotions and beliefs in terms of affects especially, we can see that her neo-Stoic identification of emotions with beliefs is mistaken, for thoughts cause emotions and are a part of them, but affects also form a part of emotions.

Nussbaum is right to think that beliefs or judgments cause emotions and constitute them, and that if we alter the underlying belief we can change the emotion, as the Stoics say. For instance, in the example (used also by Nussbaum) of the death of one's mother, suppose instead of thinking that it is a bad thing or a loss that one's mother is dead, one changes one's underlying belief to the thought that perhaps it is for the best as she suffered for a long time and died peacefully (or that it is for the best that she is dead at last as she tormented her children for years). The emotion constituted by the belief will also change as the belief changes, from grief to a peaceful (even if sad) acceptance (or joy, in case one thinks it is a good thing she is dead at last). Note in passing that while the claim that judgments or appraisals are both causes and constituents of emotions may seem to imply a problematic self-causation or auto-causation, one way out here, suggested by Agnes Moors, is to appeal to two senses of appraisal and claim that the appraisal *process* is the cause of the emotion while the appraisal *output* is a component of the emotion (Moors 2013b, 134–35), and claiming further that the appraisal output in turn causes other components of emotions such as feelings.

However, against Nussbaum, the fact that the emotion changes as the constitutive belief changes does *not* show that emotions are to be *identified* or equated with their cognitive elements, whether beliefs or judgments or seeings-as or imaginings, nor does it show that mere judgments of the right sort are sufficient for emotions, as she thinks. For emotions are also constituted by affects or feelings, as well as by desires in some cases. On Nussbaum's neo-Stoic view, grief, for example, is identical (at least for adult humans, if not for non-propositional infants and animals) with the acceptance of an evaluative, eudaimonistic proposition, to wit, that someone beloved is lost forever (Nussbaum 2001, 40–41). But while this proposition or rather acceptance of it may *cause* and *partly* constitute grief, surely grief also *feels* a certain way, a certain painful, perhaps "sinking" way. Or perhaps grief *feels* "like putting a nail into your stomach," as Nussbaum says, which is just the non-intentional, non-cognitive *feeling* or affect of grief associated with and caused by the proposition that causes and partly constitutes grief. There is something it is *like* to have an emotion, and so how can feelings or affects be left out of any account of emotions, given that emotions *feel* a certain way, the feeling being an essential and central part of the emotion? What about other emotions such as love, anxiety, fear, jealousy, hope, despair, anger, and so on? Don't these all *feel* certain ways? Doesn't love, for example, (typically) involve a "yearning" feeling to be with the object of one's love? Don't anxiety and fear involve (typically) something like a "gripping" feeling? It really seems Nussbaum's account of the emotions is too narrow and one-dimensional if it leaves affects—whether pleasurable or painful or neutral (or some species of these)—out of these and other emotions. Thus I find I must reject her view as being at best partially right.

Note that it is possible that one may not be conscious *of* the feeling or affect one has when one has an emotion, and one may not even know *that* one is having a feeling. These qualifications block a *possible* reply that someone with a cognitivist position such as Nussbaum might make, to wit, that one can have grief but lack that particular feeling associated with grief or any feeling at all. For example, someone trying to defend Nussbaum might say that we may sometimes experience guilt *without* actually feeling any pangs of guilt. In response, it could be said that in such cases one could still be having the feelings, the affect of grief or the pangs of guilt, that is, without being conscious of them. Or else one may simply not know that one is having the affect of grief or the pangs of guilt. It might be interjected at this point, on Nussbaum's behalf, that an alien species could have the same emotions as us with slightly different feels or with no feels at all, and this shows that feelings are just accompaniments to emotions, not essential to them. In response to this, I grant that alien species might have the emotions we have, though the feelings involved may be different. But this does not yet show that feelings or affects are *mere* accompaniments to emotions, not essential to them. What is needed for that is to show that there indeed *is* another species (not just that there might be one such) with our emotions but without *any* feelings at all. This, I submit, is an empirical question. Until such time as it is proven that such a species exists, we have reason (even if not indefeasible reason) to think that affects are essential constituents of emotions.

Nussbaum herself makes two points in defense of her claim that feelings are not essential to emotions (Nussbaum 2001, 61). First, she says that there are non-conscious emotional states, such as non-conscious anger or non-conscious fear of death, and as these do not involve any necessary phenomenological feelings, feelings cannot be essential for emotion-types. Second, the feeling states people claim to experience in connection with emotion-types vary greatly, and thus Nussbaum claims she herself often feels anger without having the "boiling" feeling many report, which shows that this feeling is not essential to anger. As to the first point, while I grant Nussbaum that there can be non-conscious emotions, nevertheless when these emotions become and are *conscious* and one is conscious of having them, one must, I submit, *feel* the affective or phenomenological condition that is part of them. And conscious emotions might be said to be the *central* cases of emotions, ones which non-conscious emotions are derivative and different (and thus non-affective) forms of. Note that I am *not* committing myself to the idea that there is something it is like to have non-conscious emotions, that these have a phenomenological aspect, nor am I denying that non-conscious emotions are emotions. Regarding Nussbaum's second point, one must first ask whether it is anger that she feels or some less intense state such as annoyance or irritation if the ("boiling") affect of anger is absent. Even if it is anger that she feels, I suggest there can be variations of intensity in the feelings one has, and these feelings might even be *non-conscious* and one need not be reflectively aware of them at all times. So it is *conceivable* that while angry, she feels *something like* the ("boiling" or "burning") affect of anger, perhaps as a physical affect in the form of a tension at the back of her neck or a headache the next day, as she claims about herself, even if she is not aware that she has the affect (compare Stocker 1996, 21–23). One can allow for variations in the intensity of feelings or affects felt across and within subjects at different times and places, as Nussbaum wants, yet still claim, contra Nussbaum, that *some* sort of feeling (perhaps a "loose" or "broad" or a very weak feeling) or affect *must* be felt when we feel conscious emotions such as love or grief or anger.

A final point against Nussbaum. As Jerrold Levinson (Levinson 2004) has suggested, despite what Nussbaum seems to think, the choice when it comes to theories of emotions is not just between a purely cognitivist view of the emotions such as Nussbaum's, on the one hand, and a view that sees emotions as merely thoughtless sensations or tingles or feelings, on the other hand. There is also a mixed position between these two (extreme) positions, to wit, a cognitive-affective view such as the position I have advanced above.

I.5. Paul Griffiths's Theory

Next I discuss the position advanced by Paul Griffiths (1997), whose view might seem radically different from my own stance, though I can take his claims on board, as I hope emerges below. Griffiths claims that the folk psychological category of "emotions" is a mistake, and that philosophers who write about the emotions should focus on recent findings in biology, neurology, and brain science. There is need, he claims, for an empirical investigation into the emotions. The emotion category of folk psychology does nothing to illuminate what is going on in people, suggests Griffiths. He is not, however, claiming that there is nothing going on in people who claim to feel emotions.

Griffiths allows for two different categories of emotions: "affect programs" triggered by separable low-level processes, and "higher cognitive" emotions that are shaped and "constructed" by culture. Work on affect programs is inspired by Darwin, and the theory is associated with Paul Ekman. Affect programs deal with, roughly, the occurrent instances of the English terms "surprise," "fear," "anger," "disgust," "contempt," "sadness," and "joy"; what might be called "basic emotions." These are seen by the affect program theory as short-term, stereotypical responses that involve cross-cultural facial expressions, autonomic nervous system arousal, and other elements. Cross-cultural facial expressions, claims Griffiths, require evolutionary explanations but do not imply that the emotional responses are innate. As for higher cognitive emotions, these are produced in agreement with cultural norms, and may involve subconscious conformity to cultural models. Traditional work on the emotions, Griffiths claims, also needs to take into account the social construction of emotions. Griffiths also claims that Ekman's "basic emotions" are homologs, i.e., they have shared evolutionary origins across mammals; fear, for example, can be felt by many mammalian species and has a shared evolutionary origin in their common ancestors.

I begin my criticisms of Griffiths by focusing on what he says about affect programs (p. 77): "The central idea of the affect program theory is that emotional responses are complex . . . because they involve several elements . . . (a) expressive facial changes, (b) musculoskeletal responses such as flinching and orienting, (c) expressive vocal changes, (d) endocrine system changes and consequent changes in the levels of hormones, and (e) autonomic nervous system changes. . . ." Contra Griffiths, I would suggest that (a) through (c) are neither necessary nor sufficient for emotions, as one can have an emotion as an occurrent, inner, mental state and not express it facially or musculoskeletally or vocally, and one can pretend to manifest facial or vocal or musculoskeletal behavior typically associated with emotions without having emotions themselves. As for (d) and (e), these only give us the chemical and neurophysiological *bases* of emotions, but do not tell us what emotions themselves are, as I briefly elaborate below.

While I agree with Griffiths that traditional work on the emotions needs to make room for empirical, scientific investigations into these mental phenomena as well as the social construction of emotions, I would register the following reservations for his position. Work in the neurosciences can and does tell us a lot about the underlying neurophysiological and chemical *bases* (or causes) of emotions that allow us to feel these, and it explains how emotions are realized. However, it is not clear that it *suffices* to tell us what emotions *themselves* are, how they *feel* and are manifested, what they are *constituted* by, what the affects that constitute them are, which other mental phenomena (such as beliefs, desires, affects, moods, etc.) cause and relate otherwise to them and how they do so, and so on, as more traditional work on the category of emotion tries to do. Likewise, it is not clear that the notions of affect programs as well as higher cognitive emotions, and work on these, *suffice* in themselves to tell us more about what emotions are, how they feel, and so on. About moods, Griffiths claims similarly (pp. 254–55) that these are neurochemical states of the central nervous system that modify its activity by affecting the probability that neural state transitions will take place. But here too, while we are told what *realizes* moods and explains their neurophysical and chemical bases, Griffiths does not tell us what moods are, how they feel, and so on, and in particular he ignores the *affective* side of moods, which seems so important for many moods such as elation, depression, and so on.

Against Griffiths, I submit that the category "emotion" characterizes usefully what people feel, and also helps distinguish emotions from and relate them to other mental phenomena such as feelings, moods, beliefs, desires, and the like, as I tried to do above. Griffiths is right to claim that conceptual analysis alone cannot determine the real nature of fear, for example. Nevertheless a cognitive-affective theory, such as mine, *can* and should make room for empirical research to tell us more about the neurophysiological and chemical and social constructionist causes and bases of fear, while *simultaneously* analyzing fear in terms of a cognitive element such as an evaluative judgment or belief or imagining or seeing-as, plus affect (plus desires). In any case, the onus is on Griffiths to come up with a genuine counter-example to a cognitive-affective theory that makes room for such empirical research. If Griffiths comes up with even one such case, which as far as I am aware he has not yet done, I am inclined to think that a cognitive-affective theory that respects and accommodates such research can deal with it. Until such time, I remain optimistic about the prospects of a theory that *combines* the kind of empirical work Griffiths wants with a more traditional approach to the emotions.

Indeed, in a recent essay (Griffiths 2013), Griffiths suggests that we need to integrate the approach to emotions of those philosophers who draw on the biological and psychological sciences with a more traditional approach, which sees philosophical work on the emotions as self-sufficient. Even though my view leans more toward the latter approach, I fully agree with Griffiths that integration is desirable, for while empirical science and data matter, so do philosophical and conceptual clarity, especially if philosophy can reveal truths about the mind of a different kind from those uncovered by science. I am inclined to claim that, similarly, work on musical expressiveness and in philosophical aesthetics in general must be *both* open to being informed by neuroscience, psychology, etc., without being mere armchair speculation, on the one hand, and at the same time also seek philosophical and conceptual clarity, on the other hand, without getting bogged down in empirical and psychological data. In this vein, I was amazed to discover some years back at a talk given at my institution by the McGill music researcher Robert Zatorre that a lot of psychological work about music has been about musical arousal (compare Matravers 2011, 221), and until recently empirical research into music did not acknowledge the distinction between arousal and expression, a basic distinction long-acknowledged within musical aesthetics which will be discussed in section II.5. But more about such things later.

I.6. Jesse Prinz's Somatic View

I turn now to the neo-Jamesian view put forth by Jesse Prinz (Prinz 2004) in his book *Gut Reactions* (also, incidentally, the title of a few books on gastric disorders by several different authors). Prinz tries to reconcile earlier bodily or somatic views of emotions with cognitive approaches to emotions and claims that emotions are *embodied appraisals*. He also suggests that emotions are perceptions, perceptions not just of aroused states or changes in the body as it registers things in our environments but also perceptions *through* the body of themes such as danger, loss, etc., that relate to our well-being. Fear of a snake, for example, involves pounding hearts, strained breathing, etc., and in perceiving these bodily changes we become aware of danger; fear thus tracks danger via heart palpitations (Prinz 2004, 68–69), as the heart beats with significance. Emotions, Prinz suggests, register bodily changes and thereby represent or track core relational themes (a phrase Prinz borrows from the psychologist Richard Lazarus) such as danger that pertain to our well-being.

In making a case for his view, Prinz rejects cognitive approaches to emotions, claiming that emotions are not cognitive if cognitions are taken as necessarily concept-laden and disembodied (Prinz 2004, 41). This leads to questions about how we should understand cognition, and Prinz suggests that cognitive states and processes exploit representations that are under the control of organisms, not the environment. Prinz grants that we can cause emotions by acts of will, e.g., imagining being angry, where the emotion is a concept based on memory, but he claims that our daily emotions are not cognitive but more like percepts under exogeneous control (Prinz 2004, 50).

Emotions, Prinz claims, are appraisals in that they represent organism-environment relations with regard to well-being by registering bodily changes. He claims there is no principled reason for claiming that appraisals must be disembodied. While the neuroscientist Antonio Damasio (Damasio 1994, 139) claims that emotions are perceptions of bodily changes *coupled with* evaluations, suggesting that emotions can play a role in reasoning only if they involve a cognitive element, Prinz thinks cognitive evaluations are not required here (Prinz 2004, 60).

In suggesting that emotions are perceptions, Prinz claims that they are ways of using our bodily radar detectors to literally perceive our relationship to the world. He defends his view from apparent contrasts between emotion and perception (with regard to such things as unobservables, endurance, action, indirectness, modularity, and warrant), contrasts that might suggest either that emotions are not perceptual states or that they are not perceptions of core relational themes.

Prinz's novel and ingenious approach has many plausible aspects, but I have several qualms about it. To begin with, it is not clear how *mere* bodily changes such as racing heartbeats, faster breathing, etc., and perceptions of these can *appraise* or evaluate things, creatures, situations, and the like. As the *Concise Oxford English Dictionary* tells us, to appraise something is to estimate the value or quality or price of that thing. It would seem then (at the risk of sounding like an ordinary language philosopher) that the very concept of appraisal calls for something like cognitions or judgments or concepts in order to evaluate. The neuroscientist Antonio Damasio seems to grasp this larger, philosophical point, and perhaps that is why he incorporates evaluations in his view of the emotions, as mentioned briefly above, claiming that emotions are perceptions of bodily changes *coupled with* evaluations. In contrast, it is not clear how Prinz solves this philosophical problem; indeed he even goes so far as to claim that "embodied appraisals are thoughts . . ." (Prinz 2004, 244). Of course, Prinz might claim here that what he means by appraisal is representing organism-environment relations with regard to well-being (Prinz 2004, 52); or as Magda Arnold who popularized the term "appraisal" in emotion research puts it, to appraise a thing is to see it as affecting oneself in a way that matters (Arnold 1960, 171), another notion that incidentally seems to call for evaluation and something like cognitions or judgments or concepts in order to evaluate. But notice now that when cognitive views of emotions (and cognitive-affective views of emotions such as the one I incline toward) talk about appraisal, they have cognitive evaluations in mind, involving something like concepts or judgments or cognitions, as is the case, for example, with the view of the psychologist Richard Lazarus who sees appraisals as evaluations of organism-environment relations and their significance for one's well-being. If this is right, then it looks like Prinz is talking about something quite different from cognitive theorists of emotions when he mentions appraisals. As such, one can doubt his claim that his view reconciles or "bridges the gap" between cognitive and non-cognitive, bodily theories of emotions (Prinz 2004, viii). It would seem more plausible to claim instead that Prinz is only offering us an updated version of a bodily or somatic theory of emotions, a theory that is non-cognitive rather than a reconciliation of cognitive and non-cognitive approaches to emotions. Relatedly, one might also wonder contra Prinz how *mere* physical states such as pounding heartbeats can be focused on or directed toward the environment, as his notion of appraisal seems to require, given that intentionality has traditionally been thought to be a mark of the mental (compare Carroll 2006, 219). To be sure, Prinz appeals to teleosemantics, suggesting that the content of a representation is the state of affairs which it is that representation's *function* to detect; for example, although anger is a perception of the body on Prinz's view, its function is to detect when one has been demeaned or offended against, the *nominal content* of anger being the aroused body and its *real content* being the proposition that I or mine have been demeaned or offended against. But it is still not clear contra Prinz how *mere* physical states can detect things or have intentionality without something cognitive or mental to lean on. Note also in passing that cognitive views of emotions need not be committed to cognitions being "necessarily concept-laden, disembodied states" as Prinz portrays them (Prinz 2004, 41, 50–51, 74–76), for cognitions may involve something like not very highly sophisticated proto-concepts in the case of emotions in infants and non-human animals, and in any case cognitive theorists grant cognitions are *neurophysiologically based* and so cannot be disembodied (à la Cartesian mental states, for example).

My second concern about Prinz's view pertains to his claim that emotions literally are perceptions or perceptual states. While Prinz ingeniously and quite successfully defends his view from many apparent contrasts (mentioned above) between emotion and perception in the last chapter of his book, I would register the following reservation that pertains to control and change. We can often control and change our emotions over time in ways that it is not clear apply to our perceptual experiences. To use the kind of example familiar to and used by the Greeks, especially the Stoics, and Nussbaum, someone can control and change the sadness felt upon the death of her mother to acceptance if she changes the underlying evaluative judgment from one that suggests that it is somehow a bad thing that her mother died to an evaluative judgment that suggests instead that perhaps it is not so bad after all that her mother died, for she lived a long, happy, and fulfilled life, died in her sleep, without much pain, and she had to die sooner or later anyway, and so on. Indeed, one might even change the emotion of sadness to happiness in such a case if the underlying evaluative judgment is changed to one that suggests instead that it is in fact a good thing that one's mother died, for she was wicked, abusive, and so on, assuming all this is true! Many ethical theories (such as virtue ethics as well as the ethics of love and care) and claims in fact build on this idea that we can often control and change our emotions to some degree. In sharp contrast, it is not clear how I can control and change my perceptual experience or state of, say, seeing a sunset as yellow or orange or red to one that involves seeing the sunset instead as blue or green or black (short of wearing tinted glasses or closing my eyes, both of which seem to involve a kind of cheating). This contrast with regard to control and change casts some doubt on Prinz's claim that emotions are perceptual states. Moreover, contra Prinz (Prinz 2004, 222–24), it is not clear that emotions inhabit one of the senses (such as vision, audition, and olfaction), as he claims perceptual states must do, nor is it clear that emotions are implicated in perceptual input systems, as Prinz suggests. Of course, Prinz is right that emotions reveal how we fare in the world and how situations relate to our well-being, drawing our attention to certain things in the world and compelling us to act in response. But these insights can easily be taken on board by cognitive and cognitive-affective theorists *without* making the yet to be established claim that emotions literally are perceptual states; perhaps talk of emotions being perceptions should be taken not literally, as Prinz seems to do, but only figuratively.

Third, one might wonder against Prinz if bodily changes such as pounding heartbeats are just part of the neurophysiological *bases* of emotions that allow us to have emotions rather than being constitutive of emotions themselves. Prinz suggests (Prinz 2004, 244) that most emotion researchers try to pack too much into emotions by assuming that bodily changes, propositional attitudes, action dispositions, and feelings are parts of emotions, whereas he thinks these are mere causes and effects of emotions that should not be mistaken for emotions themselves. But in the same vein, it might be objected against Prinz that bodily changes (part of the set just mentioned above) should not be identified with emotions for they are only neurophysiological causes and effects of emotions. Note in this connection that Prinz suggests (Prinz 2004, 11) that Aristotle may have identified some role for the body in his theory of the emotions, when he speculated in the *De Anima* that anger is "realized" by blood boiling in the heart. But against Prinz, it is possible that "realization" may involve the body only being the neurophysiological, subvenient base or cause (even a standard rather than an essential cause, for Prinz grants, along with Damasio, that bodily changes are not necessary for emotions as emotions may bypass the body) of the emotion rather than being constitutive of the emotion itself. Neither subvenience nor causation need amount to constitution.

My fourth and final reservation about Prinz's view pertains to his claims about moods (Prinz 2004, 182–88). Prinz suggests that moods are just a special case of emotions, and are embodied appraisals, but while emotions tell us how localized, specific events are significant for our well-being, moods tell us how our lives are faring globally and more generally. I have no quarrel with the claim that moods may inform us how we are faring overall, but doubt Prinz's reasoning for suggesting that moods are intentional; and in any case, seeing moods as non-intentional does not prevent one from granting that moods have the kind of global, informative role Prinz identifies. Prinz claims that any mental state that has the function of being reliably caused by something represents that thing; if they have such a function, then Prinz thinks moods can be said to represent just what their corresponding emotions represent and so are intentional states (Prinz 2004, 184). But against Prinz, one must wonder if there is a double conflation going on here, one between causation and representation, and the other between representation and intentionality. Causation and representation seem to be different concepts, e.g., someone may be multiply stabbed in the back and, unknown to them, this may be the reliable cause of their intense pain, but it is not clear that the pain, the mental state here, must involve representations of a knife or stabbings, etc. Even so, it seems that conceptually, representation is not the same thing as intentionality or object-directedness or about-ness in the sense that Brentano posited, e.g., realistic portraits represent their subjects, but it is not clear that they thereby have intentionality, which has traditionally been thought to be a mark of the mental rather than of such non-mental things as portraits.

I.7. A Concluding Concession

Perhaps I need to backtrack a bit; maybe I have been unfair to some of the authors discussed above. Ronald de Sousa has suggested recently that it may be possible to reconcile cognitivist and somatic views of the emotions (de Sousa 2011, xvi, 31–32). He claims that a cognitive view of the emotions is best seen as construing emotions as perceptions of value rather than as beliefs or as something epistemic (as Michael Brady seems to do in Brady 2014). On Jesse Prinz's view, as we have seen, emotions are perceptions of bodily states, and represent states of the world that are important to our concern with core relational themes such as loss and threat. Commenting on this, de Sousa suggests that although Prinz rejects the idea that emotions are perceptions of value, Prinz's own claim that emotions "track core relational themes by registering changes in the body" (Prinz 2004, 68) is very similar to de Sousa's view, for on both positions, emotions seem to tell us indirectly about things we care about.

This may well be right. If so, I am prepared to concede that it may be possible to reconcile cognitivist and cognitive-affective views of the emotions with somatic positions, after all (something that Jesse Prinz also suggested to me recently in personal conversation). This reconciliation bears on the very nature of emotions, which I have explored briefly, though it may not matter as much for theories of musical expressiveness, whether mine or that of others. Given, however, that the primary focus of this study is musical expressiveness, I hope I have said just enough about emotions, moods, and feelings—the title of this chapter—to allow us to proceed now to other things in the next chapter and beyond.

To conclude this chapter, let me sum up. I sketched a cognitive-affective view of the emotions in section I.2. In the next section, I distinguished emotions from beliefs and also from moods. Sections I.4 through I.6 critically discussed the opposing positions of Martha Nussbaum, Paul Griffiths, and Jesse Prinz. Finally, I concluded by conceding that it may be possible to reconcile a cognitive-affective view of the emotions with a somatic theory, after all.

II

Expression Theories and Arousalism

II.1. Introduction

In this chapter, I assess and reject two kinds of theories of musical expressiveness, both of which have been very important, historically, in philosophical and musical aesthetics. The first kind of theory is usually known as the expression theory, and in its simplest version maintains that to say "The music is sad" is to say that it expresses the sadness of the composer or the performer. I will critically discuss three recent versions of this theory, as presented by Bruce Vermazen, Jerrold Levinson, and Jenefer Robinson, all of whom appeal to an indeterminate agent, a persona. The second kind of theory is usually called arousalism or the arousal theory or the evocation theory, and at its simplest holds that music is expressive of the mental states it arouses in the listeners so that to say "The music is sad" is to say that the music arouses or evokes or causes sadness in listeners: it makes them feel sad. I will critically discuss this theory, and three recent "moderate" versions of it, as advanced by Aaron Ridley, Derek Matravers, and Charles Nussbaum.

II.2. Bruce Vermazen's Expression Theory

Let us begin with expression theories. It should be clear that the simple expression theory, explained very briefly above, is false for at least two reasons. First, composers and performers need not actually feel the mental state their music is expressive of. For example, Mozart wrote his joyful "Haffner" Symphony toward the end of his life when he was going through a rough time and unlikely to have felt much joy during the time he was composing this work. Second, it would seem that composers or performers actually feeling all the time the mental state the music is expressive of rather than thinking (somewhat dispassionately) about their music over several days if not weeks or months or years might seriously hamper their musical activity in some cases at least. For example, the Polish composer Krzysztof Penderecki's musical work *Threnody for the Victims of Hiroshima* is very intensely expressive of deep anguish for those who died in Hiroshima on August 6, 1945, but it seems clear that Penderecki did not feel anguish all the time (even if he felt so some of the time) while writing the work and instead spent at least some time thinking (coolly) about what musical means he would use (e.g., high-pitched clusters and harmonics on the strings) to express anguish musically.

In what follows, I focus on recent versions of expression theories, leaving aside older expression theories such as those associated with R. G. Collingwood and Leo Tolstoy, which have been extensively discussed and criticized.[1] Unlike the simple version of the expression theory just discussed, these more recent versions do not claim that music expresses or is expressive of the mental state of the composer or the performer. Instead, they typically appeal to the idea of the music being expressive of the mental states of *someone*, usually an imagined, indeterminate musical persona.

Let us first consider the expression theory put forth by Bruce Vermazen (1986), which is a theory of artistic expression in general that I discuss below as applied adaptively to musical expressiveness. The main claim that Vermazen makes is that we attribute mental states to the imagined utterer or an imagined persona (and not the actual, historical artist or composer or performer) of the musical work, so that the musical work, and not the imagined utterer, is thought to express the relevant mental states of the imagined utterer; thus the musical work may express something even though the persona is not expressing. It should be specified that Vermazen's claim is not that there *is* such an imagined utterer or speaker, but rather only that we *imagine* that there is an utterer feeling the relevant emotion of which the music is expressive.

Also, Vermazen does mean expression as opposed to expressiveness. The distinction between expression and expressiveness goes back at least to Alan Tormey (1971), and is as follows. To express a mental state is actually to *have* it as an inner state that occurs as part of one's psychology and to show that mental state outwardly. In contrast, to be expressive of a mental state is (merely) to display or exhibit outwardly the behavioral, bodily, and other features associated with that mental state without necessarily having or feeling that mental state; the performance of actors, for example, is usually expressive of mental states that they need not themselves feel. For

Vermazen, then, the mental state in question is one that the imagined persona *does* (imaginarily) have, even though the persona herself does not express it. Note also that Vermazen distinguishes the imagined persona from the feigned speaker or narrator.

What Vermazen is proposing is an expression theory of expression, which involves an imagined persona, and not an actual person; and thus it does well in avoiding the problems mentioned earlier that simple expression theories face. He claims that the basic notion of expression in linguistic utterances as well as in behavior (and also in art) is a univocal one that involves giving evidence for someone's mental states; though sometimes the evidence may be misleading (as when the utterer fails to realize her intentions in his utterance, and ends up expressing a different thought from the one she intended), and sometimes it may be intended and sometimes not intended (as when gestures, postures, or behavior may unintentionally express, even though there may be no intention to express but rather, sometimes, a failed intention to hide one's emotions).

Vermazen also tells us that the imagined persona is a *type* of person, not a particular, specific person who has the mental states in question. This is very well-expressed and I myself would say that in such experiences, the persona is an indeterminate, indefinite, and imagined *someone* whose mental state is manifested: in such experiences of musical expressiveness, we imagine someone (we know not exactly who) "in" the music is crying or wailing, etc., and that their relevant state is being expressed musically. I think it may be essential to the kind of experience Vermazen describes that who exactly the persona is remain indefinite; I suspect that this is what the reality of such experiences may involve and, moreover, one may actually need to *have* this sort of experience to grasp this point fully. This type of person, who is the persona, is constituted by our inferences to the persona's mental states as well as by certain background assumptions that we make. The persona is a fiction or a construction that only has the traits assigned to her by interpreters or listeners.

A musical work, claims Vermazen, expresses a mental property (emotions, even thoughts and beliefs)[2] if and only if it *evidences* that an imagined utterer of that work has that mental property. More stringently, a musical work expresses a property if and only if attributing that property to an utterer of the work *explains* its having the features it has; and the property is not presupposed in interpretation, i.e., my own presupposition that the persona has some feature is not evidence that the persona does indeed have that feature. Evidence exists, according to Vermazen, from which we imagine the persona's mental states. When faced with an expressive musical work, Vermazen suggests, we imagine it has been uttered by someone, and then we ask what mental states the utterer has that make him utter the work.

Vermazen's theory is one of the most impressive theories of artistic expressiveness. But I am not entirely persuaded by it for the following reasons. To begin with, I am not sure that the kind of experience Vermazen describes is the *only* sort of experience of musical expressiveness there is. There may, I think, also be other sorts of experiences of musical expressiveness, one of which may involve our animating the music itself, imaginatively projecting life and life-like properties onto it as we imagine the music itself is alive, has mental states, is sad, and is expressing or manifesting that sadness musically, as I discuss later in section VI.3. A different experience of musical expressiveness may involve our cross-categorially, imaginatively, identifying with the state the music is expressive of, as though we were that state. If this is right, then the concept of musical expressiveness Vermazen offers us may be too narrow to account for the variety of experiences of musical expressiveness and stands in need of enlargement.

My second qualm is about the notion of an utterer (or utterance, if you like) as applied to purely instrumental or absolute music. It is easy to apply this notion to literary (and possibly dramatic) works of arts, but I myself do not have sufficient grip on what it means to say that this notion applies to pure or absolute music; what does it mean to *utter* a musical work (as opposed to uttering a sentence or a poem)? Nor am I sure that we actually do imagine an utterer, as opposed to a persona, of the music; I suspect that just the notion of a persona would have sufficed for Vermazen's theory, which is perhaps too influenced by, and too close for comfort to, linguistic notions and models to be true to art and its experience. Moreover, Vermazen claims that not everything that the work expresses is something that the imagined utterer expresses, but I am not sure how we would distinguish, given that the utterer is imagined, which mental states are those that the imagined utterer is expressing—and expressing intentionally at that—and which are not.

A far more important worry is this, though it is related to my suspicion that like many twentieth-century analytic philosophers, Vermazen is far too influenced by logico-linguistic models, which he applies to art and expression. This worry concerns the role assigned to inference and explanation in Vermazen's theory. The experience of hearing music as expressive, even as expressive of (or expressing) the emotions of an imagined persona of the music, is far more immediate and direct and not as *inferential* as Vermazen's notion of evidencing suggests, though this is not to deny the crucial role of various sorts of mental processes in hearing music as expressive. I am not sure, first, that we do imagine the music as being *uttered* by someone (though we often, if not always, imagine a persona in the music); second, I am not sure that we actually do, while hearing music as expressive, regularly ask and infer what mental states the imagined utterer would have that would make him utter the musical work. Hearing music as expressive, I contend, is more direct and experiential, and not as indirect, inferential, and deliberative as Vermazen thinks.[3]

My fourth and final reservation about Vermazen's theory concerns the need for a standard of correctness regarding what exactly is musically expressed, and to sort out which traits are correctly assigned to the persona by the interpreter and which are not; one possible answer here, of course, is to appeal to conformity with a broad intersubjective agreement across appropriately backgrounded or competent listeners, and yet allow room for some disagreement between such listeners in some cases. Vermazen says that we may all construct different personae, and he does see the need for a standard of correctness when he says that my presupposition that the persona has some property need not mean that it has it. However, his theory still leaves inexplicit what such a standard of correctness would consist in.

II.3. Jerrold Levinson's Persona Theory

I next consider the theory of musical expressiveness put forth by Jerrold Levinson.[4] Levinson's view modifies and adaptively applies to music Bruce Vermazen's general view about artistic expressiveness. While Vermazen's judgment-based view, as applied to music, seems committed to the idea that we *infer* the music is expressing the emotions of an indeterminate *utterer*, Levinson rightly, I think, rejects the ideas of inference and utterer and claims we directly and immediately hear music as expressive.

Levinson's view applies the ordinary notion of expressiveness consisting of the outward manifestation or display of inner mental states to musical expressiveness and its concept, claiming that musical expressiveness and its experiences involve readily and immediately hearing the music as the manifestation of the emotions (or other mental states) of an imagined, indefinite musical persona. What this amounts to is that when we hear sad music as sad, we imagine an indeterminate persona expressing sadness musically, though the sadness need not be the persona's: it is as if an indeterminate someone "in" the music is crying, or wailing, or otherwise expressing sadness, though in a musical manner. This imagined persona, as noted above in discussing Vermazen, is a *type* of individual, not a particular individual.

Levinson's view relates quite easily to our ordinary concept of expressiveness. However, my worry is that its concept of musical expressiveness may be too narrow to be adequate, for it does not cover the variety of experiences of musical expressiveness. To be adequate, a theory of what it means for music to be expressive must cover or apply to all genuine experiences of musical expressiveness. To find whether it is adequate, a concept of musical expressiveness must be tested empirically against experiences of expressiveness: its answer to what it means to say that music is expressive must be true to the various experiences of musical expressiveness.

Reflecting on my own (possibly idiosyncratic) experiences of musical expressiveness, I find that I sometimes do imagine that there is an indeterminate, imagined musical persona that is expressing emotions musically. Most notably, I have on occasion (once in fact when I was cooking and not primarily focused on the music except as background sound) experienced the opening clarinet glissando in Gershwin's *Rhapsody in Blue* in terms of an imagined, indefinite persona that is wailing or crying through the music. Likewise, I have sometimes heard John Coltrane's music in similar terms, as if an indeterminate, imagined persona "in" the music (more precisely "in" the sound of the saxophone) is expressing emotions musically.

Nevertheless, I do not always imagine an indefinite musical persona in experiencing music as expressive. Indeed, I do not even do so most of the time. There are other experiences of musical expressiveness that Levinson's view does not accommodate, such as the experience of imaginatively animating the music itself as the very being that is alive and expressive of its own emotions; or the experience of our imaginatively identifying with the music, imagining it is expressive of our own emotions; and so on. If this is right, then Levinson's view may at best only be partially adequate as an account of musical expressiveness that is true to the experience of musical expressiveness.[5] In fact, it will emerge in chapter VI that I do not reject Vermazen and Levinson's persona view totally, but take it on board as an *option* insofar as it describes *one* (though only one) amongst the many kinds of ways in which we imagine music as sad, happy, etc., in my view. Also, as chapter VI will reveal, my own resemblance-plus-imagination or imaginationist view of musical expressiveness can also be seen as a moderate expression theory insofar as the various imaginings involved in musical expressiveness considered *as a group* have *some* link with the ordinary notion of expressiveness involving the outward manifestation of (someone or something's) inner mental states, even if not every such imagining need link strictly with this notion.

More recently, Levinson (2006) has tried to articulate his view further and defend it from objections such as the one raised above. He now claims that his basic analysis of musical expressiveness is that music expressive of emotion or mental state "E" is music heard as, or as if, someone expressing "E." While I grant that music may be heard as a human someone expressing "E," I submit that Levinson's view is too narrow in not explicitly allowing the possibility that music may also sometimes be heard imaginatively as *something* expressing "E," where the something in question need not be human but could be a being (such as the music itself as animated, as I will suggest in chapter VI) that is sufficiently human-like insofar as expressiveness goes.

In response to the objection above (raised also by Robert Stecker and Stephen Davies amongst others) that listeners do not always imagine personae when they hear music as expressive, if they do so at all, Levinson has this to say. He claims that if expressive music is readily heard as or as if expression, and if expression requires an expresser, then personae or agents, no matter how minimal, are presupposed in hearing music as expressive. Levinson also claims that listeners may not always be aware that they imagine personae in hearing music as expressive.

While I agree that we may not always be aware of our imaginings or be aware that we are engaged in certain kinds of imaginings, as shown by the kinds of imaginings involved in dreaming and daydreaming, I am not persuaded that hearing music as expressive is as monolithic as Levinson suggests. The sheer variety of ways in which we imagine things—in terms of fancying or supposing or entertaining a possibility without actually believing it or dreaming or daydreaming and so on, as will be discussed in section V.1—suggests that there may be more to the truth about musical expressiveness than Levinson's view, which may at best be part of that truth. Put differently, given various kinds of imaginings and the often unconscious or subconscious nature of our imaginings, it seems hard to believe that there is only one kind of imagining, that of a persona, involved in hearing musical expressiveness, as Levinson would have it. Inference to the best explanation suggests there may also be *other* kinds of imaginings involved in hearing music as expressive rather than just the monolithic persona view; the work of other philosophers on music (such as Malcolm Budd, Kendall Walton, Aaron Ridley, and Robert Stecker), who are also competent listeners presumably, suggests the same.

II.4. Jenefer Robinson's Theory

The last recent version of the expression theory that I want to consider here is that advanced by Jenefer Robinson (2005). Reviving the Romantic theory of expression, though not in Collingwood's version, and modifying it, Robinson claims that if an artwork is an expression of an emotion, then it is evidence that a persona (which may but need not be the artist) is experiencing or has experienced this emotion so that the persona's emotion is perceptible in the work. She also claims that the work articulates, individuates, and clarifies the persona's emotion, and in doing so it enables the audience to get clear about the emotion and bring it to consciousness.

I have two qualms about this proposed theory of expression for artworks. For starters, while Robinson is not claiming that all art is expression of the artist's emotions, it is not clear of the artworks that have an expressive connection with the emotions that they all *express* emotions even if some may do so in expressing the emotions of the artist or a persona, where to express an emotion is to have it as an actual mental state that occurs in one's own psychology as a part of it. Instead, it seems that many artworks, as entities that are without life or mental states, are only *expressive* of emotions and other mental states such as moods and feelings, where to be expressive is only to display behavior or features typically associated with mental states, somewhat in the way that actors are expressive of mental states such as fear that they need not themselves feel even though they display behavior characteristic of fear such as trembling, stuttering, etc. If this distinction between expression and expressiveness (discussed in section II.2 above when dealing with Vermazen) holds up, as I believe it does, then it seems that Robinson's view is very limited in scope in not applying to artworks that are only expressive of emotions, moods, and feelings, which appears to be the case for many musical works.

My second qualm is about the notion of a persona that Robinson appeals to. It should be clear from the reservations expressed about Vermazen's and Levinson's theories in sections II.2 and II.3 above, respectively, that I believe that the persona view, even in Robinson's version, is too narrow to cover the variety of experiences of musical expressiveness and indeed experiences of artistic expressiveness in general, even if it may cover some of them.

With regard to expression or expressiveness of emotions in music as opposed to art in general, this is what Robinson has to say. She claims that song, especially the Romantic *lied*, is the quintessence of Romantic expression. Some Romantic music, she claims, expresses emotions in her full Romantic sense, many *lieder* especially expressing the emotions of their dramatis personae. In Romantic instrumental music, she claims it is thus often appropriate to posit a musical persona, either the composer or a character created by the composer. She concludes that some pure instrumental music also expresses emotion in the full Romantic sense.

As a theory of musical expressiveness, I believe this view is severely limited. Most music is not Romantic (in the sense of that term that applies to Western classical music roughly throughout the nineteenth century), and to use that one period in the history of music as a model for other kinds of music, across the ages and across cultures and genres and styles of music, and expressiveness in them seems too monolithic. To add to this limitation, and as mentioned earlier, the persona view seems limited as an account of the variety of experiences of musical expressiveness even if it arguably captures some of them, and this compounds problems for Robinson (compare Kivy 2006). Finally, it would seem that in talking about musical expressiveness, we are not focused primarily on music with words—be it Romantic *lieder* or something else—but on purely instrumental music without words or an associated program or story. For in the case of music with words or with an associated program, it would seem the expressiveness comes not just from the music per se, which is where the problem of musical expressiveness is at its most acute, but is also at least partly derived from the attached words or the associated program, a point I will return to later in this chapter. Thus, it would seem misplaced to use music with words, even lovely Romantic *lieder*, as a model for expressiveness in pure music, as Robinson does. If anything, expressiveness in these two different kinds of music may be different in that expressiveness in music with words may involve the role of words at least to some degree, whereas this is obviously not the case for pure music.

II.5. Contra Simple Arousalism

Having discussed expression theories in three recent versions, I turn now to assessing arousalism. Here again I will begin by raising some worries for simple arousalism, and then discuss three recent versions of arousalism.

At its simplest, arousalism claims that music is expressive of the mental states it arouses in the listeners so that to say "The music is sad" is to say that the music arouses or evokes or causes sadness in listeners. Here are some general concerns about such simple arousalist theories. First, and perhaps most importantly, these theories *conflate* musical expressiveness and musical arousal.[6] Expressiveness is a property of the music *itself* (an imagined property of the music, if my claims in chapter VI especially are right), whereas the aroused response, as an emotional *effect* that music has upon listeners, is something that belongs to listeners. While expressiveness is often integral to the aesthetic character of a musical work so that we usually praise a musical work aesthetically for being expressive, arousal is usually accidental and usually not an aesthetic plus;[7] unless we are talking about marches or funeral music or other music for special, rousing occasions. Expressiveness and arousal are thus quite distinct as concepts and as phenomena, even if they are often coextensive in that we are often aroused by expressive music, and arousalism is guilty of conflating them in explaining expressiveness in terms of arousal. Second, a musical passage or piece may be expressive of a specific emotion such as sadness, and it might be heard as such, and yet it may arouse a *different* emotion in us such as pity. This is similar to what happens often in real life when we see someone as sad but find pity or sympathy, not sadness, aroused in us. Or take an example from drama: we see the scene of Gloucester's eyes being gouged out in *King Lear* as expressive of ruthless cruelty or extreme hatred, and find only extreme horror or disgust or indignation aroused in us. Third, just as we can often perceive other people as sad (or happy) *without* necessarily being aroused emotionally to sadness (or happiness) or any other emotion or mental state, likewise a musical passage or piece may be heard as expressive of a certain emotion and yet not arouse *any* emotion even in competent or appropriately backgrounded, attentive listeners who are not bored or tired or excessively familiar with the music. This may be because the music may not do a very good job of being expressive. As an example, I mention some music for TV cartoons, which often uses muted solo trumpets, using the wah-wah mute in a slowly descending chromatic passage consisting of four notes. This sort of music does not do a good job of being expressive and, even when heard on its own without the accompanying animation, it may be heard as expressive of tragi-comic emotions and yet not arouse *any* emotion in us. Fourth, arousalism reverses the order of things[8] in claiming that sad music is sad *because* it (sometimes) arouses sadness in listeners, rather than claiming that sad music arouses sadness in us because it *is* (imagined to be) sad and we imaginatively empathize or sympathize or identify with it (as animated, or perhaps with an imagined musical persona in it), thus being aroused to sadness. There is, I would urge, a partial analogy between (hearing) sad music and (seeing) sad persons, given which, this implausible reversal of the order of explanation is like claiming that sad people are sad because they sometimes arouse sadness in us, rather than claiming that sad people arouse sadness in us because they *are* sad and we empathize or sympathize or identify with them, thus being aroused to sadness. Indeed, one might wonder if, unlike the alternative explanation just sketched briefly, arousalists can explain at all why we are often aroused by music, but I shall not pursue the point further.[9]

II.6. Aaron Ridley's Moderate Arousalism

The worries raised so far in section II.5 for arousalist theories rise for what one might call strong arousalism. In addition to strong arousalism, however, there are "weak" or moderate arousalist theories which might be thought to escape at least some worries raised above for arousalism, except perhaps the worries that arousal theories conflate expressiveness and arousal, and that they reverse the order of explanation.

The first kind of moderate arousalism I want to discuss here has been advanced by Aaron Ridley,[10] and mediates between strong arousalism and resemblance-based theories of musical expressiveness that account for music's being sad in terms of music resembling either our expressive vocal or bodily behavior, or perhaps resembling the emotions themselves and how they feel. This moderate arousalism claims *not* that *every time* we ascribe expressiveness to music we must have responded to it in a particular aroused way, but instead that we would not hear music as expressive unless some of us had been aroused by music on some occasions. In other words, the claim is that arousal is *conceptually* necessary for hearing music as expressive. A second, more important, claim made by this variety of moderate arousalism is that we hear the funeral march in Beethoven's "Eroica" Symphony, for example, as expressive of heavyhearted resoluteness through ourselves coming to feel heavyhearted but resolute when we hear the music. This sympathetic mirroring response is grounded in resemblances between music and our expressive behavior, and is justifiable publicly according to whether it suits the music.

I now note some reservations about Ridley's view as presented above. First, while the claim that there is a conceptual link between arousal and perceiving musical expressiveness is certainly plausible, it is not clear that it *is* true and instead it is *conceivable* that we could have heard music as sad, say, just by perceiving resemblances between sad music and the vocal and dynamic expressive behavior of sad people, and then imaginatively projecting sadness onto music, even if we had never been aroused musically. Two partial analogies may drive this point home. It is doubtful if anyone has ever been aroused to sadness by the sight of a drooping willow tree, and yet we do see willows as sad, perhaps because we see their resembling the droopy posture of sad people and then imaginatively project sadness onto willows. It is possible that the case with music may be analogous. That is, it is possible that we may perceive music as sad without it being conceptually necessary for this that some of us should have been aroused to sadness on some occasion by the music. How, then, do we perceive sad music as sad? What may in part (but only in part) allow us to perceive these musical passages and works as sad, I suggest, are perceived resemblances between sad music, on the one hand, and the bodily and vocal expressive behavior of sad people as well as the feel of sadness, on the other hand. For instance, sad music is often slow, low, and soft, resembling the way in which sad people often walk slowly, hang their heads low, and speak very softly in low-pitched voices. Perceiving such resemblances may be the causal story that allows us to imaginatively hear music as sad, even though this does not yet tell us what it *means* to say that something inanimate and insentient such as music is sad. Second, it is not clear that Vulcans or some other species incapable of having emotions and thus incapable of ever being aroused could never see a good tragic actor's performance as expressive of sadness, based on the resemblance between the actor's performance and the behavior of sad humans in real life. To be sure, Vulcans could not experience the actor's behavior as sad in a way that is as rich and "from the inside" as ours, but this need not preclude them from *minimally* perceiving the actor's performance as sad or as expressive of sadness. The case with hearing music as expressive may be similar in that there need not be the conceptual link between it and arousal that Ridley posits.

Here is a second and much more important concern about this brand of moderate arousalism. We are told by Ridley that we hear music as sad, say, through ourselves coming to feel sad when hearing the music, and that our sympathetic mirroring response to the music can be justified publicly because it suits the music. Now it is certainly true that often we may hear music as sad, and in the most involved way, through ourselves coming to feel sad when hearing the music. But while this accounts for *one* of the many sorts of *experiences* of hearing music as sad, it does not tell us what it *means* to say that music is sad given that music is *inanimate and insentient*, which is the basic problem of musical expressiveness. That is to say, there are two related questions here: one about what is involved in experiencing music as sad, to which we are given one answer; and a second question about what it means to say, and how it can be true, that something inanimate and insentient such as music is sad, which it seems this kind of moderate arousalism has not addressed (compare Levinson 1996, 97; Stecker 2010, 169-70). The two questions are related for accounts of musical expressiveness must square with genuine experiences of musical expressiveness. Relatedly, one can ask Ridley what it means to say, as he claims, that our sympathetic mirroring response *suits* the music, to which the only answer must be that it suits the music because the music *itself* is sad.[11] But this raises the question of how something without life or mental states such as music can itself be sad, which is the basic problem of musical expressiveness and to which the only answer we are given by Ridley seems to be that what is needed to hear or experience music as sad is to have a sympathetic mirroring response that suits it. There must thus be some doubt whether Ridley's brand of moderate arousalism has even addressed the basic problem of musical expressiveness, a job perhaps better done by views that suggest that at some level we *imagine* the music is sad, that, amongst other things, we animate the music, i.e., we endow it with life and life-like qualities and imagine that it is the sort of thing that is sad. More of such matters in chapter VI.

More recently, Ridley (2004) has made the following claims about musical expressiveness. He rejects the focus on purely instrumental music that most writers on musical expressiveness (including myself) have and claims that it is false to assume that the musical is the "purely" musical, and that the purely musical is music for instruments alone. Ridley claims against this focus on pure music that vocal music is not less musical for not being purely instrumental. And he accuses most philosophers of music of having a prejudice against song and vocal music, claiming instead that thinking of songs as hybrid art forms (marrying pure music and words) is not fruitful, that most philosophers of music have a misplaced emphasis on purity of music and are wrong to think that song is "impure." Accordingly, Ridley discusses Frederick Delius's setting of Ernest Dowson's poem "Cyanara" when talking about musical expressiveness rather than taking an example from pure music.

I believe Ridley misses the real reason why most philosophers of music focus on pure or absolute music when dealing with musical expressiveness. In the case of music with words or music with an associated program or story, the expressiveness of the music (as well as musical arousal) may be at least *partly derivative* from the accompanying words or story or program rather than being a function of the music per se as is the case with purely instrumental or absolute music. This makes the problem of musical expressiveness most acute when we deal with pure music, hence the focus on pure music where words, stories, and other such things do not enter philosophical explanations of musical expressiveness. Despite Ridley's suggestions, I do not believe Kivy or Davies or Levinson or other philosophers of music believe that song is "impure" music or any less musical than pure music, even as they recognize legitimate differences between pure and vocal music; the term "pure" music may be a bit misleading here if it unfortunately suggests this to some such as Ridley. Nor do I see the prejudice against vocal music that Ridley claims most philosophers of music are guilty of; indeed, Levinson (2015) has written a lot about song. Finally, while Ridley doubts if the musical aspects of songs can be assessed in isolation from their texts, I submit against Ridley that one can and should engage in at least three kinds of assessments when it comes to songs: (1) assessments of the musical materials—melodies, harmonies, rhythms, textures, timbres, forms etc.—for themselves; (2) assessments of the text itself, and whether it works as poetry or in some other way; and (3) assessments of how the music relates to the words—whether it matches the words, and to what degree, and so on. This tripartite suggestion relates not so much to my criticisms of Ridley's arousalism, but rather to his claim that philosophers of music have unjustly avoided vocal music, and it is especially aimed at Ridley's claim that the musical aspects of songs cannot be assessed in isolation from their texts.

II.7. Derek Matravers's Moderate Arousalism

The next recent version of moderate arousalism I want to discuss is that advocated by Derek Matravers (1998). Matravers claims that expressive judgments are about the capacity of artworks to cause certain sorts of experiences involving certain emotional effects or arousal. Sad artworks are sad because part of the experience they cause in arousing feelings is similar to the characteristic experience we would have were we to see sad people; music is sad if it has the capacity to be experienced as sad through arousal. A second component of this brand of moderate arousalism is the claim that to say that music is sad (or expressive of sadness) is to say that it is appropriate to feel sad when we hear it; that music expresses that particular emotion to which our aroused feeling would be an appropriate response when, as qualified listeners, we hear the music under normal conditions.

This brand of moderate arousalism faces some problems, in addition to the problems discussed briefly above of conflating arousal and expressiveness, and reversing the direction of explanation, which I will not belabor. For starters, it is not clear that to say that a musical work or passage is sad is to say that it has the capacity to cause sadness in listeners and thus be experienced as sad; even though it may well have that capacity. This is analogous to the case of sad persons: to say someone is sad is *not* to say that they have the capacity to make others sad and thus be seen as sad; though they often have this capacity. Rather, it means that they possess a certain mental state, whether or not they make others sad or are seen as such. Analogously—and this is only a partial analogy—I would urge that to say the music is sad is to say that it is *imagined* in various ways to have sadness, in part in virtue of its structural and other properties resembling sad people in various ways.[12]

Second, there are qualms to be raised about the claim that to say music is sad is to say it is appropriate to feel sad when we listen to it. To begin with, pursuing the analogy between sad music and sad people, just as to say someone is sad is *not* to say that it is appropriate to feel sad when we see them (though it *may* often be appropriate to feel sad when we see them) but rather that they possess a certain mental state, similarly I submit that to say music is sad is *not* to claim that it is appropriate to feel sad when we hear the music (though it *may* often be that) but rather that the music is *imagined* in some way and at some level to be sad in ways resembling sad people. Moreover, even if it is *always* appropriate to feel sad (as opposed to it being appropriate sometimes to feel pity or some such emotion instead of sadness) when we hear sad music, we must dig deeper here and play the "Why" game that little children are so good at playing: *why* is it appropriate to feel sad when we hear sad music? Analogously—to return to the partial analogy between sad music and sad people—one can ask *why* it is appropriate to feel sad when we see sad people. The natural answer here, I suggest, is that it is appropriate to feel sad when we see sad people because they *are* sad, and it is very natural and human to empathize or sympathize or identify with them, thus being aroused to feeling sad. Likewise, one can claim that it is appropriate to feel sad when we hear sad music because it *is* sad, and it is very natural and human to be aroused to sadness musically when we imaginatively empathize or sympathize or identify with the music itself as animated (in the sense I explain in chapter VI) or with a musical persona in it. But now this will lead to the further and basic question how something *inanimate and insentient* such as music can *itself* be said to be sad, which is the basic problem of musical expressiveness that Matravers's brand of moderate arousalism does not answer or otherwise solve in claiming that to say music is sad is to say it is appropriate to feel sad when we hear it; instead, perhaps all we are told is that it is appropriate to feel sad when we hear sad music. In contrast, we are given an answer and a solution to this basic problem of musical expressiveness when we are told—as I will suggest in chapter VI—that amongst other things we often *animate* the music at some level, *imagining* that it is the sort of thing that is alive, has mental states, is sad, and manifests that sadness via musical gestures, development and the like.[13]

Elsewhere, Matravers (2001, 359) formulates his view as follows: "A expresses E if, among the mental states caused by A, is some non-cognitive state which stands in the right kind of relation to the appropriate reaction to the expression of emotion in the central case." And more recently, Matravers (2003, 360) claims that ". . . a piece of music is expressive of an emotion if, among the mental states caused by the music, is some non-cognitive state that stands in the right relation to that emotion felt in nonmusical cases." Besides the fact that we need an explanation here why it is appropriate to feel a certain reaction, a point I just tried to press above against Matravers, it also needs to be specified here what "right kind of relation" or "right relation" amounts to, and why it is right. Without such a clarification, it is obscure what claim is being made here.

II.8. Charles Nussbaum's View

I turn at last to the arousalism put forth by Charles Nussbaum. Drawing on various things in cognitive science, philosophy of mind, science and such, Nussbaum (2007) proposes a naturalistic theory of musical representation according to which Western tonal art music since 1650 is a norm-governed, representational practice. I will focus specifically on what Nussbaum has to say about musical arousal and its role in expressiveness, since that is the purview of this chapter.

Nussbaum claims that well-executed musical performances emotionally affect us immediately, in the manner of a friendly or loving touch that is unique to music and its beautiful sounds. He rejects formalism and advances a version of "weak" or moderate arousalism, granting that musical experience has cognitive components. On Nussbaum's view (which is very similar to that of the psychologist Nico Frijda), emotions involve tendencies toward action and are intentional but not necessarily propositional states with both mental and bodily components. In particular, Nussbaum claims that emotions are valent perceptions of objects, situations, events and such that relate to our survival (or core relational themes), involving arousal in some way as well as changes in action readiness. He also claims that music gives us affordances (in the sense of that term used by the psychologist James Gibson), i.e., possibilities for action. Making a claim that echoes Ridley's arousalism discussed above in section II.6, Nussbaum suggests that to experience emotions appropriate to a musical piece, i.e., emotions of which the work is really expressive, we must enact and adopt the plan of the work in imagination or simulation (or "off-line," as Nussbaum puts it), with the tendency for action being inhibited. Music, Nussbaum argues, regularly arouses real or "on-line" surprise and joy, and tends to cause appropriate behavior; all successful musical performances in fact arouse not just pleasurable sensations but the basic emotion of joy. Claiming that expression is (an) interpretable (sign) and thus a mode of representation, Nussbaum suggests in the spirit of the Jamesian theory of emotions that the expressive character of musical works is founded on listeners' mirroring, i.e., empathetic or simulating, responses. As for how music arouses emotions, Nussbaum claims that when we understand and accept a musical work, making its plan our own, this leads to a sense of oneness with the music, this identification in turn leading to arousal.

Having summed up the gist of what Nussbaum has to say about musical expressiveness and arousal, I turn now to criticisms. While Nussbaum's empirical approach is very welcome, and there is also a lot to agree with in his appeal to imagination and simulation as well as in his accounts of emotions and of musical touch and how music arouses emotions, it is not clear that his "weak" arousalism can escape the kind of philosophical and conceptual worries raised earlier for arousalism, especially in my discussion of Ridley in section II.6 above. First, Nussbaum's suggestion that to experience emotions appropriate to a musical work, i.e., emotions of which the work is really expressive, we must enact and adopt in simulation or imagination the plan of the work is a lot like some of Ridley's claims. And so, as with Ridley, one might wonder if this at best captures only *one* sort of experience of hearing musical expressiveness. Even if this kind of experience accounts for our recognizing and experiencing "from the inside" and in the fullest sense the emotions the work is expressive of, there are other sorts of experiences of musical expressiveness where one need not be aroused even in simulation or imagination (or "off-line"), for one can often hear music as expressive without real ("on-line") or imagined ("off-line") arousal just as we can often perceive actors as expressive or people in real life as expressive without being aroused. Second, as in Ridley's case, we must press Nussbaum further about his claims and ask *why* certain emotions are appropriate to a musical work; or, in other words, what it *means* to say that a musical work is expressive. The natural answer seems, as I will suggest in later chapters, that some emotions are appropriate to a musical work because it *is* sad, say; that is to say it is *imagined* to be sad but not really sad; or, in other words, the work is expressive in virtue of resembling in its gestures, development, and so on human vocal and behavioral expression of emotions as well as the affective feel of emotions. But if this is right, then it seems Nussbaum's position ultimately rests on or somehow leads us on to an imagination and resemblance-based view, such as mine. Third, and perhaps most importantly, one must question Nussbaum's suggestion that the expressive character of musical works is founded or somehow dependent upon our mirroring, i.e., empathetic, responses. This seems to reverse the order of things, for just as the performances of actors can be expressive even though the audience does not have an empathetic or mirroring response, and just as people in real life can express and be expressive of sadness, even though we do not feel empathy toward them, similarly it would seem music can be expressive and indeed be heard or perceived as such, as argued before, without our having a mirroring or empathetic response. Thus, against Nussbaum, mirroring responses cannot be the foundation or some sort of basis of the expressive character of musical works.

II.9. Conclusion

Here now is a summary of what has been done in this chapter. I have discussed and rejected two kinds of theories of musical expressiveness, the expression theory and arousalism. After presenting some concerns for the expression theory in general, I discussed in sections II.2 through II.4 three recent versions of this theory, as presented by Bruce Vermazen, Jerrold Levinson, and Jenefer Robinson, all of whom appeal to an indeterminate agent, a persona. I then turned to arousalism, and raised some concerns about simple arousalism in section II.5. Sections II.6 through II.8 then criticized three recent "moderate" versions of arousalism, as advanced by Aaron Ridley, Derek Matravers, and Charles Nussbaum.

In the next chapter, I examine metaphorism, very roughly described as the view that talk of musical expressiveness is only figurative. In the process of rejecting that position, I will briefly explore the nature of metaphors themselves in a way that will be used later in rebutting metaphorism.

III

Metaphors and Metaphorism

III.1. Introduction

Many passages and indeed entire works of instrumental music without words or an associated story or program are often heard and described, by many musicians as well as laypersons, as expressive of mental states such as emotions, moods, and feelings. Thus, it is not uncommon to come across musical passages or works being heard and described as sad, happy, anguished, serene, etc. Samuel Barber's *Adagio for Strings*, for example, is heard by many as expressive of grief or something in that neighborhood; which may be partly why it was played so much on the radio in the days after the assassination of President John F. Kennedy on November 22, 1963.

However, as something that itself neither possesses mental states nor indeed is alive, music cannot *literally* be sad or happy. And this has led some to suggest that music is instead only *metaphorically* sad or happy, the alleged figurativeness of musical expressiveness being further explained in terms of notions such as metaphorical exemplification or metaphorical transference or metaphorical hearing-as (Goodman 1976; Scruton 1997). In turn, many writers have extensively criticized various metaphor-based or metaphorist accounts of musical expressiveness (Budd 1985, chapter 2; Budd 1989; Davies 1994, chapter 3; Matravers 1998, chapter 6; Carroll 1999, chapter 2).

In this chapter, my main aim is to present *several* considerations against seeing musical expressiveness as metaphorical; thus, except in passing, I will try not to say too much about my own positive resemblance-plus-imagination or imaginationist view of musical expressiveness that I will discuss in later chapters (see also Trivedi 2001a; Trivedi 2003; Trivedi 2006). I also leave aside formalist, and resemblance-based approaches to musical expressiveness, both of which I will discuss in later chapters, indicating therein why I am not persuaded by these positions.

Here is a brief outline of this chapter. I begin in section III.2 by presenting some general considerations against metaphorism, claiming it is unclear what it means to say that music is *metaphorically* sad, as metaphorists claim. And I reject the metaphorist theory of Nelson Goodman, whose view is one of the two most prominent accounts of metaphorism; the other being that of Roger Scruton. I then argue in section III.3 that metaphors have *both* a literal and a metaphorical meaning, rejecting Donald Davidson's view that metaphors only have a literal meaning that is usually false and do not have a metaphorical meaning (Davidson 1984); and I argue that metaphors must be paraphraseable. In section III.4, I then offer *several* considerations against metaphorism, drawing on the conclusions of section III.3, to wit, that metaphors have paraphraseable metaphorical meanings. Amongst other things, I argue that it is not clear, contra metaphorists, that locutions such as "The music is sad" are metaphorical *to begin with*, for attempted paraphrases of this alleged metaphor fail to capture and explain its emotional content adequately without loss of meaning. In section III.5, I switch gears in my argument against metaphorism. Assuming *only for argument's sake* that metaphorists keep insisting, *despite* the arguments presented earlier, that "The music is sad" is figurative, how does one proceed further? Rather than take the notion of metaphor for granted as metaphorists usually do, I suggest one must dig deeper into the very nature of metaphors. Briefly exploring the nature of metaphors, then, my *hunch* is that metaphors, as used in ordinary language, involve resemblance plus imagination at the very least; and they may also involve a lot more, which I leave to be explored on other occasions, since I do not offer anything like a complete theory of metaphors, something which in any case is beyond the scope of a study focused primarily on musical expressiveness. I also briefly and critically survey *some* central theories about metaphors, some of which also appeal to resemblance or imagination or both. In section III.6, I then use the conclusions of section III.3 (that metaphors have paraphraseable metaphorical meanings) and section III.5 (that metaphors involve resemblance-plus-imagination at least) to present more arguments against metaphorism, especially the metaphorism of Scruton. I argue that *even if one grants only for argument's sake* that "The music is sad" is a metaphor, a further analysis and explanation of this alleged metaphor via paraphrase shows that metaphorist views of musical expressiveness lead on to resemblance-plus-imagination views of musical expressiveness such as mine, which may thus underlie metaphorist views and be more basic. For if metaphors themselves involve resemblance-plus-imagination, as suggested in section III.5, and if they have a metaphorical meaning that is paraphraseable, as suggested in section III.3, then *even if one grants only for argument's sake* that "The music is sad" is a metaphor, when you paraphrase the metaphorical meaning of that alleged metaphor then that alleged metaphor itself involves resemblance and imagination and leads onto a resemblance-plus-imagination view of musical expressiveness as being more fundamental and underlying, and in a way that eliminates the alleged metaphor, contra Scruton's claim that metaphors are indispensable here.[1] I also present other grounds for disagreeing with Scruton, and conclude by explaining why, appearances notwithstanding, I am not a metaphorist.

III.2. Against Metaphorism (Part 1)

Here is a worry for metaphorist views in general. These views all seem to replace the mystery of musical expressiveness with another mystery, that of how music is or can be said to be *metaphorically* sad or happy or expressive of other mental states. They all need to explain, perhaps via an adequate paraphrase, what exactly it *means* to say that talk of musical expressiveness is only metaphorical, no matter whether one appeals further to metaphorical exemplification or metaphorical transference or metaphorical hearing-as or any other notion that essentially involves metaphors. How does one cash out or explain such allegedly metaphorical descriptions as "The music is sad," given that metaphorists generally take the notion of metaphor for granted and do not offer theories of metaphors? What does it *mean* to use the word "sad" with its ordinary meaning (rather than a special, metaphorical meaning that would need to be clarified anyway) to apply *metaphorically* to music, as Roger Scruton suggests, where it does not literally apply? The allegedly metaphorical use of the word "sad" here must connect somehow to the ordinary use of "sad"; and while metaphorist views in general fail to make this connection clear, I will argue later that the connection involves resemblance-plus-imagination, and leads to resemblance-plus-imagination views of musical expressiveness, such as mine, as being underlying and more basic.

Perhaps metaphorists (such as Goodman and Scruton) think in general that talk of musical expressiveness and musical possession of sadness, etc., is metaphorical because of the huge influence of the linguistic turn in philosophy on twentieth-century analytic philosophers, which makes them focus on linguistic entities and descriptions. Relatedly and more importantly, perhaps they think music can only possess sadness metaphorically because, as something without life or mental states, it cannot possess sadness literally, and there can be no third option here. However, contra both literalists and metaphorists, I submit there *is* a third option here: music can be and is *imagined* in not always highly foregrounded ways to possess sadness, as I will argue later. Against metaphorists, it is *experiences* of musical expressiveness rather than linguistic descriptions of them that are primary; and rather than the descriptions being metaphorical, as metaphorists being heavily influenced by the linguistic turn in philosophy claim, what is true, I think, is that experiences of musical expressiveness involve imagination. Put differently, if you do *not* see the problem of musical expressiveness in terms of linguistic descriptions, as metaphorists heavily influenced by the linguistic turn do, but instead focus on experiences of musical expressiveness, then listeners imaginatively hearing music as sad makes perfect sense. Thus, one can reject the false claim that music possesses sadness literally, and one can also reject the metaphorist's unexplicated and mysterious claim that music metaphorically possesses sadness.

A brief word now as to why I am not persuaded by Nelson Goodman's view of expression or expressiveness as metaphorical exemplification (compare Kulvicki 2008). Applying this idea to locutions such as "The music is sad" or "The music is expressive of sadness," we get from Goodman that these amount to saying "The music metaphorically exemplifies sadness." But now the very notion of metaphorical exemplification, as used in this context, cries out for greater explication. Goodman tells us that exemplification is possession plus reference. It seems to follow that "The music metaphorically exemplifies sadness" amounts to (i) "The music metaphorically possesses sadness," plus (ii) "The music metaphorically refers to sadness."

Neither (i) nor (ii) gets Goodman very far. As regards (i), while it is clear that music cannot literally possess sadness, given that it is insentient and inanimate, what does it mean to say that music *metaphorically* possesses sadness? Absent a clear answer to this question, it seems Goodman has replaced the mystery of musical expressiveness with another mystery, that of the metaphorical possession of sadness, which itself seems to be another metaphor that cries out to be cashed out, perhaps through a paraphrase.

As for (ii), one must ask what *metaphorical* reference amounts to and whether Goodman has not here given us another mysterious metaphor that needs further elucidation. Moreover, music does not for the most part literally *refer* to things outside itself the way words or gestures refer to things.

Thus it seems usually false to say that music literally refers to expressiveness or to emotions, moods, and feelings such as sadness, and it seems mysterious to say music metaphorically refers to these things. Against Goodman, instead of referring to these things, music is better and indeed usually described as being *expressive* of sadness and other such mental states. Music is *imagined* to be expressive, as I will argue later, and it seems at worst false and at best mysterious for Goodman to say that music metaphorically refers to sadness and other such mental states.

III.3. Metaphorical Meaning and Paraphraseability

Let us now consider the issue of metaphors and paraphraseability. Here we must first discuss the related issue of whether metaphors taken as a whole only have a literal meaning (one that is usually false, except for some metaphors such as "No man is an island," where the literal meaning is trivially true), as claimed by Davidson, or whether they also have a metaphorical meaning in addition.

But first a word about the relevance of metaphorical meaning and paraphraseability to what follows. Amongst other things, I argue that if metaphors have a metaphorical meaning that is paraphraseable, when we try to paraphrase the metaphorical meaning of alleged metaphors such as "The music is sad" we either end up in doubts about whether such locutions are metaphorical in the first place, as I argue in section III.4, or else in resemblance-plus-imagination views of musical expressiveness such as mine, which may underlie metaphorist views and thus be more basic, as I argue in section III.6.

Now Davidson is right, I think, if he means that the *individual words* that constitute a metaphor do not have a special, metaphorical meaning but rather are used in their ordinary sense and in an imaginative way that points to similarities; and perhaps Davidson does mean this because he thinks that the individual words that form metaphors do not, contra Beardsley (1962), acquire special metaphorical meanings. For instance, in the metaphor "the spiteful sun," the word "spiteful" does not, contra Beardsley, acquire a special, metaphorical meaning that it does not have in nonfigurative contexts. Beardsley suggests that there is a semantic opposition or tension within this metaphor, which forces a twist of meaning so that the word "spiteful" gets a new meaning that it may not have in other contexts. But one must wonder against Beardsley here if instead the word "spiteful" is not used in its ordinary sense though in an imaginative and imagination-involving way that points to some resemblance between the sun and spiteful people. Thus, the metaphor has a metaphorical meaning that can be paraphrased as saying roughly that the extremely hot sun is discomforting and harmful just as spiteful people are, and in virtue of this resemblance we are asked to and can *imagine* the sun is deliberately so and spiteful, i.e., filled with malice and ill-will, just as spiteful people are. Besides, Beardsley needs to explain what new meaning the word "spiteful" has in this context, as he claims.

However, I disagree with Davidson if he means the metaphorical utterance *as a whole* does not also have a metaphorical meaning in addition to its literal meaning. The problem for Davidson is that he cannot allow that someone might grasp the literal meaning of a metaphor and yet not get the point of the metaphor, i.e., its metaphorical meaning (compare Moran 1987; Levinson 2001). For on Davidson's view, there is no such thing as metaphorical meaning that one can fail to grasp until that is revealed to one by correct paraphrase.

Consider as an example the famous metaphor "Architecture is frozen music" (which is sometimes attributed to Schelling, sometimes to Goethe, and sometimes to Schiller). Suppose a non-native speaker or a Venusian understands the literal meaning of this metaphor and takes it to mean that when you take the scores (whether manuscripts or printed, sheet music) of musical works and put them in deep freeze, the subsequent ice-patterns that form on paper are called "architecture." What is it that our non-native speaker and Venusian have failed to grasp? The natural and perhaps only answer is metaphorical meaning. For if it is a kind of meaning that they have failed to grasp it must be metaphorical meaning, not literal meaning which they seem to have grasped. In contrast, someone who understands the metaphor correctly grasps its metaphorical meaning, which is the object of her understanding. It may be hard but it is not impossible to capture the metaphorical meaning of this metaphor through paraphrase; which illustrates that some metaphors may be open-ended in that there may be no predetermined limit to their content and thus more to paraphrase or clarify than even the best paraphrase offered, which may go a long way anyway, and the paraphrase need not be a simple expression but can be a complex phrase or string. Here is my best paraphrase: architecture is like music in that both art forms are architectonic where form or structure matters essentially, but whereas musical structure unfolds over time when a musical work is experienced, music being a temporal art, the structure of architectural works themselves is static, not dynamic, and does not *itself* unfold over time in our experience of them (even if *we* experience it bit-by-bit over time and do not usually take it all in at once), and due to these similarities and differences we can imagine architecture to be music that is "frozen" in time, as it were. There may be more to paraphrase here, but something like this metaphorical meaning as given by the paraphrase above is, I suggest, the object of the understanding for those who grasp the point of this metaphor.

So far, I have raised one worry for Davidson's view that metaphors only have a literal meaning not a metaphorical meaning, a concern about *meaning* that the view that metaphors only have a literal meaning cannot explain adequately what it is that is understood or not understood when a metaphor is understood or otherwise. The point or metaphorical meaning of a metaphor can be grasped as expressed, without loss of meaning, by an adequate paraphrase. In particular, it is through an adequate paraphrase that conveys metaphorical meaning that one can explain the point of a metaphor to someone who has not grasped it.

To be sure, Davidson might claim here in response that grasping the point of the metaphor is an achievement, a kind of know-how or an appropriate response, without allowing that there is such a thing as metaphorical meaning. But the question that arises for Davidson is this: what is it that one grasps when one grasps the point of a metaphor, if not metaphorical meaning? It is not literal meaning, as the example above "Architecture is frozen music" shows, so what is the *object* of one's understanding if not metaphorical meaning? And what do metaphors convey if not metaphorical meaning? It is not clear Davidson has easy answers here.

Here is a second worry for Davidson's view, this time a concern about *truth*. Consider as an example the metaphorical expression "He is drowning in sorrow," said of someone who is extremely sad. One possible literal meaning of this, an obviously false one, is that he is sinking in a large body of liquid called "sorrow." Someone who does not know English too well might grasp this literal meaning of the metaphor, and yet not have grasped the point of the metaphor. The point of this metaphor is its metaphorical meaning given by the paraphrase that he is extremely sad, so very sad that his sadness can be imagined to be like a deep ocean that he is immersed in and unable to come out of, as if he were drowning in an ocean. Now while the literal meaning of this metaphor is obviously false, one must wonder *what* it is about the metaphor that is true, what the vehicle or bearer of its truth-value is, given that it is said truly of someone who is extremely sad. The natural and perhaps only answer seems to be that it is the *proposition* that expresses the metaphorical meaning or content that is true, and it is not clear in contrast that Davidson's position has an easy answer here, given his denial of metaphorical meaning. The problem seems especially acute because Davidson does allow for metaphorical truth, even though it is not clear what metaphorical truth would attach to in his view. Of course, Davidson might reply that the metaphor as a whole is true without allowing for such a thing as metaphorical meaning. But then the problem for Davidson is that it is not clear what *makes* the metaphor as a whole true, if not the metaphorical meaning or content of the metaphor (and its fit or correspondence with the world).

So much for Davidson. In passing, it should be noted here that metaphorical meaning and interpretation are dependent on literal meaning. And, it may be impossible to grasp metaphorical meaning unless one first grasps the literal meaning of a metaphor.

Let us turn now to the issue of metaphors and paraphraseability, where *note that by "paraphrase" I only mean clarifying statements*. Now, that some metaphors may be hard to paraphrase fully in a way that commands universal assent does not show that it is in principle impossible to paraphrase or otherwise clarify them. The burden of proof is on those such as Max Black who claim that metaphors need not be paraphraseable to produce an example of a metaphor that allegedly cannot be paraphrased, which those in my camp would then try their best to paraphrase (see Black 1955/2004; Cohen 2003, 72 ff). As far as I know, Black's camp has provided no such example, at least not so far. Absent such an example, I urge that metaphors must be paraphraseable if we are to be able to explain their cognitive content to those unfamiliar with them or unable to grasp their cognitive content. Otherwise, it is not clear how we would explain metaphors to those who do not understand them, and our linguistic communication would break down at least when it comes to some metaphors.

I grant, however, that there is a difference in *effect* and structure—especially communicative and rhetorical effect, and grammatical structure—between a metaphor such as "Architecture is frozen music" and its paraphrase. Such differences may account for why it is felt by some that *something* is lost in paraphrase: the information expressed by a metaphor is conveyed by its "metaphorical mode of expression," as Josef Stern puts it, which mode of presentation is not carried over in paraphrases (Stern 2000). But it is not clear that these differences in effect, structure, or mode of presentation must amount to a difference in *cognitive* content or informativeness between metaphors and their paraphrases, which is what needs to be shown by those who think metaphors can be unparaphraseable. It is also granted that it may be often hard to say via paraphrase what "exactly" metaphors in literature and poetry amount to. But the case of metaphors in ordinary language need not be the same, for the two kinds of metaphors need not be sufficiently similar. And it is alleged metaphors in ordinary language such as "The music is sad" that I am concerned with in this chapter.

III.4. Against Metaphorism (Part 2)

I now present another set of considerations against metaphorism. Let us assume, *only for argument's sake*, that "The music is sad" is indeed a metaphor. Now, how might one explain this metaphor, especially its *emotional content* or the emotion-terms involved in it? How might one explain what it *means* to say that music is only *metaphorically* sad in a way that connects the ordinary use and meaning of "sad" with its allegedly metaphorical application (or transference) to music, given that "sad" cannot literally apply to music, which is inanimate and insentient?

It seems the only way to explain metaphorical meaning here would be via paraphrase, assuming metaphors have paraphraseable metaphorical meanings, as argued in section III.3 above. And there would seem to be only three candidates for paraphrase here: (i) in the layperson's nontechnical terms so that to say "The music is sad" is to say "The music is slow in tempo, soft in volume, low in pitch, and so on"; (ii) in the technical terms of musical analysis so that to say "The music is sad" is to say that "The music is in a minor key, uses diminished chords, and so on"; and (iii) in terms of a combination of (i) and (ii) so that to say "The music is sad" is to say "The music is slow in tempo, in a minor key, soft in volume, low in pitch, uses diminished chords, and so on." None of these three possible paraphrases adequately captures the *emotional* content of the alleged metaphor "The music is sad" *without* loss of meaning. In fact, instead of explaining musical sadness in emotion-terms, all three paraphrases use *non-emotional* terms, whether technical, or nontechnical, or both. The failure of these three paraphrases to explain how "sad" applies only metaphorically to music in the sense in which we use that word ordinarily leads to doubts, contra metaphorism, about whether descriptions such as "The music is sad" are metaphorical *in the first place*. Of course, the metaphorist could offer an alternative fourth (or fifth, and so on) paraphrase that adequately explains the emotional content of "The music is sad" in satisfactory emotion-terms. But so far at least, no such fourth paraphrase has been offered by metaphorists, and thus one must doubt whether locutions such as "The music is sad," "The music is happy," etc., are figurative, irrespective of whether one appeals further to metaphorical exemplification or metaphorical transference or metaphorical hearing-as or some such notion that essentially involves metaphors. In fact, it is not clear *that* there can be a fourth paraphrase here in addition to the three offered, for by the Law of Excluded Middle, technical and nontechnical paraphrases (plus their combination) seem to exhaust the logical space available here.

Second, against the three paraphrases suggested above, it is *conceivable* that a musical passage or piece might be sad without being slow or low or in a minor key, and so on; for example, some *ragas* of Indian classical music are expressive of sadness when performed in high registers even though they are not in a minor key. And, it is conceivable that a musical passage or piece might be slow or low or in a minor key, and so on, without being sad: e.g., the theme in the rondo of Beethoven's "Pathetique" Sonata, Op. 13, is in a minor key and yet the music is expressive not of sadness but of a childlike playfulness (compare Budd 1989; Davies 1994). Third and relatedly, all of the three candidates above for paraphrase might be thought of as giving us only a *causal story* at best of what, intentionally or otherwise, makes or causes some music to be, and be heard as, sad. They do not, however, tell us what it *means*, in an allegedly metaphorical sense, for music to be sad, which is what we want to know from an adequate paraphrase of this alleged metaphor. For it is possible that someone (a super-intelligent robot or extraterrestrial, say) might grasp that a musical passage or piece is slow, low, in a minor key and so on, and yet not grasp what it is for the music to be *metaphorically* sad (or even what it is for it to be sad). Someone in this situation would thus grasp what *makes* the music sad, without knowing what it is for it to be *metaphorically* sad, for it remains to be clarified in what sense musical expressiveness and talk of it is metaphorical (compare Levinson 1996). Fourth, while (exceptions apart) we generally use metaphors deliberately, knowing fully and consciously that they are usually false when taken literally, in sharp contrast it is not clear that in hearing music and describing it in expressive terms we do so deliberately, knowing consciously that the emotion-terms we are applying to music are literally false (compare Boghossian 2002). Rather, I suggest that hearing music as expressive is often almost automatic; we often animate the music, amongst other things, and *imagine* willy-nilly, readily, and immediately that it is sad or happy etc., without realizing necessarily at the time that this is what we are doing, a claim I will return to in later chapters. This contrast suggests, contra metaphorism, that metaphors may not be involved when we hear emotions in music and describe it as expressive. Fifth and finally, it seems that experiences of musical sadness and those of musical expressiveness in general are *much* stronger, phenomenologically speaking, than metaphorism suggests. If I am right, then in hearing music as sad we imagine in various not always highly conscious ways that the music is sad so that it is often felt *as if* the music itself is sad, as if the sadness is in the music *itself,* as if the sadness is an *imagined* property of the music itself, rather than being something that the music only has in a thin, metaphorical sense, whatever that obscure notion ultimately amounts to.

III.5. Metaphors, Resemblance, and Imagination

I believe the considerations of sections III.2 and III.4 above are decisive against metaphorism. However, metaphorists may not buy these considerations, for whatever reason, and may insist *despite* these considerations that "The music is sad" is a metaphor. Does that lead us to an impasse? Not necessarily, for I believe one can open up a new front against metaphorism. To proceed further, rather than take metaphors for granted as metaphorists usually do, in this section let us first dig further into the very nature of metaphors; for we have not yet reached bedrock, as Wittgenstein would have said. And then let us see what follows *even if one grants only for argument's sake* that "The music is sad" is a metaphor. (Accordingly, in section III.6, I will draw on the conclusions of section III.3—that metaphors have paraphraseable metaphorical meanings—and of section III.5, and assuming *only for the sake of argument* that "The music is sad" is a metaphor, I will enquire further into what this alleged metaphor involves, arguing ultimately that it reveals an underlying view of musical expressiveness that is more basic than metaphorism.)

So, what are metaphors? It is doubtful this question can be answered in terms of a single, unified theory that applies to poetic as well as more prosaic metaphors. For it is not clear that metaphors in their everyday, ordinary language use are sufficiently similar to metaphors in poetry and literature to allow for a single description of all kinds of metaphors (compare Cohen 2003, 366–67; Levin 1993, 112–13). Accordingly, I leave literary and poetic metaphors aside in what follows, and focus on the everyday use of metaphors in ordinary language. This narrower focus suffices for my main purpose here, which is to reject views that claim that everyday, ordinary language ascriptions of musical expressiveness such as "The music is sad" and "The music is happy" are only figurative.

Though I do not have anything even remotely like a complete theory of metaphors, my *hunch* is that metaphors are used to point to or suggest (without necessarily asserting, as similes do) previously unnoticed and unexpected resemblances, or indeed lack thereof (often via denying class membership or identity, as in the case of metaphors such as "Life is not a bed of roses," "No man is an island," "You, Dan Quayle, are no Jack Kennedy," and so on), between two (or more) things in an imaginative way that involves the imagination both of those who coin and first use a given metaphor as well as the reader or hearer. Our faculty of reason is asked and prescribed through the use of metaphors to imaginatively compare, see, and understand one thing at least partially as or in terms of another, or in some cases as not being another or not in terms of another; though the imagining need not be conscious or even actual, and it is sufficient to be aware that we are being asked to imagine something by the use of a metaphor.[2] As Lakoff and Johnson memorably put it, metaphors unite reason and imagination and are thus imaginative rationality; though I would urge against them that metaphors are *primarily* a matter of words, even if they are right that concepts too can be metaphorical and we often think metaphorically. I sympathize with Kendall Walton's view that metaphors in context imply or suggest or introduce or call to mind possible games of make-believe (Walton 1993/2004), though I would *broaden* talk of make-believe to talk instead of imagination, for make-believing or pretending to oneself is only one kind of imagining and metaphors may also involve *other* kinds of imaginings such as fancying, or supposing, or entertaining a possibility or a proposition without actually believing or affirming it, and so on. I disagree with the "emotivist" position that metaphors are merely expressions of emotion without cognitive content, and I also disagree with the "decoration theorist" view that metaphors are merely ornamental pretty prose for what can be stated plainly, and claim instead that metaphors may serve *unique* communicative and rhetorical purposes. Because metaphors usually have a different communicative, rhetorical, and grammatical effect from their literal paraphrases or equivalents, they can be and often are used to point to things not seen yet and helping others see them in colorful, attractive, striking, and memorable ways. As a result, I am inclined to think that metaphors have both a cognitive content as well as an emotive significance, which often manifests itself in the surprise many hearers and readers feel on first encountering some metaphors. I fully grant there may be more to metaphors than resemblance and imagination and leave it to other occasions where these additional elements may be explored. For my purpose of arguing in this chapter against metaphorist views of musical expressiveness, I do not need to provide a complete theory of metaphors.

My hunch about metaphors is quite similar to the view of Samuel Levin. On Levin's view, we project ourselves into metaphoric worlds so if we read in a poem "the sky is angry," we conceive of a world where the sky is angry. I would add to Levin's view and stress the essential role of imagination in metaphors, claiming that the metaphoric worlds Levin talks of are imagined and the projection into them involves imagination. I also agree with Andrew Ortony's claim that there is similarity involved in metaphors because the terms involved share attributes (Ortony 1993, 342). And I also agree with Ortony that comparisons are of fundamental importance in understanding metaphors, though metaphors are not to be identified with similes, nor to be reduced to these. Ortony is also right, I think, to claim that metaphors stretch language, and I would suggest they do so in pointing to previously unnoticed similarities and asking us to imagine certain things.

I am in broad agreement also with Josef Stern's claims that metaphors are context-dependent (Stern 2000). Stern claims, rightly I think, that metaphorical interpretation is governed by rules and is more regular and predictable than some such as Davidson suggest when they claim that understanding and creating metaphors is not guided much by rules. I would claim that while imagination plays *a* role in creating and interpreting a metaphor, there are rules and constraints involved in creating and interpreting metaphors (rules that may well involve resemblance), just as there are often rules and constraints involved in other imagination-involving activities such as creating and experiencing artworks. Not just anything goes when it comes to metaphors. To my mind, Stern is right to claim that there is often substantial intersubjective agreement about the classification of utterances as metaphorical rather than literal, and also over the paraphrases of metaphors, which shows that metaphors are not entirely unpredictable and idiosyncratic. Most importantly, I think Stern is right to claim that context determines the interpretation of metaphors when he claims: same expression, same context, same interpretation; but same expression, different context, different interpretation. To use Stern's example, when Romeo says in the context of Shakespeare's play "Juliet is the sun," the utterance means something like he cannot live without her, that she is exemplary and peerless, worthy of worship and adoration, and so on. But when Paris utters "Juliet is the sun" in a context where Paris thinks she is the kind of woman who destroys admirers who try to get too close to her, the utterance might be used to warn Romeo not to get involved with Juliet. A somewhat different view from Stern's is that of Christopher New, who claims that the utterer's intention determines whether a sentence produces a metaphor (New 1999). Against this, I urge that the utterer's intention often only determines if a sentence is *intended* by the utterer to be taken literally or metaphorically, and as the utterer's intentions like other kinds of intentions can fail and as a metaphor can mean more than just what its utterer intends, the utterer's intentions are not *necessary* to determine if a sentence or an expression produces a metaphor, which the larger *context* of utterance determines instead. As an example, consider the utterance of "No man is an island" by someone who *only* intends it literally and fails. Nor, against New, is the utterer's intention *sufficient* by itself to make an utterance metaphorical; as an example, consider someone uttering "New York is part of the U.S.," intending it be taken as a metaphor, which it clearly is not. The utterer's intentions may often only determine that his or her meaning is not necessarily *utterance* meaning, which is what we seek here, as opposed to both utterer's meaning as well as word-sequence or literal meaning.[3]

I now briefly survey *some* of the central theories about metaphors, some of which also appeal to resemblance or imagination or both (compare Hagberg 2001). On the analogy theory often said to derive from Aristotle, metaphors involve an analogy and a transfer of name, whereby we give one thing a name that belongs to another thing. I sympathize with the appeal to analogy or resemblance in this position, though I would suggest that, at the very least, one must add imagination to this view, for metaphors point to resemblances through an imaginative use of words and in a way that involves the imagination both of those who first coin the metaphor in question as well as the speaker, hearer, and reader. Amongst other things, what makes me wary of construing metaphors *only* in terms of resemblance is the fact that while resemblance is usually thought to be symmetrical, many metaphors are asymmetrical and irreversible; for example, "Man is a wolf" makes a different point than its ordinary language reversal "A wolf is man," if this latter has a point at all.

A second position, the elliptical simile theory, sees metaphors as elliptical or condensed similes, whereby a comparison is elliptically implied by metaphors, even if not explicit, thus asserting the same thing as a simile. One problem with this view, however, is that it is not clear how a metaphor can make the very same assertion as its corresponding simile. For to say A *is* B seems to be different, in general, from saying A is *like* B. A second problem for this view is that metaphors seem to involve a *greater* appeal to imagination than do similes, as we are asked and prescribed to imagine not just that A is like B but rather imagine something more, to wit, that A *is* B due to some resemblances between them. For example, the metaphor "Man is a wolf" differs from its corresponding simile "Man is like a wolf." While the simile explicitly points to similarities between men and wolves and asks our imaginations to figure out the relevant respects of similarity, the metaphor implicitly does the same but in addition, I suggest, it asks and prescribes us to *imagine*, in virtue of the resemblances between men and wolves, that man *is* a wolf and is not merely *like* a wolf. In the case of "Man is a wolf," in virtue of various similarities (of which there may be many), we are asked to imagine identity or class membership at least, while in the case of "Man is like a wolf," the imagination is only asked to figure out the relevant respects of similarity (of which there may not be very many), but we are not asked to imagine class membership or identity.

A third view, the comparison theory, sees metaphors as conceptually comparing a primary subject to a secondary subject, so that we are asked to imaginatively compare various similarities between two (or more) things as suggested by the words that constitute the metaphor and the context in which they are spoken or written. To refer to an example used earlier and two different paraphrases given to it by Garry Hagberg, the metaphorical expression "Juliet is the sun" is fixed by the words and the context to mean something closer to "Juliet is necessary for life itself for Romeo" than to "Juliet is a fiery ball of burning gas." As may be obvious from what I have briefly indicated above, I have some sympathies for this position too, and think it is not too far from the resemblance-plus-imagination view of metaphors that I have a hunch about. Indeed, it has been suggested that this comparison theory is one species of the analogy or resemblance view discussed above that is said to derive from Aristotle.[4] It is sometimes objected against this comparison theory that it assumes that the objects being compared exist, which need not be the case, e.g., the metaphor "Sally is a dragon" (Searle 1993). In response, the existence of the objects being compared need not be real but could only be *imagined*. So, in the example here, dragons can be imagined to exist, and Sally can be imagined to be like them in being ferocious, and indeed we can thus imagine that she is a dragon; alternatively, one can just imagine Sally as a dragon without necessarily imagining first that dragons exist. And imagining existence can take various forms, e.g., imagining Hamlet exists in the sense of entertaining this possibility without actually believing it.

A fourth stance is Max Black's who claims that metaphors are not reducible to literal paraphrase and is critical of the three views mentioned so far (Black 1955/2004; 1993). Black suggests that metaphors create insightful similarities through conjoining terms in a new way, and these similarities are not preexistent. Black is right, I think, to claim that metaphors cannot be reduced to literal paraphrase. However, I disagree with Black's and also Lakoff and Johnson's claim (2003) that metaphors create similarities, and submit instead that the similarities, which are usually between *properties* of things, to which metaphors point may often preexist, and just have not been noticed or remarked on until they are indicated to us by metaphors in an imaginative and imagination-involving way. For example, the similarities in property between argument and war pointed to by the metaphor "Argument is war" were, I submit, already there before someone noticed them and pointed to them: both arguing and war involve two (or more) opponents; both can involve winning and losing; both involve attack, defense, strategy, and tactics; and so on. Call this a *moderately* realist view of the similarities involved in metaphors insofar as the similarities involved predate metaphors so long as these similarities are *in principle* recogniz*able* even if not actually recognized at a given point in time; such a position differs from a strong or extreme realist view of the similarities involved in metaphors, according to which the similarities involved in metaphors are *totally* independent of human experience, recognition, and recognizability. In virtue of these similarities that make argument to be like war, we are asked to *imagine* that argument *is* war.

Black calls his own positive stance the interaction theory of metaphor. On this view, the use of metaphors involves two thoughts of different things that are active together due to a word or phrase, and these thoughts interact to produce the meaning of the metaphor. The question that arises for Black's view, however, is whether these thoughts are not "active together" and "interacting" because hearers and readers of metaphors *compare* them when they think about metaphors. Take Black's example, "The poor are the Negroes of Europe." I take it the two thoughts involved here feature the poor of Europe, on the one hand, and the Negroes (in America) on the other hand. If these two thoughts are brought together and interact, it must be because our minds compare them and think that the poor in Europe are like Negroes (in America) in that both groups are disadvantaged, and that in virtue of this resemblance we can imagine that the poor of Europe just are the Negroes of Europe. What else could do this job of making these two thoughts interact? How else could thoughts be "active together" and "interact," without the intervention of the human mind? If Black has no easy answer here, as seems to be the case, then Black's own interaction view might itself ultimately rest on and involve something like the comparison view, a view he tries to deny, even if it is arguably not reducible to the comparison view. Elsewhere, Black follows I. A. Richards's claim that the reader is forced to "connect" the two ideas involved in metaphors. But once again, one must ask Black how readers or hearers connect the two ideas involved in metaphors except through comparison, given their juxtaposition, and so it would seem yet again that we are back to the comparison view. Besides, Black's talk of interaction is itself metaphorical and needs to be explained further, and one must wonder if it is not preferable to talk instead in terms of readers and hearers imagining certain things once some resemblances or lack thereof have been noticed due to metaphors.

III.6. Against Metaphorism (Part 3)

Let us now consider the metaphorism of Roger Scruton, and here I will draw on the claims of sections III.3 and III.5 above and argue against Scruton that *even if one grants only for argument's sake* that "The music is sad" is a metaphor, that alleged metaphor can be *eliminated* via paraphrase, contra Scruton, in a way that shows there is a view of musical expressiveness that underlies metaphorism and is more basic.

There is a fair bit in Scruton's theory that is in sync with my own resemblance-plus-imagination or imaginationist position *on musical expressiveness*, which I have not yet stated (though I stated my similar hunch *about metaphors* in section III.5) and now state, very roughly, as follows: musical passages and works are only *imagined* in various not always highly foregrounded or conscious ways to be sad or happy or expressive of other mental states, in virtue of being perceived to *resemble* various things to do with emotions, moods, feelings, and other mental states such as their vocal and behavioral expression as well as their affective feel.[5] In particular, I agree with Scruton that in hearing sounds, including musical sounds, we attend to them in a way that involves imaginative perceptions. I am also sympathetic to Scruton's claim that we hear life and movement in (musical) sounds and situate them in an imagined space, though I would put the point in terms of our animating musical sounds, imaginatively endowing them with and projecting onto them life and life-like properties in not always highly conscious ways; and also imagining life and movement in music in other ways, such as imagining that the music is expressive of our own mental states, or imaginatively identifying with the music, or imagining an indeterminate musical persona in the music, and so on. And I agree with Scruton that we irresistibly see expression where there is none, extending this habit to fish, plants, clouds, trees, landscapes, and the rest of nature, as well as to musical expression, though I would put the point in terms of our animating nature and music.

However, I disagree with Scruton when he claims that metaphors are indispensable in some contexts because we are trying to describe how the world seems from the active imagination's point of view. Against this, I submit that we can paraphrase metaphors in a way that involves the imagination, thus showing that metaphors can be dispensable. Scruton also claims that a complex system of metaphor lies in our most basic apprehension of music so that metaphor is ineliminable from descriptions of music; if you take the metaphor away, you cease to describe the experience of music. Against this, I submit that metaphors can be *eliminated* via paraphrase, as below, in a way that shows there may be a view of musical expressiveness that underlies metaphorism and is more basic, and also captures how listening to music and hearing it as expressive essentially involves the imagination.[6]

For argument's sake and *only for argument's sake*, let us grant Scruton and other metaphorists that "The music is sad" is a metaphor. Now the question is what this alleged metaphor *means*, and how the use of "sad" in it connects to our ordinary use of "sad." In other words, one seeks to know what it *means* to use the word "sad" with its ordinary meaning to apply metaphorically to music, as Scruton claims, and how one would explain this alleged metaphor to someone who does not know what it means to say that music is *metaphorically* sad or expressive of sadness.

If metaphors have paraphraseable metaphorical meanings, as suggested in section III.3 above, and if they involve resemblance plus imagination at least, as suggested in section III.5, then here is a natural candidate for paraphrase of this alleged metaphor that attempts to explain it and also how it connects to our ordinary use of "sad." "The music is sad" means that the musical passage or work in question *resembles* in its timbre, slow tempo, soft volume, low pitches, etc.; how sad people (and other animals) typically express their sadness vocally and through gestures, bodily movement, behavior, etc. (e.g., when they cry or walk slowly or talk softly in a low-pitched voice or droop physically or hang their heads low etc.); or else the music resembles in its sounds (e.g., in how it attempts to resolve its tensions, attain intermediate and final goals, etc.) the affective component or feel of sadness and our mental life in general. In perceiving these resemblances we are asked and prescribed to *imagine* (in various not always highly conscious ways) that the music is sad, either by animating it itself, or imagining a musical persona in it, or in some other way. In brief, very roughly, the music resembles *something* (and there are various things here that "something" can refer to) to do with sadness and our ordinary use of "sad," in virtue of which we imagine (in various not always highly conscious ways) that the music is sad. The above paraphrase thus gives us something like a resemblance-plus-imagination view of musical expressiveness, such as mine, which I suspect may thus underlie metaphorism and be more basic; and I add that we may imagine the music sad in the sense of fancying or supposing that it is sad or entertaining the possibility that it is sad without actually believing this, and so on, and we willy-nilly imagine music as sad or happy, etc.

It would seem then that metaphorist views lead on to a more basic and underlying resemblance-plus-imagination view of musical expressiveness, such as mine, and in a way that *eliminates* alleged metaphors, Scruton notwithstanding. For *even if one grants only for argument's sake* that "The music is sad" is a metaphor, once we dig deeper into metaphors, we find there is perhaps no way to analyze and explain this alleged metaphor and how its use of "sad" connects to its ordinary use other than to paraphrase this metaphor as above, which reveals a resemblance-plus-imagination view of musical expressiveness as underlying metaphorism.

Alternatively, a metaphorist might talk of musical expressiveness involving a metaphorical transference of concepts, as Scruton claims sometimes. To this, one must ask what metaphorical transference *means*, and what allows and underlies the transfer of "sad," etcetera from their ordinary usage to apply metaphorically (as alleged) to music if not resemblance and imagination in the manner just suggested, in which case we seem to be back to something like a resemblance-plus-imagination view of musical expressiveness as being underlying and more basic.

I turn next to a crucial passage from Scruton (Scruton 1997, 154; see also Iseminger 1999; Levinson 2000; and Budd 2005), which he uses partly to motivate his *anti-realist*—a point I return to in section VI.2 in discussing Nick Zangwill—and non-cognitivist view of musical expressiveness: "If we say the [musical work] actually possesses the sadness we hear in it, we face the question whether this sadness is the same property as that possessed by a person or another property. It surely cannot be the *same* property: the sadness of persons is a property that only conscious organisms can possess. But it cannot be *another* property either, since it is precisely *this* word—'sad'—with its normal meaning that we apply to the music . . . To say that the word ascribes, in this use, another property is to say . . . that it is not used metaphorically but ambiguously . . . It follows that the word 'sad' attributes to the music . . . no property at all."

This passage nicely contrasts my *at best* "quasi-realist" view with Scruton's anti-realism, though note I am wary of *unquestioningly* importing the realism vs. anti-realism debate into this context from similar philosophical debates about reality, truth, moral judgments, scientific theories and unobservables, and the like. For it seems to make little sense to be a realist about musical expressiveness and claim falsely that sadness etc. are *real*, mind-independent properties of the music, which after all is inanimate and insentient, or claim falsely that music literally or really possesses expressive properties. I agree with Scruton against the realist that musical sadness is not the same property as that possessed by persons, for music is without life, consciousness, and mental states. But I submit against Scruton that the sadness is an *imagined*, nonmetaphorical (and unambiguous) property of the music, one it is only *imagined* to possess as listeners willy-nilly imaginatively, readily, and immediately project it in various not always highly conscious ways onto the music due to the various perceived resemblances, as spelled out above, between music and mental states such as sadness, happiness, etc. Note that the imagined sadness of music *cannot* be the same property as the real sadness of persons; for while the latter is dependent on neuron-firings and other neurophysiological properties of those who have it, in contrast the imagined sadness of music is not dependent in this way as music *itself* has no neurophysiological properties for its imagined sadness to be dependent on. This imagined musical sadness connects via various resemblances, as spelled out above, to sadness and the normal meaning of "sad," etcetera; and it is dependent on the music's structural features, gestures and the like, either in terms of supervenience or emergence or some such relation. If we imagine music as sad based on resemblances and musical sadness is not metaphorical, then what exactly is the property sadness that we imagine the music to have? In brief response, the imagined sadness of music is not a real property or feature of it, given music is inanimate and insentient, but is a feature or characteristic *imagined* variously of it by us (in terms of animation, or a musical persona, or imaginative identification, and so on)[7] somewhat in the way (and this is only a partial analogy, given that mirages involve perceptual illusions) that we imagine or suppose wateriness (or being watery) to be a feature of the desert when we experience a mirage, even though this is not a real property of the desert. Thus I suggest it would not be too far from the truth to say we are only "hearing things" or "imagining things" when we hear music as sad. Also, very briefly, my view is *at best* "quasi-realist" (compare Blackburn 1993) in that while I suppose no independent reality or real, mind-independent properties of musical sadness, happiness, etc., for judgments of musical expressiveness to be about, as a realist might hold; I also believe at the same time that judgments of musical expressiveness can be true or false and enter into inferential relations amongst each other, the truth-value of "The music is sad" being a function, very roughly, either of the consensus of competent (but fallible) listeners imaginatively, readily, and immediately hearing the music as sad, or of the music resembling something to do with sadness, or of some combination of consensus and resemblance. If one really must see debates about musical expressiveness in the old realist vs. anti-realist terms—and it is not clear that one must do so—then my position is neither realist nor anti-realist but rather the "quasi-realist" view in between.

It must be doubted then whether judgments of expressiveness such as "The music is sad" are metaphorical; we must thus set metaphorism aside and look at other theories of musical expressiveness. However, though the considerations especially of sections III.2 and III.4 should make clear that I am not a metaphorist, section III.6 may give the *appearance* that I am a metaphorist. So I now clarify briefly why I am not a metaphorist.

First, as a careful look at the considerations of section III.4 should show, unlike metaphorists, I deny "The music is sad" is a metaphor *to begin with*. Second, while metaphorists appeal essentially to metaphors and to further metaphorist notions such as metaphorical exemplification and metaphorical transference when talking about musical expressiveness, I do not do so; instead, my view of musical expressiveness appeals to resemblance and imagination as being basic and essential, something metaphorists do not do. Third, unlike metaphorists such as Scruton, I do not believe metaphors are ineliminable when it comes to musical expressiveness, and instead suggest they can be *eliminated* via adequate paraphrase as in section III.6. Fourth, metaphorists do not dig further into the very nature of metaphors and usually take them for granted, whereas I briefly explore the nature of metaphors in section III.5.

One final clarification, as it may seem the considerations of sections III.4 and III.6 are inconsistent. In response, I am *not* trying to have it both ways by holding on to both sets of considerations simultaneously. Rather, these two sets of considerations (both of which are incidentally in the *spirit* of reductio arguments, even if not formal reductios) have an *either-or* character, and are meant to *complement* each other: if one does not work, the other should, and vice versa. Either way, you have a problem for metaphorists: either "The music is sad" is not a metaphor, or eliminating the alleged metaphor via adequate paraphrase gives you an underlying view of musical expressiveness that is more fundamental than metaphorism. A careful look at section III.1 and especially the start of section III.5 should reveal in fact that I switch gears in section III.5, *only supposing* that metaphorists do not buy the considerations of sections III.2 and III.4 as I then proceed to open an *alternate* line of argument against metaphorism in the remainder of this chapter.

III.7. Conclusion

Let me now sum up what has been done in the different sections of this chapter. I began in section III.2 by presenting some general considerations against metaphorism, claiming it is unclear what it means to say that music is *metaphorically* sad, as metaphorists claim. And I rejected the metaphorist theory of Nelson Goodman. I then argued in section III.3 that metaphors have *both* a literal and a metaphorical meaning, rejecting Donald Davidson's view that metaphors only have a literal meaning that is usually false and do not have a metaphorical meaning (Davidson 1984); and I argued that metaphors must be paraphraseable. In section III.4, I offered *several* considerations against metaphorism, drawing on the conclusions of section III.3, to wit, that metaphors have paraphraseable metaphorical meanings. Amongst other things, I argued that it is not clear, contra metaphorists, that locutions such as "The music is sad" are metaphorical *to begin with*, for attempted paraphrases of this alleged metaphor fail to capture and explain its emotional content adequately without loss of meaning. In section III.5, I switched gears in my argument against metaphorism. Assuming *only for argument's sake* that metaphorists keep insisting, *despite* the arguments presented earlier, that "The music is sad" is figurative, how does one proceed further? Rather than take the notion of metaphor for granted as metaphorists usually do, I dug deeper into the very nature of metaphors. Briefly exploring the nature of metaphors, I suggested that metaphors, as used in ordinary language, involve resemblance-plus-imagination at the very least; and they may also involve a lot more, which I left to be explored elsewhere. I also briefly and critically surveyed *some* central theories about metaphors, some of which also appeal to resemblance or imagination or both. In section III.6, I used the conclusions of section III.3 (that metaphors have paraphraseable metaphorical meanings) and section III.5 (that metaphors involve resemblance-plus-imagination at least) to present more arguments against metaphorism, especially the metaphorism of Roger Scruton. I argued that *even if one grants only for argument's sake* that "The music is sad" is a metaphor, a further analysis and explanation of this alleged metaphor via paraphrase shows that metaphorist views of musical expressiveness collapse or otherwise lead on to resemblance-plus-imagination views of musical expressiveness such as mine, which may thus underlie metaphorist views and be more basic. For if metaphors themselves involve resemblance-plus-imagination, as suggested in section III.5, and if they have a metaphorical meaning that is paraphraseable, as suggested in section III.3, then *even if one grants only for argument's sake* that "The music is sad" is a metaphor, when you paraphrase the metaphorical meaning of that alleged metaphor then that alleged metaphor itself involves resemblance and imagination and leads onto a resemblance-plus-imagination view of musical expressiveness as being more fundamental and underlying, and in a way that eliminates the alleged metaphor, contra Scruton's claim that metaphors are indispensable here. I also presented other grounds for disagreeing with Scruton, and concluded by explaining why, appearances notwithstanding, I am not a metaphorist.

Readers should bear the anti-metaphorist arguments of this chapter in mind when reading my discussion of Nick Zangwill's Neo-Formalism later in section VI.2, given that Zangwill also appeals to metaphors. Note also that I myself regard metaphorism, as represented by such excellent philosophers as Nelson Goodman and Roger Scruton, as the most formidable alternative to the kind of imaginationism I start developing from the next chapter onward.

IV

Resemblance-Based Theories

IV.1. Introduction

Some philosophers have attempted to solve the problem of musical expressiveness by appealing to various perceived or experienced resemblances between music and the vocal, bodily, and behavioral expression of various mental states, as well as perceived resemblances between music and the affective feel of mental states. Peter Kivy, Stephen Davies, and Malcolm Budd are the most prominent advocates of such resemblance-based theories of musical expressiveness (Kivy 1989, 2002; Davies 1980, 1994, 2001, 2006; Budd 1995). In this chapter, I first briefly set out these various resemblance-based theories in section IV.2. I then offer criticisms of these views in section IV.3, and rebut some objections in section IV.4. Amongst other things, I argue that while resemblance-based views give us the causal story about how various resemblances allow us to hear music as expressive, they do not explain how something *inanimate* and *insentient* such as music can be sad. In contrast, as will emerge in chapter VI, my view, which is built on perceived resemblances, does so when it claims that in virtue of our perceiving its resemblance to various things having to do with sad people and their sadness, sad music is *imagined* to be sad in various but not always highly conscious ways, one of which involves animating the music and imagining it is the very thing that is sad.

    Note in passing that one might ask about the truth of claims about musical expressiveness: why is it true, or what makes it true, that Samuel Barber's *Adagio for Strings*, for example, is sad or mournful or something like that? One might give an error-theory in answer, claiming that such truth-judgments involve an error because music cannot be literally sad. Or one might say they are metaphorically true (Scruton 1997), though it is unclear what the alleged metaphor amounts to (Davies 1994, 150–62;

Levinson 1996, 105-6) as argued in chapter III. Alternatively, it might be claimed that such truth-judgments are literally true but in a secondary sense (Davies 1994, 162-66), though here one might doubt if the literal-metaphorical distinction ultimately illuminates much (Budd 2003, 220), and also whether appeals to it are too influenced by the linguistic turn in analytic philosophy since Frege. Other possible answers may involve the suggestion that such judgments are only imagined to be true, or that they are true in virtue of resemblances between music and something to do with mental states, or that the truth-maker here is the consensus of competent (but fallible) listeners, or some combination of these. One might also step back from the entire question of truth and claim that many people's ready and immediate *experience* of music in terms of mental states has primacy over linguistic descriptions—whether literal or metaphorical—of the experience (and the truth of these linguistic descriptions), and so we should focus on that experience instead. I will return to this point later.

IV.2. Resemblance-Based Views

I begin my summation of resemblance-based views of musical expressiveness by setting out Peter Kivy's theory, which he sometimes calls the contour-convention view (Kivy 1989, 71-83). It is claimed by Kivy (who I think came very close to solving the problem of musical expressiveness) that expressive properties are "objective" qualities that are recognized or perceived in the music just as we recognize sadness in the St. Bernard's face, rather than being something the music only has in virtue of arousing or evoking mental states in listeners. Musical expressiveness is a complex, emergent quality. We hear musical sounds as expressive of sadness because we hear them as human utterances, as structurally similar to our voices when we express sadness vocally or in speech. Additionally, Kivy says musical contour or shape also resembles our expressive behavior—movement, gesture, posture, and the like. We hear sadness in music because we hear it resembling the gestures and bearing of sad people. Likewise, happy music is heard as such because it resembles the motion and gestures of happy people in being expansive, vigorous, "leaping," and so forth.

Kivy also claims that we tend to animate all kinds of sights and sounds, and cannot but perceive expressiveness in them in ways that are not always conscious or noticed (1989, 57-59; 2002, 41-43). A piece of cloth tied around a wooden spoon will be taken by children to be a doll; a circle with three short lines in it (two on top, adjacent to each other, and one below and parallel to them) is seen as a face. Likewise, claims Kivy, we see ambiguous figures in clouds, and hear gesture and utterance in the music, even though we are not conscious of our animating it that allows us to hear it as expressive. We may, he suggests, be evolutionarily hard-wired to animate things, as this is conducive to our survival; for example, seeing a stick as a snake puts us on our guard, whereas doing the reverse would be disastrous. Similarly, we may animate sounds subliminally.

The final element in Kivy's resemblance-based theory is his appeal to musical conventions (1989, 80-83). He claims it is only due to the customs or conventions of the Western musical tradition that the major scale, the major triad, and the major third are heard as upbeat, while the minor key, minor chord, and minor third are heard as expressive of grief, sorrow, etc. Likewise, musical conventions account for why chromaticism is heard as expressive of sorrow, pain, and the like, suggests Kivy. Thus, claims Kivy, contour or resemblance and convention together explain musical expressiveness, sometimes separately and sometimes jointly.

I next sum up Stephen Davies's resemblance-based view, which is quite similar to Kivy's position (Davies 1994, 221-67). Davies claims that music presents in its aural appearance or sounds what he terms emotion characteristics associated with human expression of emotions, and thus it is expressive of emotions it does not itself possess. Other inanimate or nonsentient things such as weeping willows, cars, and St. Bernards may also display features that resemble the emotion characteristics of human sadness in their overall bearing or posture or appearance, for example, and thus they too can be seen as expressive. Musical expressiveness, claims Davies, is a public, emergent, objective property of the music, one that it possesses literally, and it mainly depends on perceived resemblances between the dynamic character of music and the demeanor of the human body—its movement, gait, bearing, carriage, etc. Our experience of music is like our experience of human behavior that gives rise to emotion characteristics. Though the emotions are heard as belonging to the music, the range of emotions expressed by the music is restricted. In sum, on Davies's view, music is expressive in virtue of presenting the outward features associated with sadness or happiness in general. Music is expressive in resembling the stance, gait, bearing, carriage, and gestures of our bodies. Just as sad people often walk slowly, hang their heads low, droop in their bodily stance, and are generally subdued, similarly sad music is slow, has a downward tendency, is quiet, and so on. Likewise, just as happy people tend to skip and leap quickly and lightly and make expansive gestures, happy-sounding music is similarly lively and exuberant.

My brief summation of resemblance-based views concludes with a short exposition of Malcolm Budd's theory (Budd 1995, 133–57). Following the American psychologist Carroll Pratt (1931), Budd claims that the basic and minimal concept of musical expressiveness is that music sounds the way emotions feel. To hear music as expressive of emotion "E" is to hear it as sounding like the way "E" feels. In what ways do music and its audible features have this cross-categorial likeness with the feel of emotions? Budd answers that there are correspondences and analogies between how, for example, our desires are satisfied and tensions released, and how musical tension is resolved. Similarly, music mirrors levels of felt energy in how the lightening of musical texture is analogous to feeling floated or being excited, and it mirrors in the way it attains its intermediate and final goals how we achieve our desired ends. Likewise, there are correspondences between musical movement and some felt movements essential to certain emotions, e.g., the tremblings intrinsic to acute agitation, and so on. Perceiving these likenesses between music and the affective tones of emotions involves recognizing such correspondences and analogies, and Budd suggests we may perceive them below the level of consciousness.

To his basic and minimal concept of musical expressiveness, Budd adds various accretions or emendations disjunctively so as to capture the different ways in which we hear musical expressiveness. One accretion involves the idea of music sounding like a feeling and thus arousing that feeling in listeners. A second accretion involves music sounding like a feeling and thus inducing a cross-categorial imaginative identification so that we imagine our having the feeling that we hear the music as sounding like. A third accretion involves imagining the music we hear as an instance of the feeling we hear it as sounding like, without the feeling being ours or the composer's, though we may imagine the feeling as being that of an imagined musical persona.

Another view that should be mentioned here briefly in passing is that of Susanne Langer (1942), who claimed that music is an iconic symbol of the emotions on account of isomorphisms between music and the emotive life in general. Langer's view has been discussed and criticized extensively for over seventy years now, and I refer the interested reader to Stephen Davies's criticisms (1994, 123–34), for example, of her view.

IV.3. Criticisms

Having just summed up Kivy's, Davies's, and Budd's versions of resemblance-based views in section IV.2, I now offer criticisms of such resemblance-based theories. I begin with three broad worries that apply to such theories in general, and then advance narrower criticisms specific to the views of each of Kivy, Davies, and Budd. Note that the resemblance-based theories under discussion try *both* to account for experiences of musical expressiveness and also try to analyze the concept of musical expressiveness; Budd, for example, clearly is concerned with the concept of expressiveness when he claims that the basic and minimal concept of musical expressiveness is that music sounds the way emotions feel (1995, 135–42). Note also that I follow earlier writers on this topic going back at least to Alan Tormey (1971) in distinguishing expression from expressiveness: while expression involves actually *having* the mental states being outwardly manifested as occurrent states within one's psychology, expressiveness in contrast involves *merely* the outward presentation of behavioral, bodily, vocal, and other features associated with the mental states in question, as actors pretend to do for example, *without* those mental states necessarily being felt or otherwise present as part of one's psychology. Accordingly, I am concerned here mainly with expressiveness rather than expression, in the case of both music and our ordinary notion of expressiveness.

To begin with, one might wonder if all these theories are theories *not* of expressiveness or expression, but rather of resemblance between music and something to do with mental states such as emotions, moods, and feelings: either their vocal or bodily or behavioral expression or their affective feel. The fact is, expressiveness is a different concept from that of resemblance. While resemblance has to do with similarities or likenesses in some respect(s) between two (or more) things, our ordinary notion of expressiveness involves the outward manifestation of inner mental states. As the *Concise Oxford English Dictionary* tells us, to express or to be expressive is to represent or make known thoughts, feelings, etc., in words or by gestures, conduct, etc.; it is a person's facial appearance or intonation of voice, especially as indicating feeling; it is a depiction of feeling, movement, etc., in art; a conveying of feeling in the performance of music. When we say ordinarily, for example, that someone's eyes are very expressive, we mean that her eyes are such that they can outwardly manifest a variety of mental states. But merely resembling something, in the sense that resemblance-based theories of musical expressiveness have in mind, is not the same thing as outwardly displaying inner mental states. For the mere fact that A resembles B in some way that is perceived need not be the same thing as A thereby presenting someone or something's mental states outwardly, which is the sense of expressiveness we are concerned with. Resemblance-based views do not appear to connect in this or some other way with our ordinary notion of expressiveness, and so there must be doubt about whether they are not merely theories of resemblance rather than being theories of expressiveness. As a *species* of expressiveness (rather than expression) in general, musical expressiveness and theories of it must relate somehow to our ordinary notion of expressiveness, and as the resemblance-based views under discussion do not seem to do so intelligibly one must wonder if they are not just theories of resemblance rather than expressiveness per se. Note that I am *not* identifying musical expressiveness with our ordinary notion of expressiveness, just claiming instead that they must connect somehow.

Second, and relatedly, besides the fact that resemblance and expressiveness are philosophically and logically quite distinct as concepts, perceived resemblances by themselves are not sufficient for expressiveness, nor for hearing it, though the resemblance-plus-imagination view of musical expressiveness I favor grants that they may be (causally) necessary for expressiveness. All kinds of things may resemble either how we vocally or physically or behaviorally express various mental states or else the affective tones of these mental states, but are not thereby expressive of these mental states, even if we perceive these resemblances. For example, turtles and snails move slowly, with their heads hung low, and their bodies very close to the ground, resembling the way sad people often walk slowly, hanging their heads low, with their bodies drooping in a downward direction toward the ground. But against Kivy and Davies, merely such resemblances and perceptions of them do not have us see turtles and snails as sad, or as expressive of sadness; this is perhaps even clearer in the case of snails, as it is not clear whether their brains and nervous systems are complex enough to allow them to *have* anything like emotions even if turtles do. To see turtles and snails as sad, we need to add to the account something *more* than merely these resemblances that we perceive. We need, I suggest, to couple resemblance with imagination so that consciously or otherwise seeing these resemblances makes or allows us to *imagine*—either in a real-life, nonfictional context or else within the fictional world of a story, play, novel, film, poem, etc.—that turtles and snails are sad, or at least imagine that their slow motion is expressive of sadness, perhaps their or someone or something else's real or imagined sadness. In like manner, I will suggest later in chapter VI that to get a theory of musical expressiveness, we need to combine imagination with the various perceived resemblances between music and emotions, moods, and feelings, that Kivy, Davies, and Budd identify, rightly I think.

Here is another, admittedly somewhat speculative, example (this time against Budd) of perceived resemblances that do not suffice for expressiveness. The taste of some foods, I suggest, may resemble how emotions, moods, feelings, and other mental states feel, though these foods are not thereby expressive of these states. For example, a hot, spicy food may have a "burning" taste or gustatory "feel" that is similar to how anger or anguish feel. Likewise, a smooth, cool beverage consumed on a hot day may have a "cool" taste that resembles the affective feel or tone of calmness. Note, I am not talking about the ingestion of these foods causing mental states such as anger, anguish, and calmness in us. I am instead talking about the very taste of these foods, their phenomenological, what-it-feels-or-tastes-like aspect, their gustatory "feel," if you like. Now if there are indeed these cross-categorial likenesses between how these foods taste and how certain mental states feel, these resemblances and perceptions of them do not thereby make these foods expressive of certain mental states, nor do we see these foods as such (that is unless we somehow *imagine* these foods as being expressive of anger, anguish, calmness, and the like, combining resemblances with imagination, as I am inclined to do in the case of musical expressiveness).

I now turn to a third and arguably the most formidable worry for resemblance-based views of musical expressiveness in general. The theories of Kivy, Davies, and Budd, even when combined, give us the causal basis or grounds or mechanisms underlying musical expressiveness. They tell us what *makes* or causes or allows music to be and to be heard as expressive, to wit, perceived resemblances of various kinds between music and something to do with mental states such as emotions, moods, and feelings. Put differently, these views tell us *why* we hear music as expressive: we hear music as expressive or as sad, happy, etc., *in virtue of* various resemblances we consciously or otherwise hear between the music and something to do with mental states such as emotions, moods, and feelings. Indeed, composers, improvisers, and performers often, consciously or otherwise, exploit these resemblances to make their music expressive. However, merely giving us this causal story underlying musical expressiveness does not tell us how something *inanimate* or *insentient* such as music can be sad, happy, and the like, or how it can be expressive of such states, which is the basic problem of musical expressiveness, as stated by Kivy and Davies themselves (Kivy 1989, 6–10; Kivy 2002, 31–32; Davies 1994, x; Davies 2003, 169, 173). Granted these perceived resemblances make music sad, but how can music, a sequence or a set of sounds *without* life, consciousness, or mental states be sad or somehow have sadness "in" it, and be experienced to be so? This fundamental question is not adequately addressed by resemblance-based views; indeed, this worry was raised by Budd himself (in *Times Literary Supplement* (1981), p. 762) in a review of Kivy's vocal resemblance-based theory of musical expressiveness, and also in his essay "Music and the Expression of Emotion" (*Journal of Aesthetic Education*, vol. 23, no. 3 (1989), p. 27) before he revised his view: ". . . it is mistaken to attempt to use . . . a perceived resemblance of any kind in an elucidation of the concept of the musical expression of emotion. Such an analysis is wide of the mark, whether the resemblance is . . . between music and the vocal expression of emotion, the expression of emotion in the body, *or emotion itself*" (emphasis mine). There must thus be doubt whether resemblance-based views even address, let alone solve, the basic problem of musical expressiveness, instead of giving us a mere causal story about what makes music expressive (compare Levinson 1996, 106; Scruton 1997, 147). In sharp contrast, my resemblance-plus-imagination view, which I will advance in chapter VI, does address the basic problem of musical expressiveness in suggesting that in virtue of perceiving these various resemblances, our imagination kicks in and we *imagine* willy-nilly, readily, and immediately in various but not always highly conscious ways that the music is sad, happy, and the like, often animating it by projecting life and life-like qualities onto it, and imagining it, itself, is the very thing that is alive, sentient, and possessive of mental states such as sadness or happiness.

Having raised three broad worries that apply to resemblance-based views in general, whether in Kivy's or Davies's or Budd's versions, I now offer some narrower, more specific criticisms, beginning with Kivy's view. I am puzzled by Kivy's insistence that musical expressiveness is an "objective" property of the music that is recognized or perceived "in" the music by listeners. That seems to suggest that musical sadness, happiness, etc., are already there "in" the music, somehow prior to human beings and their experience of hearing the music, which seems false given that music itself is without life and mental states. Against Kivy, I submit that musical expressiveness is an at best "inter-subjective" property of the music, one that competent listeners (those who are attentive; not tired or bored or distracted or too familiar with the music; not tone-deaf; musically sensitive even if not necessarily trained; emotionally open; and so on) *imaginatively* hear or perceive in the music, in ways that often allow broad agreement amongst them as to which musical works and passages are sad or expressive of some negative mental state in that approximate vicinity, and which are happy or expressive of a not too dissimilar positive mental state. Musical sadness, I suggest, is *imaginatively* heard in the music in virtue of various resemblances we hear, consciously or otherwise, between the music and something to do with mental states such as emotions, moods, and feelings; similarly, I suggest the sadness Kivy claims we "recognize" in the St. Bernard's face is not something preexisting, as his view seemingly implies, but instead we imaginatively see the sadness in that dog's countenance once we see or experience preexisting resemblances between its appearance and the droopy look typical of sad people. If anything is recognized and preexisting, it is resemblances, whereas the expressiveness, sadness, happiness, etc., are imagined in virtue of perceiving these resemblances, if I am right.

Additionally, while I am very sympathetic to Kivy's claims about animation, I am inclined to go *beyond* him and claim *much* more: animating the music involves not just hearing gesture and utterance in the music, as Kivy claims, but also *imagining* at some not always highly conscious level that the music *itself* is alive, sentient, and possessive of mental states such as the one we hear it as expressive of. Animating the music on my view involves listeners imaginatively projecting life and life-like qualities, including mental states, onto the music, as I suggest in chapter VI.

As for Kivy's claims about the essential role of musical conventions in explaining the expressiveness of the minor third, the minor triad, and the minor key as well as chromaticism, I have two qualms. First, I submit against Kivy that one could offer an alternative resemblance-plus-imagination explanation of the expressiveness of the minor third, triad, and scale. When heard and compared in context *against the backdrop* of the major third—often said to be part of the harmonic or overtone series—the minor sounds like a "drooping" or "fallen off" or "crouching" or "sagging" or "sinking" or "subdued" version of the major, resembling the way in which sad people are often droopy, sagging, sinking, subdued versions of their happier selves. In virtue of perceiving these resemblances, we imagine willy-nilly, readily and immediately, in not always very conscious ways that the minor third, triad, and scale are expressive of sorrow, grief, etc. My second qualm is about whether musical conventions fix—and whether knowledge of them is really needed to hear—musical expressiveness, as Kivy claims. For I would not be surprised to find that *some* highly musical listeners from non-Western musical cultures can hear chromatic music (e.g., the opening passages of the Habanera in Bizet's *Carmen*) as often expressive of mystery or something foreboding or something like that, even though they have no knowledge of Western musical conventions. Indeed, it would not surprise me to find that *some* listeners from other cultures may also occasionally hear the minor as expressive of sorrow, grief, etc. (e.g., to use one of Kivy's examples, the brief switch from major to minor harmonization often used by Beethoven, as in bars 205–6 of the last movement of his Ninth Symphony, just before the outburst of the entire orchestra and chorus) even though they have no knowledge of Western conventions about the minor.

A fair bit of recent empirical psychological data in fact supports my claim against Kivy that musical expressiveness can be and often is perceived or heard across cultures (Swaminathan and Schellenberg 2015). For example, Western listeners can often hear happiness, sadness, and anger in Hindustani or north Indian classical music (Balkwill and Thompson 1999). Similarly, the Mafa from Cameroon who are unfamiliar with Western music can nevertheless hear sadness, happiness, and fear in bits of it (Fritz et al. 2009). In like manner, Japanese listeners can hear sadness, happiness, and anger in Hindustani music that they are unfamiliar with (Balkwill, Thompson, and Matsunaga 2004). None of this is to deny that listeners are usually better at hearing emotions in music of their own cultures than in music of other cultures (Balkwill et al. 2004; Fritz et al. 2009; Laukka et al. 2013).

More recently, Kivy has distanced himself from the resemblance-based theory discussed above, and he now claims it is an unknown "black box" how music has the emotions we hear in it (Kivy 2002, 47–48). Here, I submit that the resemblance-plus-imagination view I offer later can penetrate this "black box" and offer insightful answers; one should not throw in the towel on this topic, as Kivy seems to be doing these days.

Turn now to some specific criticisms of Davies's theory. It should be clear from the criticisms of Kivy voiced above that I am equally puzzled by Davies's claim that musical expressiveness is an objective rather than an inter-subjective property of the music. Additionally, I am not persuaded by Davies's claim that musical expressiveness is a literal property of the music, one that it somehow literally possesses. Given that music is without life and mental states, it just seems false for Davies to say that music is literally or really expressive, or that it is literally or really sad, happy, etc. Perhaps what motivates Davies's claim that music is literally expressive is his opposition to those such as Nelson Goodman and Roger Scruton who claim that music is only metaphorically expressive, or only metaphorically sad, happy, etc., a claim that needs to be elucidated, as argued in chapter III. And perhaps Davies thinks that there are only two options here—literal and metaphorical—and so his rejection of metaphor-based views of musical expressiveness leads him to claim that music is literally expressive. However, against Davies's literalism and against metaphor-based views of musical expressiveness, I submit there is at least a third option here, the option I favor which emerges if one focuses on the very *experience* of musical expressiveness rather than on words and linguistic descriptions—whether literal or metaphorical—of the experience: music is only *imagined* to be expressive, sad, happy, etc. Musical expressiveness, I submit, is not literally possessed by the music, a claim that seems just false. Nor is expressiveness metaphorically possessed by the music, a claim which seems obscure and doubtful given that, amongst other things, there seems no satisfactory paraphrase available of the alleged metaphor "The music is sad" that adequately captures its emotional content, or explains how the allegedly figurative use of "sad" in this context connects with our ordinary use of "sad" (compare Davies 1994; Matravers 1998; Carroll 1999), as argued in chapter III. Instead, I suggest expressiveness is an *imagined* property of the music, one that listeners only willy-nilly, readily, and immediately imagine the music to possess in various, not always highly conscious, ways.

To be fair to Davies, he claims (1994, 162–66) that it is literally true in a secondary sense that some music is sad, some happy, and so on. In response, one must appeal to considerations based on the history and current state of Anglophone analytic philosophy and wonder if Davies's narrow overemphasis on language and words (whether in primary or secondary senses) is much too influenced by the linguistic turn in analytic philosophy since Frege, and ultimately rests on what is now widely regarded as an outdated conception of philosophy (Williamson 2007, 10–22). While debates about theories of truth, meaning, reference, and other such topics in the philosophy of language dominated analytic philosophy in the 1970s (when Davies's views on musical expressiveness were first being formulated and were put forth soon thereafter in an essay in *Mind* in 1980), the fact is that such philosophical issues no longer dominate analytic philosophy the way they did say in 1976 (when Gareth Evans and John McDowell's *Truth and Meaning* was published and was the hot ticket, and Davies got his doctorate from London). Davies's appeal to language and literal usage is in part a *function* of those times, the heyday of the linguistic turn in analytic philosophy. Today, instead, linguistic considerations and issues do not excite analytic philosophers as much as, for example, experimental philosophy or cognitive science or data from neuroscience and other empirical sciences or analytic metaphysics or "the affective turn," a point I will return to in section IV.5.

Against Davies, the fact is that the *experience* of hearing music as sad, happy, etc., has primacy over linguistic descriptions—whether literal or metaphorical—of the experience and claims about the truth-value of such descriptions. Not only is the experience more important but it is also temporally prior to linguistic descriptions of it: we first *hear* music as sad, happy, etc., and only then describe it as such, as should be clear unless one is inseparably wedded to language and linguistic notions (such as the literal-metaphorical distinction). I now offer two additional considerations, one pertaining to little children and the second stemming from philosophical Daoism, which might be seen to support these concerns about Davies's view being too narrowly focused on the wrong things—words—rather than on the very experience of musical expressiveness. First, those who have spent a lot of time around little children (and one need not have biological children or adopt children to do so) realize fairly early on that even though little children know nothing about the literal-metaphorical distinction applied to language or about the secondary sense of literal usage, nevertheless quite a few of them (even if not all) *hear* music as expressive from a very early age.[1] As appeals to empirical psychological data are very much in fashion these days and seem to be the only thing that will convince some (including many philosophers who seem to have lost faith in their philosophical training), I now cite some data to support my claim against Davies that little children can often hear musical expressiveness even though they know neither how to use metaphors nor how to use words in a literal but secondary sense. It has been found that three- and four-year-old children can hear happiness and sadness in music (but are not so good at perceiving anger, fear, and neutrality in it), while five- to seven-year-old children can hear happiness, sadness, fear, and neutrality (but not anger) in music at levels that are above chance (Stacho, Saarikallio, van Zijl, Huotilainen, and Toiviainen 2013). Little children also regard faster pieces as happy, while they judge slower music as sad (Gagnon and Peretz 2003; Juslin and Lindstrom 2010). In fact, against Davies, even five-year-old children can hear temporal cues about emotions in music (Dalla Bella, Peretz, Rousseau, and Gosselin 2001). Also, caregivers across cultures use musical cues (such as in lullabies) to communicate with infants because they express emotions effectively (Trehub 2003). Additionally, singing works better than speech when it comes to holding infants' attention (Nakata and

Trehub 2004), so much so, in fact, that caregivers from different cultures often intuitively speak to infants in a musical manner, with high overall pitch, a large pitch range, exaggerated pitch contours, and slow, rhythmic rates (Fernald et al. 1989). My second consideration is related and stems from philosophical Daoism. Although non-Western philosophies remain less well-known, they have a lot to offer; similarly, Kathleen Higgins has argued recently that it is a loss for (Anglophone) musical aesthetics that much of it completely ignores various non-Western musics (which incidentally together constitute the overwhelming majority of the world's music of 7 billion plus people). The Daoist writings ascribed to Laozi (or Lao-Tzu, as he used to be called in the old Wade-Giles Romanization system before the adoption of the Pinyin system) and Zhuangzi (or Chuang-Tzu, as he used to be called) from around the fourth century BCE (or perhaps even a bit before) remind us amongst other things that we should not get bogged down in rigid (linguistic) preconceptions and forget the spontaneous, free *experience* of the lived life; I am told that the great American Pragmatist William James claimed likewise that percepts are more important than concepts. It is perhaps no coincidence that chapters 10 and especially 55 of the *Dao de Jing* even celebrate babies—recall my mentioning little children above—as being free of distorting, rigid preconceptions, and as able to experience things in life flexibly and spontaneously, living fully in the moment, here and now. Indeed, one might even see Daoist writings as the liberating antidote to getting bogged down in petty argumentation (as sometimes sadly happens to some analytic philosophers who miss the big picture consequently, something I have witnessed myself having been trained primarily in the analytic tradition). It might seem appropriate here to bring in claims made recently by Tiger Roholt, to the effect that the "grooves" or "feels" of rhythm in jazz, rock, etc., must be felt and comprehended bodily rather than intellectually conceptualized or grasped. But whether Roholt knows it or not, these claims in fact echo approximately 2,500-year-old Daoist warnings against over-intellectualizing things, and instead urge us to focus on the free, spontaneous experience of the lived life (Graham 1989). Witness, for example, the famous opening lines of chapter 56 of the *Dao de Jing* (lines which later passed on into Zen Buddhism): "Those who know do not speak, those who speak do not know." And witness the fact that Zhuangzi stresses the *unverbalizable* knack or know-how that skilled boatmen, swimmers, carpenters, cooks, and other craftsmen possess. Indeed, in a very famous example used in the thirteenth chapter of *The Book of Zhuangzi*, we are told about the wheelwright who *feels in his hand and thus grasps* how fast or slow he should chip with a chisel when making a wheel but cannot convey this knack in words, thus stressing the kind of bodily understanding that Roholt too seems to be after. Now while it is true that Roholt emphasizes the body as do feminists, it must be pointed out that Daoism too is seen as teaching "feminine" wisdom insofar as it stresses things on the passive, weak, female, Yin side of the traditional Yin-Yang divide (as opposed to Confucianism, Mohism, Legalism, and the other philosophical positions in classical China at that time). Thus, there is in fact more convergence here between non-Western philosophies such as Daoism and Roholt's claims—and indeed also the claims of Continental philosophers (such as the phenomenologist Maurice Merleau-Ponty, who inspires Roholt) and empirical, psychological data as well as analytic philosophers (such as myself)—than one might realize at first blush; though this is not to deny that there are also differences, which need not detain us.[2] In short, I am deeply sympathetic to and agree with Roholt's focus on the *experience* of music, even though I am no phenomenologist and my focus is mainly on musical expressiveness rather than rhythm, as is the case with Roholt.

I conclude my criticisms of resemblance-based theories by presenting one specific, minor reservation about Budd's view. The first of the three accretions to his basic and minimal concept of musical expressiveness that Budd presents seems to capture not musical expressiveness nor experiences thereof, but rather musical arousal when Budd claims that in virtue of sounding like a feeling music arouses that feeling in listeners. As such one must wonder if that accretion has any role to play in a theory of musical expressiveness as opposed to arousal. It seems Budd may here be *conflating* expressiveness, which is a(n imagined) property of the music itself and is usually an aesthetic plus, with musical arousal, which concerns the music's effect on listeners as it causes listeners to feel certain states and is not usually aesthetically and artistically good-making unless we are dealing with marches, dirges, and music for other such special, rousing occasions (compare Levinson 1996, 97–98; Scruton 1997, 145). This is not to deny that experiences of musical expressiveness are often co-extensive with those of musical arousal as expressive music often arouses mental states in listeners, nor is it to deny that being musically aroused may sometimes help us hear musical expressiveness, even though we can often hear music as expressive without being musically aroused, and we may also be musically aroused to a mental state different from what the music is expressive of.

IV.4. Objections and Replies

I now consider and reply to some objections raised by resemblance-based theorists by way of defense of their view. And I will also try to defend resemblance-based views from some objections raised by *others*.

Here is the first objection. It is claimed by Kivy that resemblance-based theorists have a reply to the worry raised earlier that perceived resemblances are not sufficient for expressiveness (Kivy 1989, 61–62). The way Kivy states this worry it is that on resemblance-based views, it would seem to follow that music should be expressive of *everything* it resembles such as ocean waves, the rise and fall of the stock market, and so on, which is clearly not the case, implying thereby the falsity of resemblance-based views and their claim that resemblance is sufficient for expressiveness. Kivy says two things in reply to this. First, he claims that it makes no sense to say that the music is expressive of ocean waves or the stock market. Expressiveness must be of mental states, and so Kivy claims the objection flouts a "logical" condition. Second, Kivy claims that there is an empirical condition that must be satisfied, to wit, that there must be some psychological connection between music and what it expresses. He claims music is expressive of emotions not just because it resembles expressive behavior but because we tend to animate our perceptions and cannot help but see expressiveness in them.

In response to Kivy, I claim two things. First and most importantly, Kivy has simply misstated and thus not addressed the objection that perceived resemblances are not sufficient for expressiveness, even if he may have stated and answered a different, not completely unrelated concern. The worry is *not* that music should be expressive of everything it resembles such as ocean waves and the stock market, as Kivy puts it. Rather the objection is that all kinds of things (e.g., turtles, some foods, etc.) may resemble our vocal or bodily or behavioral expression or the affective feel of mental states such as emotions, moods, and feelings, and we may perceive these resemblances, but merely these resemblances and perceptions of them do not make these things expressive thereby. The same holds for music. Second, Kivy's claim that there must be some psychological link between music and what it expresses, and that music is expressive not just due to resemblance but because we tend to animate our perceptions and cannot help but see expressiveness in them echoes and leads on to my resemblance-plus-imagination view. Insofar as animation is one kind of imagining, as I will suggest in chapters V and VI, and insofar as our willy-nilly imagining (in various not always highly conscious ways) that music is sad, happy, etc., constitutes a psychological link between music and what it expresses, I submit that Kivy's second claim above means that his view, as stated in this second claim, either collapses or, at minimum, leads on to something very much like my view.

A second objection comes from Davies, again by way of an attempt to answer the concern that perceived resemblances are not sufficient for expressiveness (Davies 2003, 184). As Davies states this worry, it is that resemblance alone cannot ground musical expressiveness or explain why we experience music as expressive. For resemblances can be found between music and many things in addition to the resemblances between music and expressive appearances. Davies replies that one can simply say that "this is how we hear" the music (as expressive), without being committed to explaining what mechanisms and triggers underlie this response. Many insentient things such as crude pictures of the human face, masks of tragedy and comedy, Edvard Munch's "scream" face, etc., are, Davies claims, likewise experienced as being expressive. The resemblance-based view is no worse, asserts Davies, on this count than other theories, which he claims are not in a better position to go beyond perceived resemblances.

In reply, I claim two things. First and most importantly, note that, like Kivy, Davies too misstates and thus does not address our objection. The concern is *not* about many things resembling *music*, as Davies puts it. Rather, the worry is about many things (e.g., turtles, some foods, and so on) resembling our vocal or bodily or behavioral expression or the affective feels of mental states, but not thereby being expressive, even though we may perceive these resemblances consciously or otherwise. The concern then is why the case of musical expressiveness should be any different, why perceived resemblances alone should suffice to make music expressive. Second, note that in appealing to the supposed brute fact that "this is how we hear" musical expressiveness, this is just how we are *psychologically*, Davies does not reply to the objection as he puts it and in fact tries to make the question not one for philosophers to answer. But against Davies, it is not clear that we have here a brute fact not amenable to further philosophical explanation, and one might instead be able to dig deeper and say more, building on the notion of perceived resemblances and adding something more to the picture. As will emerge in chapters V and VI, in sharp contrast to Davies's and other resemblance-based views, my view goes *beyond* mere perceived resemblances in *adding* imagination to the picture. I agree that perceived resemblances are not sufficient for musical expressiveness, and this is partly what motivates me to claim that imagination is also needed to explain how something devoid of life and mental states such as music can be heard as sad, happy, etc. If I am right, we *imagine* in various not always highly conscious ways that music is sad, happy, etc.; one of these ways involves our animating the music, imaginatively projecting life and life-like qualities, including mental states, onto it, and imagining that the music *itself* is alive, sentient, and the very thing that possesses the mental states we hear in it.

The third objection I consider here also comes from Davies (Davies 2006, 184–85). Davies is concerned to defend his view from the charge that it merely involves the presentation of the appearance of emotion but does not explain the expression of an occurrent emotion in music, a charge not too dissimilar from my claim that resemblance-based views in general do not connect intelligibly to our ordinary notion of expressiveness, and are thus theories of resemblance rather than expressiveness. Davies begins his reply by noting that though music may present unintended expressive aspects, its creator usually intends its expressive character. Where this happens, he claims we have expression in the sense of something that is created and communicated deliberately.

In brief response to Davies, I submit that what Davies gives us here is a notion of intended communication rather than expressiveness or expression. Recall my earlier example: when we say ordinarily that someone's eyes are very expressive, we mean that her eyes are capable of outwardly presenting or manifesting a variety of inner, mental states, whether intentionally or otherwise. This is our ordinary notion of expressiveness, which, unlike Davies's notion of intended communication, does not hinge on intentions.

A fourth objection (suggested imaginatively to me by Kendall Walton, playing devil's advocate on behalf of resemblance-based views) tries to defend resemblance-based views from my criticism that perceived resemblances are not sufficient for expressiveness. Recall my criticism above that even though turtles and snails resemble in their slow motion and droopy bearing the similar motion and appearance of sad people, just these resemblances in themselves, and perceptions of them, do not thereby make turtles and snails sad or expressive of sadness, nor do we see them as sad or as expressive of sadness. To this, the defender of the resemblance-based view replies that the fact that turtles and snails are not expressive is just because there is not enough resemblance here. If there were sufficient resemblance, we would have expressiveness, claims the resemblance theorist.

By way of a twofold reply, I submit, first, that there *are* enough resemblances in this case to allow us easily to *imagine* turtles as expressive, say as part of a folk tale or a children's story that might go something as follows: the reason turtles move slowly, hanging their heads low and drooping toward the ground is that the first turtles could fly, let us suppose, but were punished severely for some egregious infraction by their maker, who took away their wings, and henceforth all turtles walked slowly, with their heads hung low and their bodies drooping toward the ground, expressing their profound sadness and shame at having lost their wings forever. Second, *even if* it is true that we do not have enough resemblances in this case, here is a further claim I make by way of a second line of defense. Even if there were enough resemblances between the motion and bearing of turtles and those typical of sad people, these in themselves would not result in our seeing turtles as expressive. For the reason we do not see turtles as expressive is that we do not (usually) *imagine* that they are expressive; or, if you prefer, we do not imaginatively see them as expressive. We do not couple our perceiving their motion, bearing, and overall appearance as resembling the movement, bearing, and look of sad people with imagining, as we do with the look of the St. Bernard or the droopy appearance of the willow tree, both of which we can and do, consciously or otherwise, imagine are sad or expressive of sadness, in the sense of fancying or supposing this.

I now turn to defending resemblance-based views from criticisms raised by *others*; for I am in fact very sympathetic to resemblance-based theories, despite the criticisms voiced above. A fifth objection doubts if music really resembles the emotions, or something to do with them such as emotional behavior (Madell 2003). It should not be too hard for resemblance theorists to reply to this concern, appealing to two moves. As a first move, they can point to various resemblances between music and *something* to do with mental states, either their vocal or bodily or behavioral expression or their affective tones. A lot of music seems to sound like human vocal expression: think of rapid runs and glissandi on clarinets, saxophones, and electric guitars which often sound like someone crying or wailing, the opening clarinet glissando of Gershwin's *Rhapsody in Blue* being one example of this. In addition, a lot of music is readily and immediately experienced by many as resembling the way sad people often walk slowly: the music is slow in tempo, soft in volume, low in pitch, just as sad people often hang their heads low, droop in their physical stance and gait, and talk softly. The opening passages of the funeral march in the second movement of Beethoven's "Eroica" Symphony provide a well-known example of this. Also, along the lines of Budd's suggestions briefly mentioned above, musical passages are often heard right away, both by musicians and by laypersons, as having tension, which may or may not be resolved later, and as having points of repose as well as final resting-points—such as the tonic chord or key—which may be arrived at after intermediate goals—such as the dominant chord or key—have been reached, mirroring the way our lives often have tense moments, which may or may not be resolved, and the way we strive for and arrive at our intermediate and final goals. I might add that such intermediate goals and final resting points can be found in musical periods and styles outside Western classical music from roughly 1600 to 1900 CE. For example, Indian classical music similarly stresses the main note of *ragas*, the *vadi*, as the final resting point of music, and emphasizes another note, the *samvadi* (often a fifth higher), as an intermediate goal. The modal music of the West from medieval times and before likewise uses the *finalis* and *confinalis* of the different modes (Ionian, Dorian, Phrygian, Lydian, Mixolydian, Aeolian, etc.) as the respective final resting-points and intermediate goals for that period of Western music. Additionally, there is a second move resemblance theorists can make in reply, borrowing a leaf from those who criticize appeals to resemblance, especially when it comes to pictorial depiction. It is sometimes charged that resemblance is a very broad and vague notion, so broad that just about anything can resemble anything else in some respect: for example, unicorns and the North Star might be said to resemble each other in that they are both mentioned in this sentence. Even if their critics are right about this point, resemblance theorists can go on to claim that it should not surprise us then that music resembles mental states in *some* way, such as the ways briefly discussed above. In addition, here now is some empirical psychological data that supports these claims about music and perceived resemblances. It has been found that there are many similarities between emotionally expressive speech and music (Juslin and Laukka 2003). Angry speech, for example, involves high vocal intensity similar to the tendency of angry music to be loud. Similarly, emotions such as anger and fear which involve high arousal are expressed in both speech and music using faster tempi as compared to sadness and tenderness which are low arousal emotions.

A sixth criticism is directed specifically at Kivy's version of the resemblance theory. It might be doubted if we really animate sounds (Kivy 2002, 46–47). In reply, the resemblance theorist can offer the following two scenarios as examples of our animating sounds. Very often, while walking down quiet, empty city streets late at night, one might hear a noise. Immediately, one is on guard, thinking that the sound might be coming from another person (perhaps a potential mugger) or some creature (such as a vicious dog on the loose). It turns out, however, that the sound is only that of a leaf rustling in the wind. The second scenario is this. Often one hears a sound while going round the bend on a quiet, lonely forest or mountain trail. Once again, one is on guard immediately fearing that the sound might be coming from a creature (such as a bear) or another person (perhaps someone dangerous). It turns out, however, that the sound is only that of a branch breaking off a tree. Both these cases provide clear sonic analogs of Kivy's example of animating the stick in the forest as a snake, as this helps our survival. Now it certainly seems to be the case, as Kivy himself has suggested, that as a species we depend more on sight than on hearing for survival; and it is also true that our noise-filled modern lives are rarely filled with silence for very long. Add to this the fact that the animation of sounds may be very dim or subliminal, as Kivy has also suggested, and you start getting some sense of why it is hard to detect the animation of sounds, making some skeptical of this.

IV.5. Conclusion

To conclude this chapter, let me sum up. I began in section IV.2 by setting out resemblance-based theories of musical expressiveness that try to solve the philosophical problem of musical expressiveness: the problem of how something *inanimate* or *insentient* such as instrumental music without words or an associated story or program can be experienced and said to be sad, happy, etc. These theories try to solve this problem by appealing to various perceived resemblances between music and something to do with emotions, moods, and feelings such as their vocal or bodily or behavioral expression, or their affective feel or tones. I then raised three broad criticisms for resemblance-based views in general in section IV.3, in addition to more specific criticisms: (i) that they may be theories of resemblance rather than expressiveness, given especially that they do not seem to connect intelligibly with our ordinary notion of expressiveness; (ii) that resemblances and perceptions of them are not sufficient for expressiveness, even if they are (causally) necessary; and (iii) that while resemblance-based theories give us the causal story or ground underlying expressiveness, they do not address the basic problem of musical expressiveness, the problem of how something inanimate or insentient such as music can be sad. I believe, by the way, that these *philosophical* criticisms also apply to James Young's recent attempt to give a resemblance theory of musical expressiveness, though I have no quarrel with his appeal to psychological data to support resemblance.[3]

Resemblance-based theories of musical expressiveness appear to get a lot of things right, though, as should be clear from my attempted defense of them toward the end of section IV.4. It seems there are resemblances of various sorts between music and something to do with mental states; that we perceive these resemblances consciously or otherwise; and that resemblances account for the causal story underlying what allows music to be heard as expressive. It will emerge in chapter VI that while I do not accept resemblance-based views fully, I *build* on their insights as they form the causal foundation of my own resemblance-plus-imagination or imaginationist view, instead of throwing out the baby with the bath water, and indeed my positive view builds on my criticisms of resemblance-based views as I *add* an imaginative component that shields my view from the objections discussed in this chapter. Progress in intellectual inquiry of many sorts, including philosophy, usually involves building on the achievements of one's predecessors; and I have a lot of genuine respect for the influential work of Kivy, Davies, and Budd. Witness, for example, Newton's famous claim (in a letter to his rival Robert Hooke, who was a hunchback) that if he had seen further than others, it was by standing on the shoulders of giants, referring thereby to such physicists before him as Kepler and Galileo.

It might seem, though, that one could save Kivy's resemblance (or contour) theory if one gives it a metaphorical twist, as has been suggested recently by Severin Schroeder (2013), so a quick word about this in concluding this chapter. Schroeder claims that if we stress the metaphorical character of descriptions of pure music as expressive of emotions, then Kivy's view can be defended against objections. In particular, Schroeder suggests that given that music is dynamic and its passages change emotional character a lot as they progress, often giving us the impression of a narrative, we should use narrative or extended metaphors in describing music. These metaphors, he concludes, should be justified as mere comparisons rather than as interpretive claims about the music's contents. I will say three things about Schroeder's view (the first two of which have been stated before, even if somewhat differently). First, as lovers of wisdom, philosophers should be at least a little wary of Groupthink and philosophical fashions, rather than jump onto the bandwagon (even if that is good for one's career). Consider briefly the history of Anglophone analytic philosophy over the last eighty years or so. Logical Positivism held sway during the 1930s and 1940s, partly under the influence of the early Wittgenstein. Then, under the influence of the later Wittgenstein, ordinary language philosophy and linguistic philosophy dominated the 1950s and 1960s. Next, it was the turn of philosophy of language, and then philosophy of mind to rule. It is for future historians of philosophy to figure out what the dominant trend is these days in the early years of the twenty-first century—whether it is experimental philosophy or some sort of (cognitivized) neurophilosophy or the return of analytic metaphysics or what has been called "the affective turn" or something else— and what are mere fashions that will not pass the test of time. Anyhow, my point is this. Just as we today regard Logical Positivism and linguistic philosophy as outdated, similarly we should step back and take a look at our current ways of philosophizing. Under the influence of the linguistic turn since Frege, we analytic philosophers have been way too focused for many years on words; language; the ordinary (primary, secondary, etc.) usage of words; dictionaries; descriptions; sentences; propositions; speech acts; the literal/metaphorical distinction as applied to words and descriptions; and other such essentially linguistic items and notions. But if we step back from the linguistic turn and recognize that *experience* has primacy over words, even when it comes to the experience of musical expressiveness, then the entire literal/metaphorical distinction "falls away" (to use a Wittgensteinian metaphor) and there opens up a third way which sees musical expressiveness as somehow imagined when we first *hear* it in the music, and only then use words (imaginatively, and neither literally nor metaphorically) to describe that experience. Second, contra Schroeder's claims, if we see metaphors themselves as involving resemblance plus imagination, as argued in chapter III, then perhaps even a metaphorist view of musical expressiveness might reduce or otherwise lead onto an underlying imaginationist position as being more fundamental. Third, insofar as Schroeder appeals to narratives (in talking of narrative or extended metaphors), it must be pointed out that narratives themselves involve invention and imagination, something Schroeder seems to grant (Schroeder 2013, 16).

V

Imagination

V.1. Introduction: Different Kinds of Imaginings

In thinking of imagination in relation to music, it seems clear that the creative imagination is involved in such activities as musical composition and improvisation and also in performance as performers may often imagine auditorily how a certain passage or piece will sound if played at this tempo or at that one, or with these dynamics and articulation rather than those ones, and so on. Perhaps composers, in writing musical works, imagine musical forms, timbres, textures, and the like by creating images of these in their auditory imaginations, and then later often, even if not always, test their hypotheses about these images through actual music-making (Levinson 1992, 84–85). The same might hold true of improvisers in jazz and other oral traditions, such as Indian classical music, which call essentially for improvisation, though the auditory imagination must work much quicker here, since improvisers play or perform what they imagine, or some variant thereof, soon after imagining it, leaving aside what has been imagined prior to the commencement of the improvisatory performance.[1]

Be that as it may, before exploring the issue of how imagination applies to musical expressiveness, which will be done in the next chapter, we need to explore briefly the nature of imagination itself. Accordingly, I begin in section V.1 by briefly exploring different kinds of imaginings. Section V.2 discusses the important work on imagination by Brian O'Shaughnessy, which I draw on presenting my imaginationist view of musical expressiveness both in this chapter and especially in chapter VI. In section V.3, I briefly discuss work on children's imaginings by the psychologist Paul Harris and relate it to my imaginationism about musical expressiveness, while section V.4 deals with Gregory Currie's influential work on the imagination. Section V.5 discusses the role of imagination in music perception, and also in musical culture.

So, what is it to imagine something? What is involved in imagination? Is there one, uniform sense of imagination involved in various imaginative activities? Or are there many different senses of imagination? If there are various senses of imagining, do they all apply to musical expressiveness? If so, do they all apply in the same way or to the same degree, or are there important differences in how they are involved in hearing music as expressive? I cannot address all these questions adequately in what follows, and no doubt there are also other questions that can be raised. But I hope at least to make a start here at addressing some of these questions that are seldom raised and addressed in the work done so far on musical expressiveness by various philosophers.

We imagine things in a variety of ways, not all of which are highly conscious or foregrounded (see Ryle 1949, chapter 8; Walton 1990; Kieran and Lopes 2003). What follows is a short, nonexhaustive list of different kinds of imaginings.

The first notion of imagination that comes readily to mind is that imagination involves forming mental images in the sense of visualizing things or scenes or events or things not present, as when one tries to picture an ice-cream cone in one's mind. Such a notion of imagination is to be found in Aristotle, who claimed that imagination involves images being presented to us, and that the soul can never think without a mental image. It is also the notion of imagination favored by the Romantic tradition. Indeed, the very etymology of the word "imagination" (from "imago," meaning images or pictures) suggests a close link with mental images. Moreover, as Roger Scruton (1992) points out, images have a subjective, phenomenological character: they are like perceptions in having a sensory component; and to describe them we must refer to a perceptual experience associated with them, in terms of what it would be like to have this perception. Imaginings can also involve forming mental images associated with the other senses besides sight, such as forming an auditory image of the distinctive timbre or tone-color of a trumpet. Or forming an olfactory image of the smell of a rose, or a gustatory image of the taste of a fine wine, or a tactile image of the prick of a cactus thorn.

However, we do not always imagine in the sense of forming mental images, especially when we experience art. In particular, when reading fiction, though we may intermittently and occasionally form images, we are not always visualizing every sentence uttered by one character to another, or visualizing every metaphor. Instead, sometimes when we read fiction, we may imagine in that we suppose something is said by one fictional character to another without actually visualizing how these fictional characters look, what they wear, where they live, and so on. Indeed, there are ways of speaking in ordinary language where when we ask someone to imagine something is true, we ask her to suppose or think it is true without necessarily forming mental images. For example, to imagine that the universe is infinite is to suppose or think that this is the case, and it is not clear that one is being asked to visualize an infinite universe, if one can visualize something infinite in the first place.

There are in fact many activities that are imaginative, as Ryle (1949) stressed, and thus many different senses of imagination. In addition to imaging, these may include pretending, especially pretending to oneself or making-believe (or make-believing), something children often engage in when they play games such as imagining that a tree stump is a bear or that a block of wood is a truck even though the wooden block has no engine or tires as trucks must have (Walton 1990, 21–24). Imagining can also involve fancying or supposing something such as when we are asked to imagine the denial of a certain proposition at the outset of a *reductio ad absurdum* proof. And imaginings can also involve entertaining possibilities without actually believing or affirming them, such as when we are asked to imagine that Lincoln is the U.S. President today or that Louis XIV is the present king of France. In addition, imaginings can consist of acting or impersonating or having false beliefs or delusions such as when a deranged person has delusions and imagines she is Queen Victoria. Dreaming and daydreaming are also instances of imagining and clearly show that we need not always notice that we are engaged in certain kinds of not highly foregrounded imaginings; we are not always aware that we are daydreaming and we usually lapse into it when we do so, and we rarely if ever realize at the time that we are dreaming (compare Scruton 1992, 214; Scruton 1997, 88–92; Walton 1990, 13–21; New 1999, 69–73).

This last fact about dreaming and daydreaming points to something important about the nature of imagination and various kinds of imaginings. Imaginings can have a long or a short duration, be constant or instead be intermittent, be voluntary (in the sense of being under our control) or not so; they can be engaged in while we are involved in other activities (e.g., daydreaming in class that you are a Distinguished Professor); they can be spontaneous, non-deliberate and passive (rather than intended) or otherwise; and they can be engaged in consciously or otherwise. In what follows, it is important that the reader bear in mind that imagination is not always highly foregrounded and we can engage in certain kinds of imaginings without being aware of doing so.

Is there a defining quality common to all and only these various kinds of imaginings? Even if it is true that all varieties of imagining share a family resemblance in involving some sort of contrast with reality, clearly this is at best a necessary but not sufficient condition. For all kinds of things, such as false propositions themselves, involve a contrast with reality without themselves being forms of imagining thereby. Perhaps imagination involves new perspectives, new ways of seeing things, literally or otherwise, or conceiving, framing, and entertaining possibilities beyond known facts (Hamlyn 1994, 362; Williams 2003). However, it is beyond the scope of this discussion to define imagination, and so I leave that issue aside, assuming we have some grip on the many notions of imagination that we will need for what follows in the next chapter.

V.2. Imaginative Perceptions and Perceptual Imaginings

I now review some of the best recent scholarly discussions of imagination and relate them to my project on musical expressiveness, though I cannot do an exhaustive literature-survey here, which is not my aim anyway. Easily amongst the best recent accounts of imagination is the one provided in passing by the late London-based, Australian-born philosopher of mind Brian O'Shaughnessy (2002, 339–78), even though most aestheticians and philosophers seem to have overlooked it, perhaps because it is forbiddingly dense and difficult to read. O'Shaughnessy rightly distinguishes the question of what the faculty of imagination is from the question of what it is to imagine, i.e., to exercise the faculty of imagination. He then identifies several varieties of imaginings: (i) self-conscious propositional imaginings which involve a propositional content as we imagine-that, as in the case of a novelist; (ii) unselfconscious propositional imaginings, as in the case of dream-beliefs; (iii) imaginative perceptions, as when we look suitably at photographs or cartoons; (iv) will-susceptible perceptual imaginings, as in the case of common mental imagery; and (v) will-impervious perceptual imaginings, as in the case of visual hallucinations.

What is most relevant for my purpose of discussing imagination and musical expressiveness is O'Shaughnessy's discussion of the non-propositional, direct-object imaginative experiences involved in (iii), (iv), and

(v) above. Accordingly, I focus on O'Shaughnessy's discussion of imaginative perceptions, as in (iii) above, and perceptual imaginings, as in (iv) and (v) above. As we have already seen to some degree in chapter III and will see again later, the particular notion of imaginative perception (or imaginative hearing in the specific case of music) is applied to the experience of music by some thinkers such as Roger Scruton. So it seems appropriate to clarify here before proceeding further what imaginative perception is, generally, and how it is different from related phenomena such as perceptual imaginings. Note that while O'Shaughnessy's examples are visual, we will see auditory analogs of these later in this chapter and the next in discussing musical expressiveness.

In discussing imaginative perceptions, O'Shaughnessy tells us that these are imaginative non-imaginings where the imagination openly helps generate the internal object of the perceptual experience, i.e., what we see, as in the case of seeing photographs of a landscape suitably. When seeing a photograph of a landscape suitably, the imagination imposes a second-order interpretation upon our first-order interpretation of seeing colored expanses on cardboard. We see these expanses of color on cardboard in such a way that while remaining expanses of color, they simultaneously bring a landscape into view (or allow a landscape to be visible in these marks) in a special imaginative sense (which O'Shaughnessy does not clarify, however). There is, he claims, one complex phenomenon here with two internal objects—the colored expanses and the landscape—the latter being dependent upon the former; put differently, there is one complex experience here involving two mental representations—one of the colored expanses and one of the landscape. Thus, the phenomenon is fundamentally a seeing (an imaginative seeing, that is) rather than an imagining (or a visual imagining). Moreover, claims O'Shaughnessy, it is vital that the colored expanses on the photographic surface share *some* similarity with the landscape (as seen from a point of view) such as common contours and color-distributions. This combination of some similarity and yet some dissimilarity prompts the imagination to this imaginative seeing, though the imagination need not follow the prompt. O'Shaughnessy claims that a landscape is visible in these marks to those who know the look of landscapes and can also impose second-order imaginative interpretations upon suitable marks on surfaces. The landscape that "appears" to one is not really there; all that is literally there are the marks on the photographic surface, the cardboard, which one sees, even as one also goes beyond them simultaneously in imaginatively seeing a landscape.

There is much in O'Shaughnessy's account of imaginative perceptions that I admire and agree with, more so as analogs of many of O'Shaughnessy's claims about imagination would seem to apply well to the experience of music, especially to that of hearing musical expressiveness. In hearing absolute or purely instrumental music—music without words, or an associated story or program—as sad, happy, anguished, tranquil, and so on, it is clear we are hearing something that is not literally or really true of the music, which after all is without life and mental states. It seems plausible, then, that music is not literally sad, happy, etc., but is rather only *imagined* to be so (Levinson 1996; Trivedi 2006). If that is right, then it is possible that music may be imaginatively heard as sad in a variety of ways, given that we imagine things in many ways, as outlined above, and that we may often imagine things without being aware of it. As Stephen Davies (2006a, 190) puts it, "what goes on in people's heads as they listen attentively to music and . . . its expressive character is very varied." As we will see in section VI.3, I make claims similar to O'Shaughnessy's in discussing *one* (and only one) of the many kinds of imagining involved when we hear music as expressive, to wit, our animating the music itself, imaginatively projecting life and mental states onto it; our animating music is like our animating inanimate objects (trees, the sun, cars, trains, etc.) in comics and especially in animation films (e.g., those about Thomas the Tank Engine) when we project life and mental states onto the moving images that constitute these objects, these moving images of animation films being as much processes as are the sounds that make up musical works. Our animating the music (more on this in the next chapter) when we hear it as expressive involves imaginative perception or imaginative hearing, I claim, whereby we imagine the music *itself*—not something else such as the composer, performer, listener, or an imagined persona in the music—is sad. We really hear musical sounds in hearing musical expressiveness, and so there is aural perception or hearing going on, fundamentally. But at the same time, there is also imagining going on as we imagine readily, immediately, and willy-nilly of these sounds, in ways we are not always conscious of, that they are sad, happy, etc. Furthermore, as in the case O'Shaughnessy deals with, what prompts imaginings in the case of musical expressiveness may be resemblances of the various sorts discussed in the previous chapter between music and *something* to do with mental states, either their typical vocal or behavioral expression or their affective feel. And, greatly mirroring O'Shaughnessy's claims further, I could easily claim that musical expressiveness is heard in these sounds by those who can willy-nilly, readily, and immediately "impose" imaginative (second-order) interpretations on suitable sounds. The mental states heard in the music are not really there; they are only imagined to be in the sounds, for nothing is there besides the sounds. In the very midst of hearing musical sounds, there is thus a nonperceptual or nonaudible "going-beyond" as we imaginatively hear mental states in the music. In accordance with Scruton's claim (Scruton 2004, 184) that the "literal perception and imaginative perception can cohabit the same experience, since they do not compete," we literally hear or perceive musical sounds unfolding in time and at the same time also imaginatively hear mental states in them, as part of one and the same musical experience.

To return to O'Shaughnessy, let us now look at his discussion of perceptual imaginings, which is focused on visual (as opposed to nonvisual) imaginings. We are told there are three kinds of visual imaginings: mental imagery, visual hallucination, and "dream-seeing" (about which O'Shaughnessy does not have much to say). Mental imagery comes in many varieties, of which but one is the normal "seeing in the mind's eye." Mental images can be conjured into and out of existence at will, but they often come and go unbidden, e.g., sexual images, to use an example from Colin McGinn (2004, 14). They are will-susceptible in that even though their arrival may sometimes be unbidden, we bear a limited degree of responsibility for willing their persistence and their course. In contrast, we are usually without choice in the case of both visual hallucinations and "dream-seeing," both of which also involve some measure of weakening of one's sense of reality. Visual hallucinations can be experienced with belief (e.g., Macbeth's hallucination of Banquo), or with doubt (e.g., Macbeth's hallucination of a dagger), or with the knowledge that they are illusory (e.g., the first stages of mescaline intoxication). In O'Shaughnessy's view, visual hallucinations and perceptual imaginings generally are imaginings rather than perceptions or seeings. An alcoholic's "seeing" pink elephants, for example, is a visual imagining; it is an apparent visual experience that is the seeing of nothing rather than a real visual experience with a real presence in the visual field (as when we see pink elephants in a picture).

Once again, I find much to agree with in O'Shaughnessy's discussion, and will focus on what strikes me as most relevant for my purposes of sketching and defending an imaginationist view of musical expressiveness. One and only one kind of imagining involved in hearing music as expressive is when we imagine an indefinite musical persona—someone or something, we know not exactly what—expressing (its) mental states *via* the music, its gestures, development, and so on; more will be said about the persona in the next chapter, though the persona view has already been discussed earlier in sections II.2 through II.4 in the views of Bruce Vermazen, Jerrold Levinson, and Jenefer Robinson, respectively. What I want to stress here is that imagining a persona may involve a kind of indeterminate mental imaging, not a visual imaging but an auditory imaging. Along with the kind of visual imaging or "seeing in the mind's eye" that O'Shaughnessy describes, it is also possible, with the help of memory, to form mental images associated with the other senses besides sight so that one might form an auditory image of the distinctive timbre or tone-color of a trumpet. To be sure, many of these mental images are faint and not very precise or determinate, which also holds for the imagined, indefinite musical persona. Alternatively, one might view hearing musical expressiveness in terms of a persona as involving a kind of propositional imagining—that there *is* some agent expressing (its) mental states musically—though a possible problem here may be that propositional imagining seems to be more determinate than, and not as immediate or direct as, hearing musical expressiveness in terms of a persona, which happens readily and immediately and is indeterminate; one *hears* the sadness in the music first—someone or something is crying or wailing in the music—and only then forms the belief that the music *is* an agent's expression. Moreover, as with the visual images O'Shaughnessy discusses, nonvisual mental images can be conjured into and out of existence at will, but they often come and go unbidden and are will-susceptible. In the particular case of imagining an indeterminate musical persona, we may form this kind of auditory image without being aware of doing so, and yet the unbidden image of a musical persona may be terminated at will after we realize we are engaged in imagining it.

V.3. Children's Imaginings

I next turn to the insightful account of imagination provided by the developmental psychologist Paul Harris (2000), whose work is largely focused on the imaginings of children. I first sum up some of Harris's main claims, and then discuss their relevance to my imaginationist view of musical expressiveness.

Arguing against earlier thinkers such as Freud and Piaget, Harris claims that little children's early imaginings (from their second year onward, around the same time language emerges) and fantasies are not as disorganized and primitive as has traditionally been thought. Instead, he claims that their ability to imagine hypothetical situations and counterfactuals, as in their games of pretend play, is quite sophisticated, contributing to their cognitive and emotional development and being vital for making causal and moral judgments.

Harris suggests that children take their real world conceptual knowledge of causal powers and such into their pretend play, where they can stipulate things, suspend objective truth for make-believe truth, and imagine episodes with unfolding causal chains. They can thus engage in the same cognitive activities as us when we pretend things in a make-believe mode. Children's pretend play may be inspired by reality, claims Harris, but that does not mean that it is intended to signify or represent reality. Harris suggests that two-year-olds may understand some of the essential components of fiction and drama, and can exercise the same sort of imagination that we engage in when we entertain fictional possibilities. He claims that our disposition for fiction is thus remarkably deep-rooted, and begins to emerge around age two as speech develops. Pretend play is an early sign of our lifelong capacity to consider alternatives to reality, according to Harris.

Another aspect of children's imaginings is role-play, which Harris defines as pretend play where children temporarily act out the part of someone else, or project a role onto a doll or toy that serves as a prop, or else invent without props a creature or person such as an imaginary companion. Children thus enter into make-believe situations they create, and in ways that call for flexibility and sensitivity. Role-play, Harris claims, often depends on active simulation whereby role players project themselves into make-believe situations, this kind of simulation playing a lasting role in our mental lives. Also, young children engaging in complex pretend play with others are more likely to be better in assessing others' feelings, as their simulation skills and thus their psychological understanding improve. Interestingly, Harris reports that it is only when children impersonate animate beings endowed with mental states rather than inanimate objects (such as airplanes) that they better understand mental states. And children who engage in more pretend play are better at seeing others' perspectives. Harris contends that our absorption in fictional narratives as adults is continuous with the alter-centric role-play of children.

Harris also discusses children's emotional reactions to imaginary entities. He claims that rather than confusing fantasy and reality when they invent creatures and events in their pretend play, preschool children know full well that what they miss or fear is imaginary, and yet feel sad or fearful as their emotions are aroused by their imaginary inputs. Both children and adults can become absorbed in imaginary worlds, as we adults know from the experience of being lost in good novels and films. Harris finds (incidentally, against some philosophers such as Kendall Walton, who claim that fiction only arouses make-believe or quasi-emotions) that imagining situations can sometimes provoke genuine emotions, not just ideas of emotions, and this is common to both adults and children, who can both be driven to emotions even though they know that the relevant inputs are fictional. He also reports that adults and children adopt similar strategies when responding to fiction, those identifying with the imagined events (and imagining they are happening to themselves) being more likely to become emotionally involved than those who remained detached by inhibiting identification and reminding themselves that their inputs are not real. How can imaginary situations arouse real emotions if we know from the outset they are not real? Harris argues that this is because thoughts about the ontological status of what is depicted do not enter our appraisal system, unless the material fictionally portrayed is graphic or disturbing, in which case we remind ourselves that it is merely fictional. But why are human beings so designed that our emotions can be evoked by real and also imaginary events, and what purpose does such an emotional responsiveness serve? Harris speculates that our felt emotions have evolved to help us plan, and in imagining various alternative courses of action, our felt emotions guide our decision-making by showing what emotions we would actually feel were we to take a certain course of action. This linkage between imagination and emotion holds for fiction as well, suggests Harris, for in imagining situations from a fictional character's point, we are emotionally aroused, even though we know intellectually that this situation is not affecting us or likely to affect us. In this manner, imagination and emotion are brought together both when we make hard decisions and when we experience fiction, claims Harris. A second speculation from Harris is that if emotionally charged eyewitness reports arouse the same emotion in us, then we end up being in sync with our interlocutors and being alerted to events. Fictional inputs can engage the same apparatus that is involved in our emotional sensitivity to eyewitness account, our engagement with fiction and drama being a function of our being language users.

To conclude this summation of Harris, here are some more claims he makes. Harris claims that our capacities for language and imagination fused at some point in our evolution, allowing us to think about a variety of imaginable situations. About children, he claims that they can compare actual events with imagined alternatives, and while they usually assume ordinary causal laws apply to imagined situations, they can also imagine violations of these laws in special settings or genres, such as fairy tales and religious stories. He also claims that adults process narrative discourse in ways similar to those whereby children engage with make-believe situations.

I now turn to explaining the relevance of Harris's claims to my project. There is much in Harris's rich account that is worthy of admiration and agreement. I am no psychologist and so cannot assess Harris from that perspective, but for my purposes of talking about imagination in connection with musical expressiveness, Harris's claims are relevant in the following ways. Harris asks whether children invest their imaginative creations with a quasi-reality when they become emotionally involved with these and feel fear or sadness, or whether instead they know full well that they are only dealing with imaginary entities and situations and yet feel emotions, and ultimately favors the latter hypothesis. In the case of imaginatively hearing musical expressiveness, I want to suggest that *both* these possibilities can obtain, for we hear musical expressiveness in different ways. Sometimes we may know full well that what we imagine—say, an imagined, indeterminate musical persona—is only imaginary, and yet hear and feel aroused to emotions, or something like that. But at other times, we may become so intensely involved with the music (especially when hearing very intensely expressive music such as passages in Beethoven's symphonies and late quartets) that we may at least *momentarily* forget that what we are imagining—when we animate the music itself, say, and project life and mental states onto it, imagining it is the sort of thing that is alive and sentient—is not real, and get so absorbed in the music that we are also aroused by it. Both of these cases are similar to the one Harris suggests in that his case involves children themselves inventing creatures and events (rather than those invented by others in the stories, books, videos, and so forth, that children usually come across), and both cases of musical expressiveness also involve listeners themselves imaginatively creating—albeit, in ways that are willy-nilly and not always highly foregrounded—an indeterminate musical persona or an animated entity that is none other than the music itself, on which life and mental states are imaginatively projected by listeners.

As well, Harris's claim that imagining a situation can sometimes provoke genuine emotions is pertinent to musical expressiveness, for imagining music as sad or otherwise imaginatively hearing musical expressiveness can also, I suggest, arouse emotions or something like that, but more of these matters in the next chapter. And another similarity with Harris's claims is that as in Harris's case of identifying with fiction and its characters causing arousal, imaginatively identifying with music in various ways (either by imagining that the music is expressive of our mental states; or by imagining we are the music; or by the imagining of our auditory experience of hearing the music that it is an experience of our feeling the mental state we hear the music as being expressive of, as Walton suggests; or in some other way) can also cause arousal of mental states in listeners. Also, Harris suggests that focusing on technical and other structural details of films can inhibit arousal; likewise, focusing on structural and other details of music can thwart hearing musical expressiveness and being aroused by it.

Two final comments about Harris's claims and their relevance to my project. First, in a discussion of reasoning and make-believe, Harris suggests that while children and others may be led during reasoning from premises to a conclusion to adopt an analytic orientation that focuses on the claims of the premises themselves even if these do not fit into their experience, they might also alternatively fall back into an empirical orientation that relies on their experiences and observations in reasoning about the given premises. In the case of theorizing about musical expressiveness, I want to stress that we need *both* of these kinds of approaches or something like them. That is, we need an analytic or conceptual approach that analyzes the very concept of expressiveness, as used ordinarily and across the arts, as well as an empirical approach that is true to the experiences of musical expressiveness in capturing their variety. Second, Harris claims that the inventions of imaginary characters and scenes by children give rise to various emotions, rather than the emotional needs of children giving rise to these inventions. In the case of musical expressiveness, I want to suggest in the next chapter that the causal arrow may point in both directions. That is, imaginatively hearing music as sad in various ways—via animation, or imagining a musical persona, or identifying with the music in various ways, etc., all of which will be dealt with in the next chapter—may arouse emotions or something like them in us. But also, as I will speculate in the next chapter, our emotional needs for play, companionship (even if an imaginary companionship), and the like may lead us to imagine musical expressiveness in various willy-nilly, not always highly foregrounded, ways that may be evolutionarily hard-wired and rewarding in many ways.

V.4. Gregory Currie's View

The next writer whose views on imagination will be considered is Gregory Currie, and once again I first sum up some of his main claims and then assess their relevance for my project (Currie 2004; Currie and Ravenscroft 2002). I leave aside Currie's claim (Currie 2004, chapter 9), with which I have no quarrel, that while engaging with fiction calls for imagination, it does not always require empathetically identifying with fictional characters even though this may be required sometimes; though I would add to Currie's account that empathic responses can be intersubjective in being in principle shareable and also often justifiable as appropriate or otherwise. It is instead claims made jointly by Gregory Currie and Ian Ravenscroft that will concern me here.

Currie and Ravenscroft start with the function of imagination that enables us to project ourselves into other situations and see things from or think about other perspectives. This role of imagination in play, pretense, and fiction allows our recreative minds to recreate the mental states of others, be they actual persons or fictional characters or our past, future, or counterfactual selves. It is this faculty of recreative imagination (as opposed to creative imagination) that underpins perspective-shifting, hold Currie and Ravenscroft, and is the focus of their study. Recreative imagination (or imaginative projection), they grant, is only one kind of imagination, and it involves states that are like beliefs, desires, and perceptions (and thus can mimic and substitute for these), but are also variously different from these. With regard to imagery, or perceptual imaginings, they claim that imagery in its various modes is related to its perceptual counterparts, and is perception-like. Visual imagery, e.g., is like visual experience in having a visual character, auditory imagery like hearing things in having an auditory character, and so on; and these are all perception-like imaginings. They distinguish the character of an imagining from its content, i.e., what it is that one is imagining. Imaginings that have beliefs and desires as their counterparts are propositional imaginings. Also, imagining-that is belief-like; imagining preserves the inferential patterns of belief. Interpreting narratives works by commingling beliefs and imaginings.

Amongst other things, Currie and Ravenscroft distinguish between beliefs, belief-like imaginings, and desire-like imaginings. Imaginings are doings while beliefs are not; also beliefs are constrained in having to form an internally rational whole whereas this need not hold of imaginings, e.g., we can imagine that Desdemona has been killed while believing there is no such person. As well, imaginings are usually of very limited duration and do not have the motivating force of belief. But imaginings depend on beliefs for their wide content. Currie and Ravenscroft caution that the dependence of imaginings on other mental states should indicate that we should not expect much of a definition of imaginative states, as defining beliefs, desires, and perceptions has been hard. Regarding desire-like imaginings, they postulate these since in imagined situations, especially in response to fiction, we often desire things we do not actually desire (given that real desires often motivate actions). Desire-like imaginings, e.g., wanting Desdemona to be saved, also explain the emotional effects of imagination. Desires and desire-like imaginings are differently constrained in that desires can be unreasonable or unjustified if they do not connect with facts in various ways, but desire-like imaginings, e.g., wanting Desdemona to be saved, are not similarly undercut as unreasonable by facts such as that Desdemona does not exist.

Mental imagery is a form of recreative imagination, grant Currie and Ravenscroft, though in the case of visual images it need not, following Wittgenstein, Ryle, and Sartre, involve seeing mental pictures. Imagery is sometimes under voluntary control, sometimes not, as in the case of dreams, illusions, etc., and it can come and go independently of us. Images are usually indeterminate in some way, and are sometimes particular, as in the case of many visual images, but often not so. Visual imagery or visualizing is not imagining that one *is* seeing, and it is confusing to use "imagining seeing" as equivalent to "visualizing," claim Currie and Ravenscroft, for visualizing is not in general imagining seeing. Rather they claim that where "imagining seeing" refers to visualizing, it should be read as "imagining, in a seeing like way, (P)"; likewise they suggest that belief-like imagining is not imagining believing something but instead imagining, in a belief-like way, P. A new kind of visual imagining they are open to but not committed to is one where an act of seeing is *itself* imaginative, as imagination penetrates the seeing itself: filmic imagining may involve this as one sees recorded screen images of actors and sets, and in that very act of seeing visually imagines fictional characters and locations, e.g., I see a screen image of Olivier on a set, and that seeing has another counterpart, seeing Hamlet at Elsinore. Alternatively, one might think of filmic imagining as a nonperceptual imagining the content of which is closely tied to the content of perception. Currie and Ravenscroft follow Ryle in denying that pretending to do F to A is in general a matter of doing F to an imagined A. While pretending and imagining are both broadly recreative states, they are contra Ryle not to be identified as pretending is behavioral (you pretend to do something *by* doing something else) while imagining is mental. There can be imagining without pretending (and its overt behavior), and there can be pretending without imagining, e.g., by some actors and deceivers (though imagining may help them).

Next, Currie and Ravenscroft clarify that supposing is belief-like imagining and to be distinguished from desire-like imaginings, e.g., we can suppose for argument's sake that female infanticide is good in the sense of forming the relevant belief-like imagining without bringing desires and desire-like imaginings into play. Fantasy is treated by them as a species of imaginative response and is indulgent imagining. They deny that imagining is a kind of introspection even if imagining can be about inner states. Also, they claim that a capacity for imagination (as in the case of the first cave-painters, possibly) need not signify a theory of or a special awareness of one's own inner life.

As well, there is a fundamental difference in Currie and Ravenscroft's view between propositional imaginings (which have beliefs and desires as their counterparts) and perceptual imaginings (which have perceptual states as their counterparts and involve mental images), though both importantly explain our mentalizing. They appeal to a notion of cognitive conservation in claiming that in simulating S's reasoning, one should appeal to *just the same* beliefs or information that S appeals to. And they claim that while it is not clear that visual and perceptual imaginings are cognitively conservative beyond the input stage (given current uncertainty about how much vision and visual imagery share neural and other mechanisms), in contrast the conditions of cognitive conservation can be met by propositional imaginings when we reason by the same inferential route from the same premises to the same conclusions.

Currie and Ravenscroft also argue that some delusions may be unrecognized imaginings, claiming in particular that the schizophrenic's delusions involve an irrational loss of the distinction between what is believed and what is merely imagined, as she finds it hard to see that what she imagines is merely imagined. Finally, they claim that emotion can cross over into imagination in ways peculiar to it, and the pleasures of imagination depend on this as we imagine in belief-like ways that the events of fictional works are happening to people. Currie and Ravenscroft claim that emotions are perception-like sensitivities to relations between the world and how we want it to be, and thus carry egocentric information; they also believe that emotions rely on perceptions, bodily sensations, and beliefs. We have genuine emotional responses to what is merely imagined because imagination takes inputs from perceptions, beliefs, and desires, and also their respective counterparts. In the case of our responding emotionally to tragedies, they suggest that emotions in response to imagined scenarios collide with emotions in response to the real-world narratives that report those imagined events. Disagreeing with both Hume and Walton, they claim that while there is an unpleasant aspect to one's emotional response to tragedy, this contributes essentially to the work's overall positive impact rather than detracting from it. We experience a tension between our negative emotional responses to tragedy and the other aspects of our engaging imaginatively with the work, a tension we value and enjoy. Our imagining, e.g., that Desdemona dies, frustrates our desire-like imagining that she live and causes a negative emotion, but simultaneously our real desire that the play go well is satisfied and so we also feel positive emotion. We have a (higher-order) desire that the play generate this conflict of emotions, and when the play does so our desire is congruent with the world, a tragic emotion being a quasi-perceptual awareness of this congruence. In this sense, Currie and Ravenscroft maintain, a tragic response is equally a response to the work itself and also to our responses to it; cultivated responses to tragedy may thus have a self-congratulatory air about them.

There is much insight in Currie and Ravenscroft's account to learn from.[2] I would like to clarify for starters, however, that what they mean by imaginative projection or recreative imagination, to wit, recreating others' mental states, is quite different from what I mean in section VI.3 when I claim that in animating music we imaginatively project life and mental states onto the music. For projecting life and mental states imaginarily onto something inanimate and insentient such as music in the sense that I have in mind need not involve recreating anyone's mental states—be it other people or fictional characters including an imagined, indeterminate musical persona or our past, future, or counterfactual selves—in the sense that Currie and Ravenscroft have in mind.

A second point I want to make is this. Currie and Ravenscroft make many plausible claims about imagination in relation to some of the arts—literature, theater, film, etc.; and claims about imagination and the other arts such as representational painting have also been made by other philosophers such as Walton. But they do not have anything to say about some other arts such as music, abstract visual art, and so on (compare Todd 2003, 421). Is it completely implausible to think imagination may also be involved when it comes to these other arts, especially—for my purposes—music? Of course, it may not be recreative imagination—the kind of imagination that Currie and Ravenscroft focus on and which involves recreating the mental states of others—that is involved in creating, performing, and listening to music (unless one is recreating the mental states of the composer, or performer, or an imagined musical persona, or one's own self). But it could easily be creative imagination (the kind of imagination that led the great Argentine writer Jorge Luis Borges to create the fictional character of Pierre Menard) that is certainly involved in composing, improvising, and perhaps also performing music, or indeed some other kind of imagining when it comes to our engagement with music, broadly speaking. Notice also that appealing to imagination across the arts in our experience of them also leads to a theoretical unity across the arts on this point, for it is not clear why, of all the arts, the abstract arts—music, abstract visual art, etc., which precisely because of their abstract nature would often seem to engage our imaginations—should stand alone in not involving the imagination in some way in our creative, performative, or sensory experience of them when the other arts seem to do so. In fact, I would not be surprised if it is harder to discuss and indeed detect imagination in relation to music than in the case of the other arts (and perhaps this is partly why not as much has been written about imagination and music as has been written about imagination and the other arts), both due to the abstract nature of music as an art as well as due to the elusive nature of imagination, given that many imaginings are not highly foregrounded.

On a different point, Currie and Ravenscroft wonder if there may be one kind of visual imagining where imagining may penetrate the seeing so that the act of seeing itself may be imaginative, e.g., filmic imagining may involve this as one sees recorded screen images of actors and sets, and in that very act of seeing visually imagines fictional characters and locations. But ultimately they remain open between committing to this kind of visual imagining and an alternative that sees filmic imagining as a nonperceptual imagining the content of which is closely tied to the content of perception, without being part of or penetrating the seeing. In the case of music, however, I want to suggest that there is a kind of hearing that is penetrated by the imagination so that the very act of hearing musical expressiveness is imaginative in that one hears sounds and *simultaneously* imagines mental states such as emotions in them, mental states which are not really in the sounds but only imagined to be there. What makes Currie and Ravenscroft hold back from committing to perception-penetrated-by-imagining in the case of vision is an evolutionary concern, that vision must have evolved to help identify predators and prey, and any creatures *that* imaginative would likely not have survived. But here are at least three alternative possibilities that push back against this evolutionary concern. First, at least in the case of hearing as opposed to seeing, I suggest that it is possible that perception-penetrated-by-imagining may actually have *helped* us survive in that, say, an unidentified sound heard as coming from behind a bush or round the corner may also be simultaneously and immediately imagined (in the sense of being fancied or supposed) to be the sound of a threatening creature and thus immediately put us on guard. Second, it is also possible that perception-penetrated-by-imagination may have come about *later* in our evolution as a species, as we (or Mother Nature) eliminated many dangerous species and other threats slowly and became more secure in our existence as a species. And, third, it is equally possible that perception-penetrated-by-imagination may arise not ordinarily when our survival is at stake but only under special circumstances, such as when we engage with the arts, be it music or film or something else. Indeed, the last of these three possibilities in fact ties in with the second possibility, for if the arts came about later in our evolution as a species (the earliest cave-paintings after all only go back about thirty thousand years or so) and developed over a long time as we evolved slowly, it is very likely that the maturing of the arts happened as we were becoming more secure in our existence as a species, even if not in part facilitated by this latter.

Currie and Ravenscroft's claim that schizophrenia involves a loss of the distinction between what is believed and what is merely imagined may be relevant to imagination and musical expressiveness in the following way. We do not believe that something without life and mental states such as music is really sad, but instead only imagine this, I submit, and this may well be a belief-like imagining, following Currie and Ravenscroft. But sometimes in the very experience of hearing very intensely expressive music, I suggest we may get so caught up with the music that we may lose sight of or forget this distinction at least momentarily, so that it feels very strongly *as if* the music itself is sad, which we may even believe for half a moment before realizing that this cannot really be. Relatedly, Currie and Ravenscroft claim that while beliefs are normally generated by perceptions or by other beliefs, imaginings are internally generated and this is what most saliently separates imaginings from beliefs. While this may be generally true, it needs to be noted nevertheless that at least some imaginings may in part also be based on perceptions or beliefs, e.g., filmic imaginings seem to be based on perceiving moving screen images and our beliefs about them, and imagining music as sad seems to be based on perceiving or hearing musical sounds (and their various resemblances with something to do with mental states and their expression), if I am right.

One final point, this time about Currie and Ravenscroft's claims that emotions are perception-like sensitivities to relations between how we want the world to be and the world itself, sensitivities that is to congruences or lack thereof between ourselves and the world. They also claim that infants and various nonhuman animals can experience emotions, even though it is doubtful whether they have beliefs. The cognitive-affective view of emotions I advanced in chapter I can take both of these claims on board. I grant that emotions tell us how we feel about the world, how we want it to be, and how it is; it is another issue as to whether we are self-aware or sensitive enough to cognize what our emotions are telling us about ourselves and the world. As for infants and nonhuman animals, I granted above in section I.4 when discussing Nussbaum that the cognitive aspect of emotions need not be evaluative beliefs or judgments, strictly speaking, but could instead be seeings-as or imaginings.

V.5. Imagination, Music Perception, and Musical Culture

To conclude this chapter, I have not said much here by way of a positive conception of imagination, beyond what I said briefly in section V.1 and then surveying some of the best recent philosophical and psychological writing on imagination. This I admit is in part because I myself do not have a complete grip on this very elusive but pervasive and important mental phenomenon, nor is it clear that anyone has uncovered all there is to the imagination, a faculty that weakens in many of us over time as we pass from childhood into adulthood. So I proceed to the next chapter and to talk of imagination and musical expressiveness on the assumption that we have just enough of a grasp on imagination for what follows.

It would, however, be awfully remiss of me if in discussing imagination in relation to music, I said nothing about two things: (i) how imagination might be involved in our basic perception of music, and (ii) how imagination might play a role in the construction of musical culture. Accordingly, I discuss these things below in concluding this chapter; though any readers dying to proceed to my positive views on musical expressiveness can safely jump ahead to the next chapter at this point.

There is an ongoing debate over whether music perception is (ineliminably) informed by spatial concepts applied metaphorically or imaginatively to sound. Roger Scruton claims that metaphors involve a deliberate transfer of a term or concept from a central context to something known not to exemplify it. In this way, metaphors bring dissimilar things together in a highly imaginative fusion (Scruton 1997, 80-96). Metaphors are indispensable, holds Scruton, when how the world seems depends upon our imagination being actively involved with it, and this is the case with musical experience. For example, sounds do not literally rise and fall, but we often hear music move this way. Moreover, Scruton claims, musical motion and other musical qualities are aspects or tertiary qualities (which, following Locke, are powers of objects to affect other objects, such as the power of fire to melt wax). These musical qualities, Scruton holds, are only perceived by rational beings *via* certain exercises of the imagination involving the metaphorical transfer of concepts from other contexts, and so we hear music under indispensable metaphorical descriptions. In hearing sounds, Scruton suggests, we may thus be on the "listen-out" for imaginative perceptions, hearing sounds and also simultaneously hearing the life and movement in them that is music, situated in an imagined space and organized in terms of such spatial concepts as "up" and "down," "high" and "low," "rising" and "falling," and so on.

Malcolm Budd believes an alternative to Scruton's account of the experience of hearing sounds as music can be offered that does without metaphors and the spatial and other concepts Scruton appeals to (Budd 2003, 211). Budd suggests that one can hear the distinctive timbral character of a note without appealing to a metaphorical description transferred from another domain (Budd 2003, 213-14). Turning next to pitch and melody, Budd rejects as untenable Scruton's claim that without reference to space, tones would no longer be heard as moving away from or toward each other. Continuing to chords, Budd argues that if melody cannot tenably be explained in terms of sounds being heard under spatial concepts, as Scruton thinks, then it seems unwarranted that we hear tones simultaneously (as chords) in terms of tones heard imaginatively as arranged spatially. Finally, as for rhythm, given that Scruton here bases his view on beat, as being comparable to the heartbeat, Budd claims that the idea should not be one involving spatial movement but rather of something contracting and dilating, as in the case of the systole and the diastole.

Budd's own positive suggestions on these matters are as follows. Arguing that the literal/metaphorical distinction may obscure things, Budd refrains from claiming like Stephen Davies (1994, 235-36) that it is literally true that melodies move up and down. He suggests instead that melodic movement from tone to tone is merely temporal, not spatial, given that relations between tones are due to their positions on the pitch continuum, which is not itself a spatial dimension. "Movement," Budd thinks, does not only mean change in spatial location, but can also mean change along a nonspatial continuum or with reference to a particular variable (Budd 2003, 219–20). As for rhythm, to hear it, Budd claims, may involve imagining the pulsations of life (Budd 2003, 221).

Scruton (2004, 185–86) responds to Budd's criticisms first by trying to clarify what it means for an experience to "involve" a metaphor. While admitting that we may be up against a sort of bedrock in this dispute, he suggests that seeing a dog, for instance, involves the concept of a dog applied in judgment, whereas seeing a dog in a picture involves the concept of a dog applied in an "unasserted thought" and thus figuratively. It is in a manner similar to the latter, claims Scruton, that we apply the concept of movement to pitches in hearing a melody, since pitches cannot literally move. Scruton also disagrees with Budd's claim that spatial metaphors can be dispensed with in hearing music, and claims in opposition that we must hear music in terms of up and down, toward and away, mirroring, inversion, forward, backward, same direction, and so on, to make sense of it. Finally, Scruton contends that Budd's suggestion that musical movement is temporal rather than spatial is itself metaphorical, and is the same metaphor of movement that Scruton (2004, 187) is trying to explicate. Scruton grants that merely temporal *Gestalts* may be broken down preconceptually into temporal chunks experienced as unified wholes without appeal to movement, but thinks that this level lies below the experience of music.

In this debate, Budd seems right to object to Scruton with regard to timbres and musical movement. For, *against* Scruton, the distinctiveness of a timbre might be heard under very different metaphorical descriptions or under none at all; for example, the literally shrill and piercing timbre of an oboe holding a high note might be heard as such even by little children incapable of understanding metaphors. And one can hear melodic or musical movement without appealing to Scruton's spatial metaphors. For example, a melody can be heard as moving from the leading note to the tonic in the familiar musicological terms of melodic tension and resolution (or melodic drive or yearning) that we literally hear in the music, or in some such terms that describe the experience without essentially referring to spatial features; musically untrained listeners unfamiliar with notions of musical space might be especially inclined to do so, or else they might hear the music as moving from the "unpleasant" to the "pleasant." For example, the supertonic and the leading note have a melodic tendency to go to the tonic, the subdominant to the mediant or the dominant, and the submediant to the dominant. There are also notes of emphasis, such as the tonic in tonal music, the *finalis* in modal music, and the *vadi* (or main note) of Indian *ragas*. And there are notes of secondary emphasis such as the dominant in tonal music, the *confinalis* in modal music, and the *samvadi* (often a fifth higher than the *vadi*) of Indian *ragas*. Similarly, there are notes or points of melodic tension and repose. Such features might be especially important in the experience of a lot of essentially monophonic music, such as Gregorian chant and many non-Western musics, where melody is not just an important element but virtually all there is to the music, barring such things as background drones, pitched rhythmic accompaniment, and the like.

As argued earlier in sections III.5 and III.6, it might also be asked against Scruton whether ordinary language metaphors at the very least point to or suggest objective resemblances (or lack thereof in the case of negative metaphors such as "No man is an island," "Life is not a bed of roses," etc.) in certain respects between two or more otherwise very different things, in virtue of which we are prompted to imagine (or not imagine, in the case of negative metaphors) one thing as, or in terms of, another. If such a resemblance-plus-imagination conception of metaphors is right, and metaphors can in principle be paraphrased, then any allegedly metaphorical description of musical motion, expressiveness, and so on, might be explained away *via* paraphrase in a way that involves resemblance and imagination and, *contra* Scruton, dispenses with the metaphor. It is also possible that musical experience may be organized by concepts that do not apply literally but might only be *imagined* (willy-nilly, readily, and immediately, and in ways that need not be highly foregrounded) to apply to sounds as we hear them, and in a way that need not, *contra* Scruton, invoke or involve metaphors at all.

Finally, I turn to the second issue I mentioned above, to wit, the role of imagination in the construction of musical culture. In an important book, Nicholas Cook (1990) has suggested that sonata form, large-scale Schenkerian tonal structures, thematic unity, serial transformations, and other such staples of music theory are not directly audible, but are rather ways of imagining sound as music—"a repertoire of means for imagining music" (Cook 1990, 4)—that constitute musical culture—"a tradition of imagining sounds as music" (Cook 1990, 223). *Against* Cook, however, many music theorists would contend that their aim is to understand how music actually works rather than merely create fictive or imaginative accounts of music that do not correspond to listeners' auditory experience (Huron 1995). Indeed, though Cook rejects such claims, it has not infrequently been held that listeners may aurally apprehend sonata forms, serial transformations and the like not directly but rather indirectly or subconsciously, contributing thus to coherent and unified musical experiences that may consequently please and satisfy (Réti 1961; Schoenberg 1978).

Of particular interest to our topic of music and imagination, leaving Cook's main thesis aside, is his rich discussion of the different aspects of musical imagination. Cook recalls Jean-Paul Sartre's example of imagining a thimble wherein our image synthesizes within a single awareness the front and back, inside and outside of the thimble, even though in real life we would have to alternate between different viewpoints to see all of the front and back, the inside and outside of the thimble, and could not see them wholly at the same time (Sartre 1972, 105). Analogously, Cook suggests that both musically trained and untrained listeners can imagine experiences of musical works in ways where all that is heard sequentially is integrated into a single, heightened experience that captures all features of the music, even though there is something illusory about this (Cook 1990, 89). Likewise, Cook follows Sartre's example of imagining the Pantheon where our image is simply "many-columned" rather than one that has a determinate number of columns (Sartre 1972, 100–1), and suggests that we may similarly simply imagine the sound of Dietrich Fischer-Dieskau's voice, say, in at least a partly generic way (imagining the mellowness of his voice, the emphasis of his articulation, etc.), without specifics as to whether he sings loud or soft, what syllable he sings, whether he sings the beginning of a note or its middle or end, and so on (Cook 1990, 90). Similarly, in trying to recall a familiar musical work, Cook claims we might form generic images of harmonic gracefulness and orchestral luxuriance rather than specific sound-images with these properties (Cook 1990, 92). All these cases, Cook claims, following Sartre, involve "the illusion of immanence," that is, the illusion that what is imagined is there before one.

Cook also suggests that a lot of imagery used by musicians in producing or playing music is kinesthetic or even to some degree visual. For instance, imagining music as fingered a certain way, or writing in a certain fingering as imagined, is one of the ways whereby musicians imagine or represent the music they play (Cook 1990, 74–85). Likewise, in trying to recall one musical work while hearing another very different and structurally incompatible musical work being played on the radio, though the work being heard interferes with auditory recall, nevertheless a skilled keyboard player might recall the other work by "playing" it on a silent keyboard, consciously focusing on the movements of her fingers, hands, and arms.

Alternatively, a work might be recalled *via* visual imagery of its score—as when a pianist plays a work from memory and remembers what comes next by "seeing" it halfway down the next page—or else visual imagery of the keyboard. The imagery of the voice can also help sometimes in imagining a musical work. For example, reading a score in a library where one cannot sing aloud and is without a piano, one might sense the virtual or even actual tensing of the throat as the vocal line hits a high note or plumbs a low note, and thereby grasp something of the melody's expressive character. *Sotto voce* singing while performing by jazz musicians or the kora players of West Africa or the great classical pianist Glenn Gould provides a similar sort of security that comes from vocal awareness. There are, then, according to Cook, many sorts of images—kinesthetic, visual, notational, vocal, etc.—besides the auditory in terms of which musical works may be represented or imagined, and musicians may first analyze or deconstruct musical works in these different ways before reconstructing them as wholes. Finally, Cook suggests that a composer may conceive or imagine the basic analytical framework of a musical work in her head before writing the autograph score. Then the composer elaborates the framework and ties together all sorts of details, just as an experienced public speaker may have the framework (the basic points, etc.) of her lecture and some specific details (illustrations, jokes, etc.) worked out in her head before elaborating the framework and tying the details together in the course of writing her lecture.

V.6. Conclusion

Let us sum up what has been addressed in this chapter. I began by exploring different kinds of imaginings. Section V.2 then discussed work on imagination by Brian O'Shaughnessy, which I related to my imaginationist view of musical expressiveness. In the next section, I looked at work on children's imaginings by the psychologist Paul Harris and related it to my imaginationism about musical expressiveness, while section V.4 dealt with Gregory Currie's influential work on the imagination. Finally, I discussed the role of imagination in music perception, and also in musical culture.

To reiterate, I have claimed that there are many notions of imagination and many kinds of imaginings. These range from fancying to supposing to pretending to oneself (or make-believing, or making-believe if you prefer) to imaging to entertaining a possibility or a proposition without actually believing it to dreaming to daydreaming, and so forth. Also, imaginings are not always highly foregrounded and can be conscious or otherwise, short or long, voluntary or not so, intermittent, and so on.

VI

Imaginationism

> ... philosophical theories and analyses tend to consist, on first reflection, of . . . vacuous truisms that hardly need stating, but that, on further reflection, and developed into systems of assertions and inferences, come to be seen as foundational beliefs, casting light on the superstructure they support.
>
> —Peter Kivy (2002, 7)

VI.1. Introduction

Pure or instrumental or absolute music without words or a program is not *really* or *literally* sad or happy, as it is often said to be. It is only *imagined* to be so. This is the view I try to advance in this chapter.

I take it that to be really or literally sad or happy, a being or a thing must be able to have mental states such as emotions, moods, feelings, beliefs, desires, and the like. And to have mental states, a being or a thing must be able to have underlying neurophysiological brain states such as neuron firings. To have these in turn, a being or a thing must, in the standard case, possess life.

It should be self-evident to anyone who has the slightest familiarity with elementary biology that music has neither mental states nor underlying neurophysiological brain states, nor is it alive. Accordingly, it follows that, as something without life and mental states, music cannot really or literally be sad or happy. And that leads us to the puzzle of musical expressiveness, the puzzle of how something insentient and inanimate, such as pure music, can be heard as sad or happy, how it can be said to be such, or at any rate to be expressive of sadness or happiness or other mental states.

In this chapter, I begin in section VI.2 by rebutting Formalism (very roughly, the view that music cannot have emotional or affective content or otherwise "represent" affect) about music. Section VI.3 advances my imaginationism about musical expressiveness, especially the central claim that often we animate the music. Section VI.4 then discusses why we engage with music in this way, and the rewards of doing so. I then proceed in section VI.5 to discuss the question of whether music can arouse emotions. Section VI.6 then defends my imaginationist view from various objections that several people have raised to me.

VI.2. Against Formalism about Music

Before I proceed to set out *how* we imagine music to be sad or happy in various not always highly conscious ways, and the various rewards of these imaginings that may partly explain *why* we do so, I want to deal briefly with objections from those who lean toward Formalism, very roughly the view that music cannot have emotional content or otherwise "represent" emotions. The locus classicus of Formalist objections is, of course, the great Czech-born Viennese critic Eduard Hanslick's *On the Musically Beautiful* (Hanslick 1986). Accordingly, it is on that work that I focus here. Note that I discuss Hanslick because Formalism is an important approach to musical expressiveness, being in fact one of the six main alternatives (besides expression theories, persona theories, arousalism, metaphorism, and resemblance-based views) to my imaginationism. I do *not* engage with Hanslick "only" because Neo-Formalists such as Nick Zangwill and Robert Kraut do so, but rather because Hanslick is staking out an important position in a pioneering and ingenious way that I greatly respect.

Hanslick's main negative thesis is that it is *not the defining purpose* of music to represent feelings. And his main positive thesis is that beauty in music comes from its form, which is also its content, not from its connection to feelings, nor from its being said to represent feelings, nor from any extraneous or extramusical connection. It is perhaps only fair to see Hanslick as reacting against the late Romanticism of his contemporaries Liszt and (especially by the time of the eighth edition of *On the Musically Beautiful*) Wagner, who invested music with substantial programmatic capabilities (see Grey 2011).

I proceed to discuss Hanslick's arguments that music cannot represent definite feelings or emotions. Hanslick gives a variety of arguments to support his views. I take three of his arguments to be salient, and consider them in turn.[1]

The first argument we are given is that music cannot represent specific feelings or emotional states, because specific feelings and emotional states depend on ideas, judgments, and the like that constitute their conceptual essence. As music cannot represent or otherwise convey ideas and judgments that are essential to emotions, it thus cannot represent those emotions or definite feelings themselves, argues Hanslick.

In response to Hanslick's first argument, the first thing to note is that Hanslick talks about and denies explicitly the *representation* or portrayal of feelings and emotions, rather than the *expression* or expressiveness and arousal of these. This gives us some room to ask whether he would distinguish representation from expressiveness and arousal. If so, one can ask whether Hanslick would only deny musical representation of emotions and definite feelings rather than their expressiveness and arousal by music, which I would have no quarrel with, as I grant that music is not primarily representational. I turn to my second and *much more important* qualm about this argument. Hanslick is right to think that emotions and definite feelings call for ideas or judgments, which would form their cognitive, intentional component according to the cognitive-affective theory of emotions put forth in chapter I. Even so, this still leaves room for *non-intentional* feelings or affects as well as moods, going back to my discussion of feelings or affects in section I.2, and also the distinction between emotions and moods made earlier in section I.3, and thus allows for the possibility that music may be expressive of and arouse these non-intentional, non-cognitive mental states rather than emotions or "specific feelings." If that is right, then it still makes sense to try to solve the philosophical puzzle of musical expressiveness, which now becomes the genuine puzzle of how something insentient and inanimate, such as pure or instrumental or absolute music without words or a program, can be said to be expressive of *feelings and/or moods* (such as sadness and happiness) rather than full-fledged emotions. (Incidentally, the philosopher Ronald de Sousa, known internationally for his work on the emotions, once attended my Philosophy of Music class at Brooklyn College, and raised the same worry about Hanslick, independently of anything I said.) A third concern about this argument from Hanslick is that despite his argument, the *experience* of many listeners, both laypersons as well as the musically trained, is that a lot of music is often heard readily and immediately as being sad or happy or as expressive of some mental state, and as often arousing these. For example, the opening passages of the second movement (Fantasia-Adagio) of

Weber's Clarinet Quintet in B-flat, Op. 34, are heard by many competent listeners as sorrowfully pensive, or something like that. In contrast, the opening passages of the last movement (Allegretto grazioso) of Brahms's Piano Concerto No. 2 in B-flat, Op. 83, are heard by most such listeners as cheerful and lightly skipping, or something in that approximate vicinity. It seems hard to ignore this data from listeners' experiences of music, and we need to explain, against Hanslick, why listeners experience music as sad or happy, even if this experience is argued to be ultimately illusory, which in any case is not what Hanslick claims.

I turn now to a second argument in Hanslick, an argument from disagreement according to which different listeners simply do identify the same musical passages as having different emotional content. While one listener says a certain theme has love, another thinks of yearning, and a third feels piety. Hanslick claims that while there is this disagreement about feelings, so that no one knows what feeling is actually the content of the music, in sharp contrast there is often agreement about the beauty of a musical theme or work. He concludes that music cannot represent feelings, as the feelings in question are perpetually debated.

There are two things to be said in response to this argument. First, even though there is often disagreement about what mental state a musical work or passage is expressive of, often there is a broad agreement amongst competent listeners about the expressive content of some musical works and passages. To take a well-worn example, most competent listeners hear the funeral march from Beethoven's "Eroica" Symphony as expressive of grief or sadness or heavy-heartedness—something in that ballpark, at least. It would be incorrect to hear this movement as expressive of glee or light-heartedness, and I venture that hardly anyone including perhaps people outside the West who are unfamiliar with Western music does so; here I refer the reader back to the empirical, psychological data supporting cross-cultural perceptions of musical experiences that I cited in section IV.3 against Kivy. Second, the *mere* fact that listeners disagree about the expressive content of a musical work or passage does not show that there is no fact of the matter, as Hanslick seems to think. For it is perfectly possible that one of the parties in the dispute is right and the other(s) wrong. It is possible that one (or more) of the parties is inattentive or musically insensitive, or unfamiliar with the style and idiom of the music to a significant degree, or tired or distracted or perhaps even tone-deaf and so on, and these factors might account for why they do not hear the music in the correct way as regards its expression.

I conclude this discussion of Hanslick with a consideration of the third salient argument given by him. Hanslick claims that the same musical works often have been and can be set to texts of opposing emotional content. This adaptability of musical themes, he seems to think, shows that expressiveness is not intrinsic to a musical theme or passage or work, and is thus not part of its content. The only contents of music, claims Hanslick, are its "tonally moving forms," in his famous phrase.

Despite this argument from Hanslick, it really must be doubted whether just about *any* music can be set to any text whatsoever. To return to our well-worn example, it really is not clear that the funeral march from the "Eroica" Symphony can be successfully set to joyful words, given its melodic and harmonic structure, tempo, timbres, orchestration, and the like. If this is right, then one might claim, *pace* Hanslick, that at least for some music, its expressive content is not a widely variable function of the words that might be set to it but is rather something intrinsic, or at least something that is *imagined* to be so, as I suggest below. Consider a second example. Take the melody of "The Star-Spangled Banner," and try to sing sad words to it. Instead of singing "Oh, say can you see" to the first phrase, try to sing "Oh, I am so sad." Against Hanslick and his third argument, the effect will be *incongruous*, given that the melodic phrase itself is mostly a rising broken chord in a major key, and reaches its highest note at the very end (where one tries to sing the word "sad") of the phrase. The new words are sad but the melody and the music do not match the words or otherwise *sound* sad, hence the incongruity.

It might be thought, however, that more recent Formalists (about music), who one might call Neo-Formalists, have better arguments than what Hanslick gives us. Therefore, I now discuss the Neo-Formalism of Nick Zangwill and Robert Kraut (Zangwill 2015; Kraut 2007).

There are many strands in Zangwill's multifaceted position, and I take four of them to be central: Formalism, Metaphorism, Aesthetic Realism, and a certain Ineffabilism. I refer the reader back to my concerns about Metaphorism in chapter III, and many (if not all) of the arguments I advanced in that chapter will apply also to Zangwill, especially my claim that imagination and imaginationism may underlie both metaphors and metaphorism as being more fundamental, after all. Additionally, some of the central strands in Zangwill's position seem to be in tension with his Metaphorism, and it is not clear how these can all be held together *coherently* as part of one overall position. First, it is not clear how Aesthetic Realism—which Zangwill takes to be the view (2015, 4) that beauty exists independently of the pleasure through which we know it—and Metaphorism can be maintained consistently, as Zangwill holds. In general, if one is an Aesthetic Realist, one (typically) thinks some aesthetic property P (such as beauty or elegance) is possessed by (or true of) some object O in a mind-independent way. So, on the Aesthetic Realist view, it would seem to be literally (or really) true that O is P or O has P (say, O is beautiful). That is not a metaphorical description, despite Zangwill. Compare here, very roughly, the situation with regard to other sorts of realism, focusing on but three kinds of realism: metaphysical realism, mathematical realism, and moral realism. Metaphysical realists think the world exists independently of us, our thoughts, perceptions, etc., in an objective way so that it is literally—not metaphorically—true to say the world exists mind-independently. Mathematical realists about numbers think similarly that the number 5 exists (out there somehow) regardless of our minds so it is true literally—not figuratively—that the number 5 is real. And moral realists think that certain moral features or properties are real in a mind-independent way so that it is literally factual or true—and not metaphorical—that certain actions or agents or situations or institutions have a certain moral status (whether good or bad, right or wrong) in virtue of possessing these features. Compare also the situation with regard to properties such as height (size or extension being a mind-independent primary quality at least since Locke): to say truly of someone that he is 6'3" tall is to assert a literal truth that is not metaphorical. It is not clear then, against Zangwill, how one could be *both* a realist and a metaphorist about music or aesthetics or indeed in general about other things, properties, and domains. Indeed, I suspect it is not just a coincidence but rather due to sound philosophical reasons (such as the ones just discussed) that neither of the two most famous and distinguished metaphorists about music and art—Nelson Goodman and Roger Scruton—is a realist; Goodman was in fact a Nominalist about properties in general, and Scruton says explicitly that he is anti-realist when it comes to music and its expressiveness, as we saw earlier in section III.6. Second and relatedly against Zangwill, it is not clear likewise how one can consistently be *both* a Metaphorist and an Ineffabilist, as he seems to be in many places. If one is an Ineffabilist about music (or anything else for that matter), then one holds that music (or that thing) cannot be captured adequately in linguistic descriptions, whether literal or metaphorical. Put differently, Ineffabilists believe that words, whether literal or metaphorical, simply fail to do justice to music (or the thing or domain in question), which is thus ineffable. It would seem then that Zangwill cannot be both a Metaphorist and an Ineffabilist. Perhaps Ineffabilism really is Zangwill's considered position—as seems to be confirmed midway through his book (2015, 112–16) when he claims that music is elusive—and so Metaphorism must go. That would also help Zangwill's overall position become consistent insofar as Aesthetic Realism and Ineffabilism are certainly compatible, unlike Aesthetic Realism and Metaphorism as argued earlier.

Zangwill sets up the contrast between literalist and metaphorist accounts of musical expressiveness (2015, 41–59). He proceeds to reject the obviousness of literalist views about descriptions of music in terms of emotion, thus paving the way for metaphorist views such as his. Claiming that descriptions of music in terms of "delicate," "balanced," and so on are metaphorical, Zangwill suggests that having a unitary account of all descriptions of music—whether about expressiveness, or about height, motion, and the like—is commonsensical and has the virtue of simplicity. So, claims Zangwill, uses of "angry" and other emotionally charged terms as applied to music must also be metaphorical; though here I would suggest against Zangwill that "angry" can instead be applied imaginatively to such inanimate and insentient things as clouds, music, etc., and in any case imagination underlies metaphors and metaphorism, as I urged in chapter III. Zangwill goes on to claim that emotion descriptions of music are usually metaphorical descriptions of music's aesthetic properties, and the function of music is to generate aesthetic properties such as beauty and elegance. Here now is my response to Zangwill's claims. First, to reiterate what I have said before, especially in chapter IV, I reject the literal-metaphorical binary as too focused on words and too influenced by the linguistic turn in Anglophone analytic philosophy. Instead, I urge we focus on the very experience of musical expressiveness, the experience having primacy over words and linguistic descriptions. And that experience involves imagination, I submit, so that emotions are only imagined to be part of the music and neither literally nor metaphorically there. Second, against Zangwill, it is possible that the expressive and nonexpressive properties of music may be so different (even if not completely unrelated) that to seek a unitary account may be oversimplified. Pluralism may well be more defensible here; though I will not pursue this thought further. Third, and more importantly, one might argue for a different sort of unitary account from the one that Zangwill urges for parity's sake. On this alternative view, imagination rather than metaphors would be involved *both* in ascribing expressive properties to music and also in ascribing nonexpressive properties such as height, space, and motion to music; indeed, some such view has been proposed very recently by Andrew

Kania (2015). In fact, if my arguments in chapter III to the effect that imagination underlies both metaphors and metaphorism are right, then all allegedly metaphorical descriptions of music (whether about expressiveness or about height, space, motion, etc.) would collapse or otherwise lead on to a unitary *imaginationist* (rather than metaphorist) view, against Zangwill.

As for Zangwill's Aesthetic Realism, here are two concerns. First, music and musical works are created and can also be destroyed or otherwise cease to exist, as I have argued elsewhere (Trivedi 2008). As such, the very art and practice of music seems to be dependent on human beings and their minds. Accordingly, not just music but also therefore its properties—whether they be expressive properties or properties having to do with music's motion (slow, fast, etc.), or height (up, down, etc.)—would seem to be mind-dependent (even if the aesthetic properties of nature might be mind-independent). That goes against Zangwill's Aesthetic Realism, which claims that music's properties are in some sense (that remains to be explained) mind-independent (Zangwill 2015, 14–16) and are "really" in the music; whether we can describe them or not. Second, against Zangwill's too narrow aesthetic conceptions of music and art (Zangwill 2015, 46–48), it is not the *function* of a lot of music to generate aesthetic properties; as anyone who has formally studied music even for a little bit knows only too well. A lot of avant-garde, experimental twentieth-century (and later) Western classical music such as many works by the likes of Milton Babbitt, Pierre Boulez, Karlheinz Stockhausen, Luigi Nono, Luciano Berio, and others is neither beautiful nor elegant, nor is it meant to be so; just as a lot of avant-garde art over the last 100 years or so going back to Duchamp's *Fountain* does not aim to generate aesthetic properties such as beauty, elegance, and so on. And yet these works are music and/or art; and in fact they have influenced later developments in music and art history. It is a different, evaluative matter as to whether these works are artistically and aesthetically good or bad, great or terrible, or something in-between. Those who would deny the status of music and/or art to such works (perhaps simply because they do not like these works or judge them to be terrible) seem guilty of *conflating* the classificatory, nonevaluative question of whether these works are music and/or art in the first place with later, evaluative questions about their artistic and aesthetic worth. These examples show against Zangwill that beauty, elegance, and other aesthetic properties are not *necessary* for music. Nor are such aesthetic properties *sufficient* to be music, as shown by the case of beautiful waterfalls that make beautiful "musical" or music-like sounds yet are not music, strictly speaking, for they are not artifacts. None of this is to deny that aesthetic properties are very important to music, even if not central in the way Zangwill means.

Turning to Zangwill's Formalism, he argues that it is not essential for music to possess, arouse, express, or represent emotions (2015, 27–40). Right away, it must be pointed out here against Zangwill that no respectable philosopher of music—including those such as myself who think that music can be expressive of emotions—thinks that music *must* essentially express or arouse emotions, for there is a lot of music that does not express or arouse emotions; think, for example, of some passages in Bach's and other Baroque keyboard music as played on the harpsichord, where beyond the formal beauty of the music it is not clear that emotions must be involved. Even many moderate arousalists such as Ridley and Matravers grant that music need not arouse emotions, as we saw earlier in sections II.6 and II.7. Also, given that music is devoid of life, it cannot possess mental states. And it is not clear that music can represent emotions, given that music is not primarily representational and has very limited ability to represent even with the help of words or a title, as Peter Kivy has argued (Kivy 1991). But to return to Zangwill, he concludes that emotion plays no role of any significance in what music is and in our experience of it, and that emotion is a complete distraction in thinking about music. In response, some music is deeply expressive, I (and many others) contend: think, to mention only a few examples, of many passages in Beethoven's symphonies and late quartets, such as the funeral march in his Seventh Symphony (also used as background music for the finale of the 2010 film *The King's Speech*) or the dramatic opening passages of his String Quartet in F Minor, Op. 95 (the "Serioso" quartet) or the last movement of the Op. 135 F Major String Quartet. Think also of the ancient Greek musical modes (Ionian, Dorian, Phrygian, Lydian, Mixolydian, Aeolian, etc.) and how they are associated in Book III (esp. 398c–403c) of Plato's *Republic* with various emotions and moods. It is also well to mention a non-Western example, the *ragas* of Indian classical music and how they are associated with different emotions and moods (as well as with different times of day and sometimes also with seasons). And think too of music and its affective qualities and powers being put to various uses—across the ages and in different cultures—in marches, wedding songs, funeral dirges, work songs, lullabies, and so on. I will say something shortly in my discussion of Kraut about why some might fail to hear any music as expressive at all on any occasion; though one might wonder if missing expressiveness in the kinds of musical examples just cited and instead treating these passages and works as purely formal is to fail to be fully human, to fail to have the rich experience of hearing or perceiving emotion in music just as we often perceive emotion or affect in the other arts and in life, making music continuous with the other arts and with life (despite many other differences). As well, *without* being a Formalist, one can grant Zangwill's claim (2015, 8–12) that absolute or purely instrumental music has aesthetic priority or fundamentality over other kinds of music in that without absolute musical beauty there would be no beauty or value in other kinds of music, but not vice versa.

I turn now to Robert Kraut's Neo-Formalism. Kraut notes that some listeners, such as Kraut himself, never hear emotional content in music, and wonders if this is due to musical insensitivity or due to an excessive focus on music's technical aspects or simply because the emotions are not there in the music. As we will see soon (if you have not already gleaned this), in my view, emotions heard in the music are only *imagined* (and often projected) to be in the music (in ways that can be shared intersubjectively) in an aural appearance but are not really or literally there; so perhaps Kraut might not disagree with me as much as might seem initially. However, let us follow Kraut and ask: why is it that some people (even some highly musical listeners) never (or almost never) hear music as expressive, or at least make such claims? At least four possible explanations suggest themselves in answer. Perhaps a failure of imagination is involved in their cases, especially if I am right that imagination is involved in hearing musical expressiveness. Or (as some of my students suggested to me in our Philosophy of Music class) maybe their perceptual, cognitive, affective, and other systems are wired differently (and perhaps deficiently) from those of the rest of us who often (though not always) hear music as expressive, though this remains to be confirmed empirically. If so, then the emotion-deaf—to use one of Kraut's terms—would be like the color-blind, as Mark Wilson (2006, 49) suggests. A third possibility is that maybe some listeners are too indoctrinated by musical formalism to be able to hear music as expressive on any occasion. It is certainly true of many who have a lot of musical training that they lean toward musical formalism and focus solely on musical structure (as I myself did and was taught to do when I studied composition, counterpoint, harmony, and music theory) to the exclusion of affect, as shown by Stravinsky's formalist sympathies and his famous remark (which Kraut also discusses) to the effect that music by its very nature is unable to express anything (Stravinsky 1936, 83–84), a remark which still leaves open the possibility that music may be *expressive* of mental states, going back to the expression-expressiveness distinction; though we should also note against Stravinsky *both* that many other great composers from Mozart to Tchaikovsky believed in music's affective content, and also that artists are not always the most rigorous philosophical thinkers when it comes to art and music, including their own works. And a fourth possible explanation is that these listeners do hear music as expressive on some occasions at least, but are simply never aware of this and hence their claims. As to which of these four suggestions is true, take your pick, and one might also combine some or all of these four.

VI.3. How We Imagine in Relation to Music

With that discussion of musical Formalism behind us, I turn now to my own positive solution to the problem of musical expressiveness.

If I am right, the solution to the problem of musical expressiveness is, at least at root, very simple, and indeed, intuitively very attractive. In a nutshell, it is this. Music is only *imagined* to be sad or happy or some other mental state. And it is willy-nilly, readily, immediately, and imaginatively heard or perceived to be so in various ways, as our imagination generally kicks in right away on hearing expressive music. These various ways of imagining are *not always highly foregrounded or conscious*, for we are not always *aware* that we are engaged in imaginings, as shown by the cases of dreaming and daydreaming, which are various kinds of imaginings. What allows us to imagine in various not always highly conscious ways that music is sad or happy or some other mental state are various resemblances between the music, its development, its gestures, its movement and so forth, on the one hand, and, on the other hand, our vocal and behavioral expressions of emotions, moods, feelings, and other mental states, and also resemblances between music and the inner feel of the affects or feelings involved in these mental states, all of which we came across in our discussion of Kivy, Davies, and Budd in chapter IV. Put differently, music is *imagined* in various not always highly conscious ways to be sad or happy or some other mental state *in virtue of* our perceiving it resembling the vocal and behavioral expression of various mental states as well as their affective feel. This, then, is a brief summary of my resemblance-plus-imagination view about musical expressiveness, resemblance being the causal foundation that allows the various imaginings whereby we imagine in various not always highly conscious ways that music is sad or happy, and hear and perceive it to be so, the listening being tied in with the imagining. In what follows, I will often abbreviate and refer to my view simply as an imaginationist position. Note that analogies between musical expressiveness and human expression are at best partial by my lights, for acts as well as perceptions of human expression may not call for imagination as much as hearing musical expressiveness does if I am right.

On my view, the sadness or happiness (or some other mental state) we hear in the music is an *imagined* property of the music: a musical passage or work is sad (or is expressive of sadness) if competent listeners (those who are musically sensitive, informed to a minimal degree, and so on) are disposed under standard conditions (they are not bored or tired or distracted or satiated by the music, and so on) to hear as imaginatively sad. It is also an *intersubjective* property of the music, one that is shared across competent listeners who can all, more or less, correctly hear the same musical passage or work in similar expressive terms. Expressiveness, especially as applied to landscapes, has also been said by Richard Wollheim to be a projective property (Wollheim 1993), with which I have no quarrel, though I would say we *imaginatively* project life and life-like emotional properties onto music and landscapes, and thus experience them as expressive. Roger Scruton describes expressiveness as a tertiary property of the music (Scruton 1997). This too may be right, as expressive music has the power to arouse mental states in listeners, tertiary properties, following Locke, being powers to produce changes in other objects, such as the power in fire to melt wax; in the case of music, vibrations might be thought to be the primary properties and sounds the secondary properties. Peter Kivy, finally, claims musical expressiveness is a complex, emergent property of the music;[2] this too is something I would not take issue with, for I think musical expressiveness is dependent (in terms of emergence or supervenience or some other relation) on the music's structural features, gestures, development, and so on, though expressiveness is neither reducible to these nor always predictable from these in a formulaic way.

I turn now to sketching briefly the various ways in which we imagine music to be sad or happy, this being an account of *how* we imagine music to be sad or happy. In the next section, I will try to explain *why* we imagine music to be sad or happy, sketching various rewards of doing so that might partly explain why we do so. Note that the imaginings involved in hearing music as sad or happy may be spontaneous, ready and immediate, and we may engage in them right away without being aware that we are doing so. It should also be noted that the imaginings involved in hearing music as expressive are guided and constrained by the music's structural features, gestures, etc., so that not everything is subject to the idiosyncratic whims of listeners; e.g., slow, soft music that is low-pitched and in a minor key is unlikely to be heard by most competent listeners as happy or something in that approximate neighborhood. This shows the listener is not free to hear just about anything in the music legitimately, and it shows that musical expressiveness is somehow dependent (perhaps in terms of emergence or supervenience) on the music's features, gestures, and such. Note also that it is musical passages rather than entire musical works themselves that are more likely to be imagined to be sad or happy, though this is not to deny that musical works as a whole too can be heard and imagined as sad or happy.

The first way of imagining music to be sad or happy is that often we may *animate* the music without always being aware that we are doing so. *Imaginatively, we project and endow the music itself with life and life-like qualities including mental states* in such cases, similar to the way in which our species often animates and imaginatively projects life and life-like qualities onto inanimate and insentient things such as comic strip characters (cars, the sun etc.), clouds and rocks (seeing angry faces in them, for example), the elements (the sun, the moon, wind, rain, the ocean, fire, etc.) as our pagan ancestors in ancient Greece, Rome, Egypt, India, Japan, Scandinavia, and elsewhere did. Animation films provide an even better example as the moving images (of cars, trees, cartoon people and such) onto which we project life and mental states are dynamic processes (rather than static things) that unfold over time, just as musical passages and works do. Animating the music is, I suggest, very similar to what we do when we see comic strips or animation films and imagine, within the world of the comic strip or the animation film, that the talking and expressive cars, trees, sun, etc., we see in them are *themselves* sad, happy, etc. Imagine, for example, seeing a car within a comic strip or in an animation film, depicted as having sparkling, happy eyes (the headlights) and a smiling mouth (the radiator), and going at a gallop at 75 miles per hour on wide, empty roads on a lovely, sunny day, when we see the sun too as smiling (or at least depicted as such). We do not think the car and the sun are literally happy or expressive, nor do we think they are metaphorically happy, nor do we see them as expressive of the mental states of their creator(s), nor do we suppose they are expressive of any mental states they might arouse in us, nor do we think they are expressive of the happiness of imagined, indeterminate "automobile" or "solar" personae that are somehow in the car and the sun, respectively. Instead we *imagine* the car and the sun are *themselves* happy within the fictional world of the comic strip and the animation film, imagining that they display *their own* happiness within the world of the comic strip or the film. Imagine now that the car—let us call her "Donna"—is damaged and splutters within the world of the comic strip or the animation film. We imagine in such a scenario that it is Donna the car itself (or herself, if you like), and not something other than it, that has been damaged and is expressing its sadness visually. When the car is then fixed and back in racing condition, within the world of the comic strip and the animation film, we imagine that it is Donna the car itself that, restored to health, is now expressing its happiness visually by means of a smiling mouth (the radiator) and eyes (the headlights). I am sure, by the way, that children, who often have greater and fresher imaginations than many grown-ups, will agree more readily and immediately than will many grown-ups that we imagine it is comic-strip and animation film cars themselves that are sad, happy, etc.; if in doubt, ask a child who or what we see as sad, happy, etc., when we see comic-strip and animation film cars depicted as such.

To illustrate all of this further, it will be helpful, at least for a little bit, to move away from music precisely because of its abstract and often intractable nature, and consider two drawings, the first of which depicts a glorious day and represents the sun as smiling, and the second of which depicts a witheringly hot day and represents the sun as angry. In such instances, we see representations of the sun showing it as smiling or as angry. But *who* is it that is smiling or angry: *whose* emotions are expressed pictorially? There is not an imagined, indeterminate "solar" persona that is distinct from the sun and "in" the sun or in its pictorial representation, and who we imagine is smiling or angry; nor do we think that the mental states expressed belong to the artist or to the viewer(s); nor do we imaginatively identify with the smiling or angry sun so that we might say that it is our emotions that are imagined to be expressed pictorially. Rather, it is the sun *itself* that is smiling or angry, that is, we *imagine* the sun itself, as depicted, is alive and smiling or angry. We imaginatively project life and mental states onto the sun, as depicted, as we animate it even though we know it is inanimate. The causal story behind this that allows us to do so involves resemblances between the faces of smiling or angry people and the features of the sun (the eyes, mouth, and forehead) as depicted by the artist.

Animating the music, in my view, involves a very similar (if not an abstract instance of the same) kind of imagining, except that it is harder to detect musical animation due to both the abstract nature of music as an art as well as the fact that we engage in various imaginings without always noticing at the time that we are doing so. While animating, we imagine musical passages (and works) *themselves* to be the kind of thing that is alive, is sentient, is sad (or happy or some other mental state), and is an audible thing or being which expresses this sadness through presenting an aurally apprehended auditory appearance which consists of musical gestures, development etc., as we imaginatively project life and life-like qualities including mental states onto the music without necessarily being aroused to these first, as Wollheim might claim (Wollheim 1993). It seems as if the music *itself* is sad (or happy) as the sadness (or happiness) expressed musically is felt as belonging to the music itself, and not to something other than the music such as the composer or the improviser(s) or the performer(s) or listeners or a musical persona. We may, but need not, imagine in such cases that the music is not music but instead something of the *sort* that can have mental states, for it is also possible that we can know at one level that the music is music and yet imagine at another level that it is animate. Also, it is not that we imagine the music as a probably very reduced person. Rather, the music itself is imagined to be a being that may or may not be a person, though it is definitely closer to the mark to say the music is imagined to be a person-like being than it is to say that it is a probably very reduced person; and sometimes our imagined animation of the music may be more specific, in that we may anthropomorphize the music so that the music is imaginatively experienced not just as the very being but as the very *person* that is crying, wailing, dancing, etc., in the music. As well, we imagine the music is sad without necessarily having to imagine first that the music has the kind of physiological or neurological states (or complex, functional organizational states, for that matter), which seem necessary for mental states on many current theories of the mind. This is similar to the way in which children can imagine or make-believe (i.e., pretend to themselves) that a block of wood is a truck without necessarily having to imagine first that the block of wood has an engine, a fuel tank, and so on; indeed, one can, somewhat prosaically and unimaginatively, point out to a child that the block of wood cannot be a truck because it lacks an engine or a fuel tank, and yet the child can continue to imagine that it is a truck. Incidentally, I believe my talk of animating the music echoes a similar suggestion made by the Italian Renaissance philosopher Marsilio Ficino (1433–1499) who claimed in his music-spirit theory that music is like a living spirit or an animal that itself moves (Walker 1958).

As an example, consider the opening passages of the second movement of Beethoven's Ninth Symphony in D minor, Op. 125 (also used memorably in Stanley Kubrick's film *A Clockwork Orange*, based on Anthony Burgess's novel). We hear these passages, I suggest, as expressive of a vigorous and exuberant joy that is almost manic; or something not too far from that. But whose vigorous and exuberant joy is being expressed musically? Often in hearing the music as expressive in these terms, it is felt as if it is the music *itself* that is exuberantly joyous, not something other than it such as the composer or improviser(s) or performer(s) or listeners or a musical persona. We imagine often that the music *itself* is alive and possessive of mental states, that it is exuberantly joyous, and that its joy is manifested through the sounds we apprehend aurally.

Note in passing that I believe that analogies between, on the one hand, comic strips and animation films and, on the other hand, artworks such as music, paintings, etc., are more apt than those with St. Bernards, willow trees and such used by Kivy and Davies when talking about musical expressiveness. For unlike artworks, St. Bernards and willow trees are not *artifacts* that might be thought to have expressive features intentionally as a result of creators' efforts or otherwise, whereas comic strips and animation films clearly are artifacts; and comic strips or at least some (e.g., Tintin, Asterix, Calvin and Hobbes) of them (arguably) are art. Here is a second reason why focusing on artifacts such as comic-strip and animation film cars, suns, etc., may have lessons for discussions of expression in the arts. I wonder if focusing narrowly on music, paintings, photographs and such may bog us down when dealing with expression. Instead, if we also look at *other* instances of expression—ones that are less abstract and more familiar to us from everyday life—we may well find at least *some* insights that may also apply to expression in the arts. In this vein, I suggest that besides looking at expressive depictions in comic strips and animation films, we also examine other everyday instances of expressive representations such as decorative coffee mugs shown as ferocious or happy; I especially have in mind a particular coffee mug I once saw, which involved a life-like depiction of the handle as the nose, and carvings of eyes above the nose and a huge smile below the nose. Indeed, I also believe that music is continuous with other things in life, as my mentioning such things as comics and ancient world religions above shows.

Notice now that the problem of musical expressiveness—the mystery of how we hear something inanimate and insentient such as pure or absolute music to be sad, happy, etc.—is solved in perhaps the simplest possible way by talk of our animating the music: we imaginatively project and endow the music with life and mental states, without always being aware at the time that we are doing so, and that is how we hear something *devoid* of life and mental states such as music as sad, happy, etc. Moreover, the very simplicity and directness of the experience of animating the music may well make it the most common experience of musical expressiveness, whether we know it or not.

Now there is something else that is also noteworthy about this first kind of imagining that distinguishes it from the other kinds of imaginings involved in hearing music as sad or happy. In the case of animating music to be sad or happy, the music *itself* is *imaginatively* experienced and felt to possess and thus *express* sadness or happiness or some other mental state through sound, through musical gestures, development, and the like. Note that I say express rather than be expressive of, keeping in mind the distinction between the two: to express a mental state is to actually have a mental state as an occurrent part of one's psychology and to reveal that, whereas to be expressive of a mental state is to merely exhibit behavior associated with that mental state, the way actors do, for example. So in the case of music being animated to be sad or happy, we *imagine*, even if we are not always aware of this, that the music *itself* and not something *other* than the music (such as the listener or the composer or the performer on an indeterminate, imagined persona in the music or something else) is sad or happy, we *imagine* that it is *expressing* musically the sadness or happiness that it is *imagined* itself to have. And this might happen especially in the case of extremely intense music, such as passages from Beethoven's late string quartets and his symphonies. In the case of the other kinds of imaginings (described below) involved in hearing music as sad or happy, in contrast, music might only, at least in the usual case, be imagined to be *expressive* of mental states that it itself is not imagined to possess, but perhaps are imagined to be possessed by something else, such as an indefinite musical persona.

This leads us nicely on to a second kind of imagining involved in hearing music as sad or happy, one that involves an imagined, indefinite musical persona.[3] In this kind of imagining, we may imagine, again not in a very highly foregrounded or conscious way, that it is *as if* someone, we know not who precisely, is crying or wailing or laughing or otherwise expressing sadness or happiness or some other mental state through the music, its gestures, development, and the like. A variant of this kind of imagining might involve the idea that *something*, perhaps a human-like being or some other sentient creature that is not a human someone (but yet is perhaps sufficiently like humans in terms of emotional and related capacities), is imagined to be expressing its mental states through the music, which might be thought to be expressive of these states. And a different variant may involve the idea that an imagined, indeterminate persona in the music is simply expressing sadness, happiness, or other mental states through the music, *without* said mental states necessarily belonging to anyone, whether real or imagined. At any rate, in imagining a musical persona, we may form an auditory image and imagine that it is as if someone or something, we know not exactly who or what, is crying or wailing or laughing or dancing in the music. For example, I have sometimes heard the opening clarinet glissando in Gershwin's *Rhapsody in Blue* as being expressive of someone's sadness, in virtue of the timbre or tone-color of the rising clarinet resembling the sound and rising shape of human wailing; I once had this experience while I was focused on cooking (and in fact, at the time I used to be deeply skeptical of claims about a musical persona) and the music was playing softly in the background, which illustrates the point made above that we can be engaged in imaginings while doing other things. On other occasions, I have heard some of John Coltrane's music in terms of a musical persona. Note that the persona is not a specific person or entity but is instead a *type* of person, we know not who exactly. Also note that imagining one persona can often be sufficient to hear music as expressive. It might be objected here that it is unclear what it means to imagine someone else (or no one) as feeling a certain emotion in such a way as to connect this imaginatively with one's perception of an artwork; in brief response, surely we can *imagine* Othello feels jealous in the sense of supposing this, or entertaining this possibility without actually believing it (given that we know Othello is not real), and this can be connected with our perception of Shakespeare's play, either while reading it or witnessing a performance of it.

Now how is this second kind of imagining—that in terms of an indeterminate persona—different from or otherwise related to the first kind of imagining described above, to wit, the kind that involves animation? First, the imagined musical persona is a mediating someone or something between the music itself and the listener and is somehow "in" the music, thus being conceptually and philosophically *distinct* (even if not detached) from or other than the music rather than being the music itself. Second, the experience of imagining a mediating musical persona is thus not as direct and immediate an experience of musical expressiveness as that of animating the music. And third, in imagining a musical persona, it is the persona and not the music itself that is (usually) imagined to have the mental states heard in the music, whereas in animating the music, it is *the music itself* (and not something other than or distinct from it such as a persona or the composer or performer or listener) that is imagined to possess the mental states we hear in it.[4]

A third kind of imagining involves the idea of imaginative identification. In some cases, *we* may imaginatively identify with the music we hear, imagining that it is expressive of *our* own mental states. A variant of this might involve our imaginatively identifying two experiences: the auditory *experience* of hearing the music and its sounds as expressive may be identified with the experience of our *feeling* the mental state we hear the music as being expressive of, i.e., we may imagine of our experience of hearing the music as expressive that it is an experience of our feeling or having the mental state we hear the music as being expressive of (compare Walton 1988; Walton 1994; Budd 1995, chapter 4). Note that this experience does not involve an actual arousal of emotions or mental states as has sometimes been thought (Matravers 1998, 137–40), but rather involves at best an imagined arousal. It might also be objected here that this kind of experience focuses too much on the potential involvement of the listener, and also that it is unclear how the music might be linked to the listener in such a way, for we would have to imagine things about the sounds (e.g., their being produced by or being part of the listener) which we normally do not imagine. In brief response, first, this kind of imagining is not essential but is an *option* that we may sometimes engage in, at least on my view, and so I doubt it focuses too much on the listener or asks too much of her; second, it involves an imaginative identification of *experiences* as noted earlier; and third, we are not imagining things about sounds per se but rather imagining of *our auditory experience* that it is an experience of our undergoing the mental state we hear the music as expressive of. To return to the different kinds of experiences of musical expressiveness which involve imaginative identification, on other occasions, we might imagine the music to be an *occurrence* or instance of the mental state we hear it as expressive of so that we may simply identify it with said mental state without having to imagine anything further than that such as that the mental state belongs to someone; though one might wonder if this is an experience not of expressiveness (understood as the outward manifestation of someone's mental states) but rather of what it is to experience music as *emotional*. And sometimes we may identify with the music itself, and imagine while the music lasts that we *are* the music, a claim made also by Malcolm Budd (Budd 1995, 168);[5] there is thus an intimate link between the music and ourselves *in our imaginations*.

There may, I think, also be other ways of imagining music to be sad or happy, and while I cannot exhaustively catalog them, here are a few more possibilities. Sometimes, we may hear the music and *imagine* it as being expressive of the *imagined* sadness or happiness of the musical instrument(s) we hear, say a violin or a clarinet or a piano or a band or orchestra. In such cases, we may be animating the musical instrument(s) we hear, imagining it (them) to possess the sadness or the happiness that the music is imagined to be expressive of through its sounds, gestures, development, and the like. Witness, in this vein, talk of wailing violins, and consider as an example the wailing violins in the Polish composer Krzysztof Penderecki's musical work *Threnody for the Victims of Hiroshima*. In a work such as this, we do not experience the violins as being only metaphorically or figuratively wailing nor can violins as something that do not have voices or life literally wail. Instead, in virtue of the extremely high-pitched cluster harmonics on the violins resembling human screams, we are asked to and do *imagine*, not always very consciously, that the violins are *themselves* wailing, thereby representing the extreme agony and anguished screams of the people in Hiroshima when the atomic bomb was dropped there on August 6, 1945. A second example of this is of course the famous George Harrison song, "While My Guitar Gently Weeps," during the playing or auditioning of which one might hear the music *as if* it is the guitar itself (not the music itself as animated nor a persona in it nor the songwriter nor the performer nor the audience) that is weeping; at any rate, one might often get this feeling while playing or improvising on a guitar, and again not in a literal or metaphorical way.

In other cases, we may hear musical passages as *resembling* certain other things or phenomena, and thus imagine (them to be) those other phenomena. For example, certain (rapidly) descending soft musical passages, as played on the piano or a harp or a dulcimer or a glockenspiel, may resemble the sound of a brook. This may be due to the timbre or tone color of the musical instrument(s), the tempo of the music, and the descending, cascading musical shape of the passage respectively resembling the timbre, pace, and descending form of a brook. And thus we might *imagine* when hearing such passages that we are hearing a bubbling brook.

There may also be other ways of imagining musical expressiveness besides the ones adumbrated above. This should not surprise us at all, given the variety of ways in which we imagine things, as discussed briefly, and given the fact that we may often imagine things subconsciously or unconsciously, without necessarily being aware at the time that we are engaged in certain imaginings that are not very highly foregrounded or conscious; as Stephen Davies puts it, "what goes on in people's heads as they listen attentively to music and . . . its expressive character is very varied"

(Davies 2006a, 190). I thus conclude this brief outline of my resemblance-plus-imagination or imaginationist view of musical expressiveness by urging the reader to explore other ways of hearing music as expressive in the very experience of hearing emotions, moods, and feelings in the music, with yet another reminder that these imaginings need not be highly foregrounded or conscious. The abstract nature of music as an art may also contribute to why these imaginings are not always easy to detect. Note also that the listener needs to be attentive, not bored or distracted or tired or sated by the music, musically sensitive and not tone-deaf, musically familiar at least with the style or idiom of the musical passage or work in question, and so on, though she need not have much formal musical training. In detecting such imaginings, it might also help to play musical instruments, perhaps improvise on them, and reflect on the very experience of hearing music as sad or happy. Careful readers will have noted, by the way, that my view tries in part to reconcile various resemblance-based views (associated with Kivy, Davies, and Budd) with various imagination-based views (associated with Walton, Levinson, and Robinson). Note also that each and every one of the various imaginings briefly described above may be *optional* rather than essential to hearing music as expressive: these different imaginings are not individually necessary to hear music as expressive though one hears music as expressive through such imaginings, and each one of these imaginings may be individually sufficient for hearing music as expressive thus showing the disjunctive (rather than monolithic) nature of an imaginationist view of musical expressiveness.

Before proceeding to the next section, there is one thing I wish to address. In a recent essay, Vincent Bergeron and Dominic Lopes (2009) cite data from the psychology of music perception to suggest that visual and auditory information combine in our perception of musical expression. Thus, they claim that music's expressive properties are not just sonic but rather audio-visual, and so music too may not be just sonic. By way of brief response, I can grant them that often hearing musical expressiveness may be helped by attending live musical performances (which, historically, used to be the only way to hear music before the advent of recording technology) and seeing performers' faces, bodies, movements, postures, gestures, and the like. In this sense, Bergeron and Lopes seem to be right that visual and auditory information may *often* combine and thus contribute to our perceiving music as sad, happy, and so on. However, while fully acknowledging the genuine importance of empirical data, let us also remember and use philosophers' time-tested conceptual tools to ask first if this kind of audio-visual combination is *necessary* to perceive musical expressiveness, and also if it *sufficient*. First, increasingly, most of us hear music (including music that is new to us) not as much via live performances, where we can see the performers, but rather mostly through the use of technology such as iPods, radios, computers, the Internet (including online music stores such as iTunes), MP3 players, Walkmans, old-fashioned CDs, boom boxes, audio cassettes, LPs, and the like, where we do not get the kind of visual information Bergeron and Lopes seem to have in mind. And yet many of us often do perceive and hear musical expressiveness, despite the absence of this sort of visual information. Consider this too. If you blindfolded some competent listeners for many days at a time and took them to several live concerts and played all sorts of music for them, would they never hear musical expressiveness for they did not get the kind of visual information Bergeron and Lopes cite? That seems doubtful. And think about this too. Just as the blind can make and use pictures (Lopes 1997), similarly many great musicians have been blind and yet have created (and presumably heard) some of the most expressive music, despite not having had the kind of visual information Bergeron and Lopes appeal to; as examples, I can mention Stevie Wonder (blinded soon after birth), Ray Charles (blinded during childhood), and J. S. Bach (blinded toward the very end of his life) as well as the blind fifteenth-century CE Indian musician and poet Surdas. Recall also my discussion of animation toward the end of section IV.4 where I mentioned hearing a sound as we go round the bend on a quiet forest or mountain trail or on empty city streets at night, and right away we project life and mental states onto the sound in a purely sonic way that does not involve visual information as we suspect the sound may be coming from a bear or a potential mugger or a vicious dog on the loose. All of this goes to show, against Bergeron and Lopes, that seeing musical expression may not be a necessary condition for perceiving or hearing musical expression. Second, turning to sufficient conditions now, nor is it clear that visual cues suffice when it comes to perceiving musical expressiveness correctly, for they could be faked and thus mislead or otherwise distract us. For example, some passages in J. S. Bach's keyboard music, as played on the harpsichord, are not very expressive if they are so all. And yet a performer could put on a fake smile (or a frown) while playing them, thereby possibly tricking some listeners to perceive some positive mental state such as happiness (or else some negative mental state) in the music.

VI.4. Why We Imagine in Relation to Music

So, *why* do we imagine music to be sad or happy? And what *rewards* do we get out of doing so? Though I do not have complete answers to these two hard questions, I sketch answers to them, answers which are not unrelated.

I believe Peter Kivy may be on to something when he suggests that we may be evolutionarily hardwired to animate things in a way that is conducive to survival (Kivy 2002, 41ff). To borrow Kivy's example, it is better for us that we tend to animate the stick or broken branch on a forest trail and see it as a snake rather than see the snake as a stick and accidentally step on it, only to be bitten. Kivy suggests that likewise it may help us survive to animate sounds in addition to sights, though the animation of sounds may be dim or subliminal, whereas the animation of seen forms is something we are conscious of, more so as sight is more important for human survival than hearing. I adduce the following examples (which I have mentioned twice before, once toward the end of section IV.4 and once in the preceding section) in support. Often when we are about to go round the corner on a quiet street or go round the bend on a mountain trail, we might hear a sound. We will tend to animate this, imagining the sound to be made by someone or something coming toward us. This puts us on our guard, the animation of sound being thus conducive to our survival.

But more needs to be added to Kivy's evolutionary story, which I think is incomplete, for animation is only one kind of imagining, and only one way of imagining music to be sad or happy, as I hope the discussion above shows. Additionally, there are also at least six rewards involved in imaginatively hearing music as sad or happy, which may explain *both* why we imagine it to be sad or happy *and* what we get out of it.

We may animate music, and indeed imaginatively enliven various nonliving things in nature (such as clouds), simply because it engages our imaginations playfully and freely. We may just enjoy doing so. This, then, may be one reward of hearing music with imagination, namely, the reward of pleasure.

Imagining the music as sad or happy may thus also rejuvenate us psychologically and otherwise, taking us away from our everyday mundane concerns and transporting us temporarily to a different realm.[6] This is very similar to the kind of rejuvenation we feel after we engage in animating faces in clouds. After being engaged in such pleasurable and creative experiences, we return mentally and otherwise refreshed to our everyday lives. This, then, would be a second reward of imagining music to be sad or happy, a reward of rejuvenation.

A third reward has to do with identification. As we imagine the music to be sad or happy, and especially as we animate it to be so, we may imaginatively *identify* with the music, or with an imagined persona in it. In doing so, we may be psychologically reassured in realizing that we are not alone in feeling certain mental states that the music also is imagined to possess and express or else be expressive of.

Through identification with the music we may manage to rid ourselves of negative emotions such as sadness, anger, fear, and the like. For example, listening to particularly angry passages in Mussorgsky's *Night on a Bald Mountain* or in Stravinsky's *The Rite of Spring* may purge us of aggression, as we imaginatively identify with the music, perhaps feel ourselves aroused to very aggressive mental states, and able to give vent to them. The ensuing catharsis, then, may be a fourth reward of imagining music to be sad or happy or some other mental state.

Identification has something to do with our fifth reward, which might more correctly, however, be said to be a reward of fellowship. This time, however, the identification is not with the music but rather with other listeners who also imaginatively hear the music as sad or happy. This shared experience across listeners may lead to bonds being forged among listeners. Such listeners enjoy a fellowship among humans who are musically and emotionally sensitive, reminded that they are not alone in being able to imaginatively hear the music as sad or as happy.

A sixth reward may have to do with knowledge of emotions, moods, feelings, and other mental states.[7] As we imaginatively hear music to be sad or happy or some other mental state, we may reflect on these mental states. Separated from the real-life contexts of these mental states, where they are often accompanied by desires, motives, actions and the like, we may be able to reflect on these states in a detached and thus more insightful manner, perhaps coming to know better what these mental states are like, what situations they arise in, what causes them, how they manifest themselves, and so on. Sometimes, imaginatively hearing these mental states in the music may arouse us to these or other mental states, as I suggest later, and this kind of arousal too may contribute to our knowledge of these mental states via imaginatively hearing music as expressive.

There may also be other rewards of imagining and animating music to be sad or happy in addition to the six I have noted. But what I want to suggest now is crucial, even if it remains to be confirmed by further empirical research. Philosophers can often see possibilities that others cannot envision (and may sometimes regard as weird), possibilities which are later realized or confirmed by others, often in other disciplines; witness, for example, philosophers' talk of many worlds and possible worlds for quite some time now, and the more recent similar discussions in astronomy about a multiverse or multiverses. As a philosopher, I thus suggest possibilities that may be confirmed by neuroscience and the other sciences, either say through finding neural pathways or links between the regions of the brain associated with imagination and emotion, or maybe by finding that the parts of the brain associated with the imagination are activated when we hear musical expressiveness, or perhaps in some other way.

We get these and other *rewards* of pleasure, rejuvenation, identification, catharsis, fellowship, and knowledge from animating and imagining the music to be sad or happy or some other mental state. They are what we get *out of* imaginatively hearing the music to be sad or happy. But these rewards may also partly explain *why* we imagine the music to be sad or happy, thus showing how the answers to the two questions I began this section with are not unrelated. Because of these and other rewards, imagining the music to be sad or happy rejuvenates us, connects us with others, and so forth, thus aiding in our survival. And this may connect to Kivy's evolutionary story. We may, I suggest, be evolutionarily hardwired to imagine and animate things, for doing so makes our existence more enjoyable, rejuvenates us, and connects us to others, aiding and enhancing our survival in these and other ways. It is not that we deliberately and consciously pause and think, and then decide to imagine and animate the music as sad or happy. Rather, these and other imaginings just happen to us as our imaginations are activated willy-nilly by music; we engage in these imaginings spontaneously, nondeliberately, and passively. We cannot help but imaginatively hear music as sad or happy, given music that appropriately and sufficiently resembles our vocal and behavioral expressions of mental states as well as the affective feel of these mental states. We can no more help imaginatively hearing music as sad or as happy than we can help seeing faces in clouds or in rocks. A good example of this latter is the (recently damaged) New Hampshire cliff "Old Man of the Mountain." Due to the high degree of resemblance between these rocks (even in their now damaged state) and human faces, we imagine we see a craggy, old face in them. We cannot help but imagine seeing the face in these rocks, and likewise I suggest we cannot help but imaginatively hear music as sad or happy. Readily and immediately, we imaginatively hear the music as sad or happy. And we do so because we are human, for which we should be thankful.

VI.5. Musical Arousal

Having dealt with musical expressiveness, both how we imagine music to be sad or happy and why we do so, I want to turn now to musical *arousal*.

By my lights, this is how musical arousal happens. As we imaginatively hear music to be sad or happy or some other mental state, we may animate it or imagine an indefinite musical persona in it or identify with it in not always very conscious ways. We may imaginatively empathize or sympathize or identify with the music as animated or with the persona in it, even if we are not aware of these imaginative acts of identification or empathy or sympathy. This in turn is what leads to musical arousal, being moved *by* and along *with* the music we hear so that we feel sad or happy or something else, even as we hear the music as being sad or happy or some other mental state. The case is *partially* analogous to arousal in real life, when we see other people in pain or in joy or in some other mental state, and *merely* seeing that they are so can suffice to arouse us to pity or sorrow or joy or some other mental state as we empathize or sympathize or identify with them, their mental states, or their situations. Musical arousal is also *partially* analogous to the way in which we feel for fictional characters in novels, stories, plays, and films. We read about or see these characters as sad or happy or in some other mental state. As we get acquainted with their situations and their conditions, we may empathize or sympathize or identify with them, their mental states, or their predicaments, which is what causes us to be aroused. Note that we need not be aroused to precisely the *same* mental state that we hear the music as imaginatively possessing, just as we need not feel the same mental state that we see in other people in real life or in fictional characters. So, just as we may sometimes feel sad when we see sad people and sometimes we may feel pity and sometimes some other negative mental state, similarly hearing sad music may arouse us to sadness or pity or some other negative mental state.

But it might be objected, along with Kivy, that music cannot arouse garden-variety emotions in us.[8] At best, says Kivy, music can only arouse in us aesthetic emotions, such as awe or wonder or exhilaration or excitement at the beauty of the music. Though he grants that some music can be deeply moving, Kivy claims we are not emotionally moved by it to the emotions we hear it as expressing. We cognize or hear or perceive emotions in the music, but do not ourselves feel those garden-variety emotions when we hear such music with sympathy.

In response to this objection, the first thing to be said is that whatever mental states music arouses in us, the affective or feeling aspect of those states is very similar to the affective or feeling component of emotions. Often when we hear music, what is aroused in us *feels* very much like what we feel when we have real-life emotions, and indeed, there are some (including myself) who are moved to tears by the intense sadness as well as by the beauty of some music, such as some passages in the Beethoven symphonies and late quartets. In fact part of the reason why some people (especially very young and very inexperienced listeners) may *avoid* sad but beautiful music, despite its immense beauty, may be precisely *because* it makes them sad, or at least arouses in them something that *feels* very much like real-life sadness. In contrast, other listeners (sophisticated, experienced, sensitive listeners) may be musically aroused to sadness and yet find *both* aesthetic and emotional rewards in hearing sad, beautiful music.[9] This is partially analogous to the case of sad but well-made weepy movies such as *Schindler's List*, which many people often shun, as they do not wish to be aroused to sadness or other negative mental states or even to feel something like them, just as they try to avoid sadness and other negative mental states in real life. In contrast, other viewers may get both emotional and aesthetic rewards from seeing such sad, weepy films, even if these make them feel something like negative mental states.

At this point, the objector might raise the concern that even granting that what is musically aroused *feels* like real-life emotions, nevertheless music cannot strictly arouse such emotions because emotions must be *about* something and thus must have intentionality to be emotions, and it is not clear what musically aroused "emotions" can be about. In response, note that musically aroused emotions can have an intentional object in that they can be about the music's features when the music is animated or an imagined musical persona in it is imaginatively heard as being sad or happy or some other mental state. The sadness or pity or some other negative mental state aroused by music can be focused on or directed toward the music itself as animated or on its persona, as well as the sadness (or some other mental state) these are imagined to possess. When we imaginatively identify or empathize or sympathize with the music as animated or with the persona in it, the emotion musically aroused in us takes as its intentional object the music itself as animated or the persona in it, and also the plight that these are imaginatively heard as being in. This is partially analogous to the way in which when we feel sadness or pity or some other mental state for people or for fictional characters, our mental state is *about* these people and their situations. None of this is to deny that music may arouse not just intentional mental states such as emotions but also non-intentional moods and feelings. And this is also not to rule out that musically aroused mental states may *also* arise due to the beauty of the music, and that they can *also* be about or directed toward the aesthetic features of the music, in addition to its expressive features.

A different worry might go something like this. Emotions require not just a feeling or affective component as well as intentionality, they also require a cognitive component in the form of a belief or a judgment. Now even if the claims made above show that what is musically aroused involves a feeling or affect and has intentionality, it is not clear that it has a cognitive component. Accordingly, it is not clear that music can arouse emotions. Moreover, while real emotions such as anger or fear motivate us to actions such as fighting or fleeing, it is not clear that musically aroused anger makes us fight or that musically aroused fear makes us flee. Thus, once again, it seems music cannot arouse real emotions, this time because what is musically aroused lacks the motivating aspect of real-life emotions.

In reply to this double worry, there are two sorts of moves one can make. The first move would be to grant that what is musically aroused neither involves full-fledged belief nor motivates us to action. At best, then, music only arouses *quasi-emotions*, which resemble emotions to a great degree in terms of both their feel and their intentionality, but do not have the cognitive component of emotions, nor the motivational force of emotions. The second move would be to insist that music *does* arouse emotions, for what is aroused musically does involve, after all, a belief component. When we are aroused to sadness by sad music, we *believe*, even if not very consciously, that the music itself is sad, that the music as animated or else its imagined persona is sad. Indeed, it is this belief or judgment involved in the mental states musically aroused in us that may account for the intentionality of these states. It is *only because* of their constituent cognitive component that musically aroused states are *about* the music itself as animated or its imagined persona being sad. As for the motivating aspect, it might be said that musically aroused sadness often makes some listeners cry, musically aroused anger often causes aggressive feelings in some listeners (especially as a result of listening to marches or other martial music) that may *predispose* them to fight even if they do not actually end up fighting, and musically aroused fear may often result in some listeners beginning to cower or tremble even if they do not actually flee. Perhaps the reason why these listeners do not fight or flee is that a moment's reflection shows them that the external *situation* is not real, and does not warrant fight or flight, even though what they *experience* emotionally is really enough.

For myself, I oscillate back and forth between these two moves but cannot decide between them, though I lean more toward the latter these days. So I end my discussion of this issue here, with the hope that future research, including empirical work, will settle the issue whether music arouses emotions or at best only quasi-emotions. I do note, however, that a lot of recent empirical work concludes, against Kivy, that music can indeed arouse bona fide emotions in listeners (Krumhansl 1997; Nussbaum 2007, 204–14). It has been found, for example, that heard and felt musical emotions are often associated (Evans and Schubert 2008; Hunter, Schellenberg, and Schimmack 2010). As well, more empathetic people are more likely to feel the emotions they hear in the music (Egermann and McAdams 2013), and in fact people who score high on the openness-to-experience personality dimension are more likely to feel actual emotions, especially positive ones, in response to music (Liljestrom, Juslin, and Vastfjall 2013). Also, people from different age groups often use music to enhance their moods, or to relax, or to be better motivated (Chen, Zhou, and Bryant 2007; Getz, Marks, and Roy 2014; Juslin and Isaakson 2014; Laukka and Quick 2013; Shifriss, Bodner, and Palgi 2014). Additionally, physiologically oriented studies show that listening to music can arouse one emotionally, judging by changes in electrodermal activity, heart rates, and breathing rates (Gomez and Danuser 2004, 2007; Rickard 2004). Brain imaging also reveals that music can activate patterns associated with emotional arousal in the limbic system (including the amygdala and the hippocampus) and also parts of the paralimbic system (Blood and Zatorre 2001; Brattico et al. 2011; Menon and Levitin 2005). Studies also show that sad music can induce negative emotions (Garrido and Schubert 2015), and it has even been argued that sad music can induce real sadness accompanied by increased levels of prolactin, which is a comforting hormone released during episodes of sadness (Huron 2011).

VI.6. Objections and Replies

In this concluding section, I want to reply to some possible objections to my imaginationist view of musical expressiveness, and various parts of it. Readers need not plow through all the objections and replies here and can instead safely jump around, for the most part. In case any readers find these objections and replies unnecessary and tiresome, I should add that several of these objections have in fact been put to me over many years by various people acknowledged in the Introduction.

But first I want to hark back to the quote from Kivy with which I began this chapter. I submit that my view that music is not really or literally sad or happy but is only imagined to be so has, in accordance with Kivy's quote, the character of looking prima facie like a vacuous truism that hardly needs stating. But further reflection on my view in all its details may reveal there is more to it than appears at first blush.

A first objection to my view goes something like this. Rocks cannot be literally or really happy or sad, and thus it is doubtful that they can be *imagined* to be happy or sad. Similarly, music as something inanimate cannot be imagined to be sad or happy or some other mental state, since, like rocks, it cannot be literally sad or happy. Therefore, my imaginationist solution does not work, as it presupposes something implausible at the outset.

In reply, it *is* possible to imagine rocks to be sad or happy. If rocks had features *sufficiently resembling* human expressive behavior, say facial (or some other bodily) expressive behavior, then we could imagine them to be sad or happy or some other mental state. A good example, one I mentioned earlier, is New Hampshire's "Old Man of the Mountain," where the degree of resemblance with human faces is so high that we can imagine these rocks to be an old man. Even a lesser degree of resemblance might do. In the Museum of Fine Arts in Boston, there is a display of Chinese scholars' rocks. For centuries, these rocks have been used in their studies by Chinese literati, who contemplate them and imagine them to be various things and also imagine various things in them, depending on their respective resemblances. For instance, a rock that is roughly oval in shape, and has three slits in it—two adjacent small slits on top and a larger slit that is placed significantly below the small slits and curves facing upwards—might be imagined to be a happy individual or else a happy face. I dare say many people, especially children, seeing such a rock in a museum may well imagine it to be a happy, smiling rock. If this is right, and if rocks can be imagined to be sad or happy despite being inanimate and insentient, there is no reason why this would not hold analogously of music as well. Given sufficient resemblances between music and our vocal and bodily expressive behavior as well as the affective feel of mental states, we can and do imagine music to be sad or happy or some other mental state.

Here is a second objection, a very good one; which was actually put to me by Hanne Appelqvist. On my view, expressiveness is an imagined property of the music. This seems to be different from the claim made by Kivy, Davies, and others that expressiveness is a *perceived* property of the music itself, a property that is somehow in the music and is heard therein by listeners in a ready and immediate way (Kivy 1989; Kivy 2002; Davies 1994). Accordingly, it would seem that my view cannot account for how expressiveness is heard as belonging to the music itself, and thus the resemblance-based view of Kivy, Davies and others is superior to my imaginationist position.

In response, on my view, hearing or perceiving music as sad or happy (or some other mental state) necessarily involves imagination. We *imaginatively perceive* or hear expressiveness to be a property of the music itself. Thus I do not deny that expressiveness or emotions are often perceived to be in the music, but instead only couple such perceptions with imagining; recall my discussion of imaginative perceptions and perceptual imaginings in section V.2, with special reference to the work of Brian O'Shaughnessy. In fact, my view is superior to Kivy's (and perhaps also Davies's) position in that I can explain how expressiveness or emotions can be said to be perceived qualities of something *inanimate* such as music, how they can be *in* the music, or belong somehow *to* it. Kivy now concedes it is an unknown "black box" how music embodies or exhibits emotions as perceptual qualities (Kivy 2002, 47–48). In contrast, I do not throw in the towel but instead try to penetrate this "black box" by building on Kivy's and others' resemblance-based views and claiming that the expressiveness or emotions we perceive or hear as qualities of the music itself (or as being embodied or exhibited by the music) are not really or literally in the music, which after all is inanimate, but only *imaginatively perceived* to be there. On my view, resemblances allow us to imagine in various not always highly conscious ways the emotions we hear in the music so that sad or happy music is imagined (and animated) in various acts of auditorily imaginative perception to be (the kind of thing that is) sad or happy. Music is thus imaginatively perceived to possess sadness or happiness, so that these and other mental states are only imagined to inhere in the music.

A third concern is perhaps more a demand for clarification than a direct objection to my view; and was made by Lydia Goehr. There are two main components of my view, resemblance and imagination. Which of these is more important, and which is prior? That is not clear, and needs to be addressed.

My reply is as follows. Resemblance is *causally* prior to imaginings, resemblance being the causal foundation that, in my view, allows the various ways of imagining music to be sad or happy. As for the question about which is more important, resemblance or imagination, that is not a question I am much concerned with. Or insofar as I am concerned about the question, I would say both resemblance and imagination are equally important. Both are necessary and neither is sufficient by itself for expressiveness.

A fourth objection to my view goes like this. My view *naturalizes* resemblances between music and the vocal and behavioral expression of mental states as well as their affective tones. But these resemblances are not there to be discovered in the first place, as some sort of objective property. Accordingly, my resemblance-plus-imagination view does not hold up, since its causal foundation—musical/extramusical resemblance—does not exist.

Here is a reply to this objection. The kinds of resemblances I have in mind are of various sorts. Some sad music moves slowly, is soft in volume, and low in pitch, similar to the way in which sad people often walk slowly, hang their heads down, and talk softly and at a low pitch. An example of this, one mentioned earlier, is the opening of the second movement (Fantasia-Adagio) of Weber's Clarinet Quintet in B-flat, Op. 34. We hear the music—the strings—moving slowly, and it is soft in volume, and at a low pitch, and this resemblance with the expressive bodily behavior of sad people allows or causes us to imaginatively hear the music as pensive. When the clarinet enters, its timbre and long notes sound like human sighing or wailing, and this resemblance with our vocal expressive behavior, together with the measured pace of the music, also induces us to imagine the music is sorrowfully thoughtful.

Some other music may resemble the way our mental states *feel* in that, for example, the way musical tension is resolved may mirror the way our mental states feel when some inner turmoil in our lives is resolved. Music may also strive for and reach intermediate and final goals (say, respectively, modulating to the dominant key, and then returning to the tonic at the end of the work) the way we strive for and arrive at these in our inner lives.

These different sorts of resemblances highlight ways in which music provides sonic or auditory *analogs* of our vocal and bodily expressions as well as the affective feel of mental states. It is important to remember that these resemblances are not always noted consciously. Now it would be one thing if I *alone* made these claims about resemblance, in which case they might be thought to be idiosyncratic. But in making such claims, I am echoing similar claims made earlier by resemblance-theorists such as Peter Kivy, Stephen Davies, Malcolm Budd, and Paul Boghossian, and also by Aaron Ridley.[10] Of course, this emerging consensus amongst philosophers and aestheticians writing about musical expressiveness does not prove once and for all that these resemblances exist and are perceived subconsciously or unconsciously, for we could all be collectively mistaken. But still, this intersubjective agreement does give *some* support to my view insofar as the philosophers variously supporting resemblance-based views of musical expressiveness might be thought to be competent listeners and Humean true critics who have spent years thinking, reading, writing about, and listening to (if not also playing) a lot of music of different kinds. Recall also that I dealt with a similar objection (Madell 2002) in section IV.4 and cited some empirical data (Juslin and Laukka 2003) in support of resemblance. To this, I will add that it has been found that happy speech in English and Tamil has larger pitch intervals than sad speech just as happy Western and South Indian music involves larger pitch intervals, supporting vocal resemblances between expressive speech and music (Bowling, Sundararajan, Han, and Purves 2012).

Here is a fifth worry for my position. It might be thought that we need to answer the question *whose* mental states the music is expressive of or expresses. But not all the various ways of imagining musical expressiveness that I described briefly earlier can be seen as providing answers to this question. In reply, first, maybe we do not always need to answer the question whose mental states the music is expressive of. There is no reason why music could not just be expressive of certain mental states merely by exhibiting behavioral features associated with those mental states *without* those mental states necessarily (being imagined as) belonging to someone or something. For example, music could simply display the upbeat behavioral features of joy such as moving quickly and thus be expressive of joy, without the joy belonging to someone or something. In any case, note, secondly, that many of the ways of imagining musical expressiveness that I briefly described earlier do answer the question *whose* mental states the music is expressive of or expresses. Thus the music might be imagined to express the mental states of the music itself as animated, or it might be imagined to be expressive of the mental states of an imagined persona, or it might be imagined to be expressive of our mental states when we identify imaginatively with the music, or else it might be imagined to be expressive of the mental states of the musical instrument(s) as animated. In this way, unlike some alternative theories (such as the simple resemblance-based view, as I argue below), my view maintains *some* link with our ordinary concept of expressiveness as involving the outward manifestation of someone's or something's mental states.

Here is a sixth objection. It might be claimed that my imaginationist view is deficient in not making room for cases of conventional expressiveness, where the expressiveness is due to musical conventions rather than due to resemblance-plus-imagination, as I claim. For example, it might be claimed that the interval of the minor third and so also the minor triad are expressive of sadness due to convention rather than resemblance or imagination or a combination of these.[11]

In response, the interval of the minor third and the minor triad are heard, I submit, in contrast to or against the backdrop of the more consonant major third and the major triad, which of course are part of the harmonic series. In relation to these, the minor third and the minor triad sound "fallen" or "sinking" or "sagging," as the mediant note in the minor is a semitone lower than that in the major. Compared to the major third and the major triad, then, the minor third and the minor triad do not sound as "confident" or "bold," and indeed sound like "fallen" or "sinking" or "sagging" versions of these. Now while it may be tempting to say that the minor third and the minor triad are only sad and heard as such due to musical conventions, what undermines such a position is that people without formal musical training who are not familiar with musical conventions can also often hear the minor third and the minor triad as sad or melancholy. Instead, *contrasted* with the major third and the major triad, which may be aurally felt in the background as they are part of the harmonic series, I suggest the minor third and the minor triad might be heard as resembling the posture or voice of someone or something that is (sadly) drooping or sinking or sagging, and we may perceive this structural resemblance subliminally without being aware of it. Is it beyond the realm of possibility to suggest here that these resemblances in turn may cause and allow us to imaginatively hear the minor third and the minor triad as if, say, a droopy or subdued person or being is musically expressing its droopy sadness or depression, even if we are not aware of this imagining? If this is right, then we may have a resemblance-plus-imagination explanation of the sadness of the minor third and the minor triad.

A seventh concern for my view might be raised by defenders of resemblance-based views. It would appear that my position conflates expression and expressiveness whereas these need to be kept distinct. But I deny this charge by making two related claims. First, as said earlier, it is only in the case of our animating the music and imagining that it itself is sad or happy that I claim that music might be imagined to *express* mental states. In all the other kinds of imagining music as sad or happy, whether these involve an imagined persona or an imaginative identification or something else, I claim that music may be imagined only to be *expressive* of mental states. In this way, I do distinguish expression from expressiveness and do not conflate them. Second, I submit that if you focus and reflect on the very experience of hearing music as sad or happy and on the phenomenology of this experience, then often, though not always, the music *itself* (and not a persona in it or something else other than the music, such as the listener or the composer or the performer) may be heard as the very thing that is sad or happy, and not merely as something that presents in its aural appearance certain characteristics that we associate with various mental states such as sadness or happiness. If this is right, then I think the best way to explain this would be to talk of our animating the music, imaginatively endowing it itself with life and life-like qualities. This leads to the claim that only on those occasions when we animate it may music be imagined to express mental states rather than just be expressive of them, which preserves the distinction in principle between expression and expressiveness.

But here is a worry for simple resemblance-based theorists that I raise by way of counterattack. The problem to be solved is either about musical expressiveness or about musical expression. If the former, then resemblance-based theories fail to link somehow with our ordinary notion of expressiveness as involving the outward manifestation of inner states, and these theories must provide *some* such link, for musical expressiveness is a species of expressiveness in general. The reason why these theories fail to link with the ordinary notion of expressiveness is that they analyze musical expressiveness *solely* in terms of music's resembling something to do with mental states (either how these are vocally or behaviorally manifested, or the affective feel of these mental states) but do not *in any way* connect these mental states as being the inner states, at least sometimes, of someone or something. In contrast, my view provides at least *some* link with the ordinary notion of expressiveness in that the mental states the music is imaginatively heard as being expressive of are often, though not always, imagined to be the inner states *of someone or something*, whether the music as animated or an imagined musical persona or even ourselves. On the other hand, if the problem is about expression, then resemblance-based views do not explain how something *inanimate* and insentient such as music can be said to be sad or happy, and instead give us only the causal story behind expression.

Here is an eighth worry for my position. When discussing our animating the music and imagining that it itself is alive and sad or happy, I suggested that we may, but need not, imagine in such cases that the music is not music but instead something of the sort that can have mental states, for it is also possible that we can know at one level that the music is music and yet imagine at another level that it is animate. To this it might be objected that we cannot imagine things that are logically or metaphysically impossible, and thus these kinds of imaginings are to be ruled out on these grounds.

By way of brief response, it is not clear why, when we animate the music, we cannot (a) imagine sometimes that music is not music but instead something of the *sort* that can have mental states, and also (b) imagine on other occasions that the music itself has mental states and is animate even though we know, and possibly imagine, at another level that it is music, similar to the way in which we often animate and imagine comic strip characters to be alive and sad or happy, even though we know at another level that they are not really so. If I am right, then contra the objector, it is even possible to imagine logically impossible things such as round squares, *not* in the sense of imagining that involves forming mental images or visualizations, but rather in the sense of imagining that involves supposing or fancying something, or entertaining a proposition without believing it. I take it there are various senses or notions or varieties of imagination.[12] In one of these senses of imagination, we can imagine that there exists a round square by supposing or fancying that there is such a thing that in some world somehow has the attributes both of being round and being square. Indeed, a highly imaginative author might even write a quite delightful short story or a novel imagining and involving a fantastic Lewis Carroll-like fictional world full of logical puzzles and absurdities that is also a cross with an E. A. Abbott-like fictional world of geometrical figures (as in his novel *Flatland*) where readers are asked to imagine, *without imaging*, by entertaining the proposition, which they do not have to believe, that there exists, say, a jovial character called Mr. Round-Square who has an impish sense of humor and delights in surprising people, not in the least by the mere fact of his existence! In this fictional world, we are asked to *entertain* the idea that Mr. Round-Square rings people's doorbells at 3 a.m., rousing them from deep slumber. When they wake up groggy and grouchy and open the door, rubbing their eyes, Mr. Round-Square exclaims, "Aha! You didn't think I existed, did you? But here I am at 3 a.m., and you are not dreaming!" If this is right, then contra the objector, we may sometimes even be able to imagine logically impossible things, at least in some senses of imagination. Furthermore, metaphysically impossible things should not be as hard to imagine as logically impossible ones. This, I submit, smoothes the way for the two kinds of imaginings (a) and (b) mentioned above that may be involved in animating the music itself as sad or happy or something else.

A ninth concern for my view might go something as follows: it is unclear if the postulated forms of imagining really exist, for they would seem to be nonpropositional imaginings that are part of a single and unified experience where we both hear the sound and also notice their expressiveness. In reply, as Levinson has suggested, we readily and immediately hear music as expressive, to which I would add that we also do so *willy-nilly*, sensitive, competent listeners being under suitable circumstances (when they are not tired or bored or distracted or too familiar with the music at hand, and so on) no more able to help hearing music as expressive than we can help seeing faces in clouds or in stains on walls (or, to use some of Kivy's examples, we cannot help but see a circle with three lines in it as a face, or a stick in the forest as a snake), perhaps because we may be evolutionarily hardwired to do so. Accordingly, I believe it is right to claim that we hear musical sounds and their expressiveness in *one* experience as our hearing is coupled with various imaginings. Indeed, recall my earlier discussion of O'Shaughnessy on imagination in section V.2, where I suggested, following O'Shaughnessy, that the mental states heard in the music are not really there but rather are only imagined to be in the sounds, for nothing is there besides the sounds; and I suggested that in the very midst of hearing musical sounds, there may be a nonperceptual or nonaudible "going-beyond" as we imaginatively hear mental states in the music. I also went on to quote Scruton's claim that the "literal perception and imaginative perception can cohabit the same experience, since they do not compete" (Scruton 2004, 184), for we literally hear or perceive musical sounds unfolding in time and at the same also imaginatively hear mental states in them, as part of the same musical experience. As for the kinds of nonpropositional imaginings involved, I also suggested in section V.2 that hearing music as expressive in terms of an imagined, indeterminate musical persona may involve a kind of imaging, not a visual but rather an auditory imaging that is nonspecific as we imagine someone or something, we know not who, is crying, wailing, and the like through the music.

Relating to the ninth concern just addressed, here is a tenth worry. It might be claimed there are no such nonpropositional imaginings among the commonly accepted forms of imagining, such as visualizing, supposing, daydreaming, or imagining seeing or feeling something, and so claims about imagining and musical expressiveness do not gel. In response, note that this brief, nonexhaustive list of imaginings includes those that are either *visual* (e.g., visualizing, imagining seeing something, daydreaming) or those that are *propositional* (e.g., supposing). As such it is not clear that this list will apply easily to musical expressiveness, which would seem to involve auditory, nonpropositional imaginings at least, perhaps of the sort discussed before. As for imagining feeling something, this kind of imagining can apply to hearing musical expressiveness when we imagine of our auditory experience of hearing the music that it is an experience of our having the feeling we hear the music as expressive of; we may thus imagine feeling the emotion or mental state we hear the music as expressive of.

An eleventh objection might be this. To hear music as expressive involves the projection of an imagined expressiveness onto the music as a (seemingly) real feature of it, which is then there to be perceived. If so, the recognition of the expressiveness of the music will be perception-like rather than imaginative, even if it originates in some sort of imagining. Here is my response. We *imaginatively hear* music as expressive, the hearing or perceiving *being intimately coupled with* or tied to the various imaginings mentioned above; we imaginatively project and hear the music as sad, and it is not really or literally sad. This intimate link between hearing and imagining seems to be part of the experience of musical expressiveness, and it is not clear why this is a problem. Indeed, recall again my discussion of O'Shaughnessy on imagination in section V.2, and my suggestion there that animating the music involves a kind of imaginative perception (whereas imagining a musical persona may involve a perceptual imagining).

Here is a twelfth objection. Imagining seems to be essentially an instance of agency, allowing us to control what we imagine at least in principle. But we never decide whether to hear a musical passage as expressive or which mental state we hear it as expressive of, something causally determined instead by how the music sounds to us. In response, it is not clear that imagining is essentially always an instance of agency under our control. For there can be *involuntary* and passive imaginings not entirely under our control (See Walton 1990, chapter 1; McGinn 2004). Dreaming and daydreaming constitute examples of involuntary imaginings not entirely under our control. Another example of involuntary imaginings is provided by fiction, where when reading a novel the trajectory and content of readers' imaginings are determined, for the most part, not by them but by the novel or story itself.

A thirteenth objection—call it the "incredulous objection"—may be that my suggestion that we animate the music itself is a simplistic or otherwise oversimplified solution to the problem of musical expressiveness. After all, if the solution is really as simple as that, how could it have eluded us so far? In response, I suggest that the fact that we often animate the music without realizing this is what we are doing and also the abstract nature of music, these two things together make it hard to detect this kind of experience. Furthermore, I suggest that flirtation with metaphor-based views (and also literalist views), under the influence of the linguistic turn in philosophy, and also flirtation with arousalist views, and thus with our aroused reaction to expressive music, may have led us away from focusing on the very experience of hearing music as expressive, thus missing recognition of animation.

Here now is a line of possible objections coming from the persona theorist that might, taken together, be seen as a fourteenth objection to my view, especially to my talk of animation; and the objection was in fact put to me by Jerrold Levinson when I was his doctoral student. The experience of animation suggests that the music itself is imagined to *have* mental states and is also imagined to *express* mental states. But the two features should be kept distinct as involving *distinct* things, as claimed by persona-based views that maintain it is the persona that (usually) *has* the emotions and the music that is imagined to *express* them. In response, I see no problem with one and the same thing both having and expressing mental states. I see no reason why there cannot be a partial analogy between music and persons (and indeed other animate beings) in this respect: sad music can be like sad persons who both have and express sadness, with the difference that, unlike persons, music is only imagined to have and express emotions.

The objector may continue at this stage and say that the analogy is not a happy one, for sad persons have certain features in virtue of which they express sadness. My response is that music too has certain features, sonic features, in virtue of which it expresses sadness and is heard as doing so. These causal features are the various sorts of resemblances discussed above as well as musical gestures, musical properties, and their development, and so on.

But, the objector may continue, the analogy does not hold up because while music is the sum of these organic features that make it expressive, persons are not the sum of the features in virtue of which they express their sadness. There are two possible responses I can make in reply to this objection, a less promising one and a more promising one. The less promising move is to defend some sort of principle of organic unity as applied to music, claiming that music is not the sum of the sonic features in virtue of which it is expressive, but rather an organic whole. I do not find this move very plausible. The more promising move is to claim that even if music just is the sum of these features, that need not be a problem for the analogy between music and persons is only partial.

A fifteenth objection is this. We often say of our behavior that it *itself* is exuberantly joyous. So, how is the music being joyous different from behavior being so? How is it that we do not animate behavior that we often say is itself joyous, but we often do animate the music itself on my proposal? My response is this. We do not animate behavior for we do not need to do so. For, with the exception of fictitious oddities such as the Cheshire cat's smile, there is no such thing as disembodied behavior: there is always a behaving agent associated with behavior of whom we can say in response to the question "*Whose* behavior is exuberantly joyous?" that her or his behavior is exuberantly joyous. In contrast, to answer at least sometimes the question *whose* exuberant joy music is expressive of, given that music is inanimate and insentient, we do need some sort of agent of whom we can say that her joy is being expressed musically. On the proposal above, often the agent is imagined to be ourselves and often the agent is an indefinite, imagined musical persona. But very often the agent is the music itself, animated in the manner suggested above as the very being or thing that is exuberantly joyous. Note though, as already granted in dealing with the fifth objection above, that we do not always need to answer the question "*Whose* mental states the music is expressive of?" for music could just be expressive, i.e., exhibit features behaviorally associated with a mental state, without expressing anyone's or anything's mental states.

VI.7. Conclusion

Summing up, here is what I have said in this chapter. I discussed and rejected Formalism about music in section VI.2, including the classic formulation given by Hanslick as well as more recent Neo-Formalists such as Zangwill and Kraut. Section VI.3 put forth my imaginationism about musical expressiveness, especially the central claim that often we animate the music, imaginatively projecting life and life-like qualities such as mental states onto the music, which we imaginatively endow with these. Section

VI.4 then discussed why we engage with music in this way, and the rewards of doing so. In section VI.5 the question of whether music can arouse emotions was discussed, with some reference to Peter Kivy. Finally, in section VI.6, I defended my imaginationist view from various objections that several people have actually raised to me.

Summary and Conclusion

Let us take stock. So, what is this book about? Before we get to that, though, it might seem, as indeed suggested by a reader for this press, that I need to address Andrew Bowie's criticisms (2007) of how analytic philosophy focuses on expression.

Focusing on writers in the German tradition (from Kant, to the German Romantics, to Wagner, Wittgenstein, Heidegger, and Adorno), Bowie's main claims are that music can teach philosophy—rather than the other way round—about such things as language, ethics, metaphysics, truth, communication, meaning, subjectivity, and so on. That is a very different project from mine, as should be obvious. Indeed, Bowie himself seems to suggest as much (2007, 14) when he says: "My focus is largely on German philosophy and music . . . I could . . . add to the list of things I fail to discuss at all, or do not discuss in any detail. These include . . . such topics as Hanslick, the specifics of the analytical philosophy of music. . . ."

However, I am sympathetic to what Bowie is saying (albeit, from the Continental philosophy perspective) if he thinks that understanding musical expression can help us understand other engagements, including general communication (language, gestures, speech acts, and so on). It may well be true also that understanding musical expression may help us grasp expression in the other arts and in life, and it may also help us understand affective states and cultivate empathy. To some degree, though, these may be matters for further empirical research, and so I am happy to leave things there for now.

Additionally, many things that Bowie says seem to be broadly in sync with my claims and as such I can take them on board, as the following four quotes from Bowie should show. For example, Bowie suggests (2007, 9) that the ". . . world is constituted partly in terms of socially instituted norms relating to, but not wholly determined by, the causal pressure of nature. This is the crucial point, because issues such as the 'location' of emotions with regard to music, which often lead to fruitless disagreement if one tries to show how a musical object has 'affective properties' in the way that physical objects have physical properties, look different in this perspective." Here, my claim that mental states such as emotions are projected onto music by listeners echoes Bowie. For I regard musical expressiveness not as an objective property (like the physical properties of physical objects) nor as a purely subjective (and idiosyncratic) property, but rather as an *intersubjective* property that involves interactions between music and listeners. Likewise, Bowie claims (2007, 10) that ". . . the problem for 'philosophy of music' is that it must rely upon whatever other philosophical assumptions are adopted by the person producing it . . . this leads . . . to the uninviting situation in which 'the philosophy of music' just limps behind whatever philosophical bandwagon happens to be running at a particular time. . . ." Here, I am sympathetic to what Bowie says, and in fact my discussion in chapter IV of how Stephen Davies's view may be too influenced by the linguistic turn in philosophy resonates with Bowie's claims (as does my suspicion that some current musical aesthetics may be too focused on neuroscience, which has been dominant lately). Similarly, Bowie (2007, 20–21) writes: ". . . consider the question of where the emotions with which music is often associated are said to be located . . . Kivy claims . . . these are 'perceived properties' of the music itself . . . The term 'perceived properties' is already strangely equivocal, involving the subject's perception, but trying at the same time to suggest that what is perceived is somehow objectively there. Emotions, though, pertain to subjects, so how can they intelligibly be said to be properties of music?" Here, I am in broad agreement with Bowie for my claim is that emotions, expressive properties, and such are not objectively in the music but are rather intersubjectively *imagined* and imaginatively perceived in various ways to be there; though it is not clear that the question of "location" makes sense. In like manner, and finally, Bowie (2007, 23) approvingly quotes the great German musicologist Carl Dahlhaus (1988, 331): ". . . [the music] seems melancholy . . . Melancholy appears as an—*intentional, not real*—determination of the object . . . The expressive character *inheres, looked at phenomenologically*, in the object, but *exclusively in the actual relationship to a subject.*" Here, I have added italics for emphasis, and once again what Bowie and this time Dahlhaus say largely parallels my claims. For I claim similarly that it *feels* to listeners that musical expressiveness, melancholy, etc., are in the music, but they are not *really* there and are instead a *function* of our listening to and interacting with the music, in ways that involve the imagination.

So, then, what is this book about? It is mainly about the problem of musical expressiveness. And what is that problem? It is this. Many musicians and laypersons (even if not all) often hear many musical passages and works as sad, happy, etc. But purely instrumental music without words or an associated story or program is *devoid* of life, consciousness, and mental states. So how can it be heard in terms of such mental states (and said to be so)?

Right away, at least six main approaches present themselves as solutions to our problem, and each solution comes in different versions as we have seen. A first view, Formalism, denies the problem and claims very roughly that music is without any emotional or affective content; this solution was discussed and rejected in chapter VI. A second position, the expression theory, maintains very roughly that sad music is expressive of the sadness of the composer or the performer; this approach was briefly dealt with in chapter II. A third option, the persona theory, claims very roughly that sad music is expressive of the sadness of an indeterminate, imagined agent in the music, the music's persona; I discussed this view in chapter II. A fourth take, Arousalism, claims very roughly that sad music is expressive of the sadness it arouses or evokes or causes in listeners so that to say that the music is sad is to say it makes us sad; this position was dealt with in chapter II. A fifth approach, Metaphorism, holds very roughly that to say music is sad is only to use a metaphor; I criticized this view at length in chapter III. Finally, a sixth solution, the resemblance theory, tries to explain musical expressiveness very roughly in terms of experienced resemblances between music and various things to do with emotions, moods, and feelings, such as their vocal, behavioral, and bodily expressions as well as their affective feel; this view was discussed in chapter IV.

So, what is my solution to the problem of musical expressiveness? I have argued that music is not really sad, happy, etc., but is only *imagined* to be so in various ways that are not always highly foregrounded, and which are causally built on the foundation provided by the different kinds of resemblances that resemblance theorists have discussed. In particular, I have said that often we animate the music, imaginatively projecting life and mental states on to the music as we endow the music with these and hear the music itself as sad, happy, etc. Animating the music in this way is central to our hearing music as sad, happy, etc., though there are also other ways in which we hear music as sad, such as the one that involves imagining an indeterminate musical persona.

It should be obvious that my view in part—and only in part—reconciles and incorporates aspects of the expression theory, the persona theory, and the resemblance theory, even as it builds on these and adds an imaginative component to give us a more comprehensive solution. For I grant that many ways of hearing music as expressive involve the idea, which is at the heart of the expression theory understood broadly, that *someone's* (or *something's*) mental states are expressed or manifested outwardly through the music, even if only in the imagination, and this someone can vary from the music itself as animated to a musical persona and so on. As this shows, I also grant that sometimes we may imagine a musical persona in hearing musical expressiveness. And I concede that experienced resemblances of different kinds exist, are heard, and form the causal foundation of hearing music as sad, happy, etc., in various imaginative ways.

It is also worth noting that I briefly explore the nature of related notions such as emotions, moods, feelings, metaphors, and imagination, not just for their own sakes—which are important, of course—but also to use in my main argument. For example, the distinction between emotions and non-intentional moods and feelings that I made in chapter I was used against Hanslick in chapter VI. Likewise, my hunch that metaphors may involve resemblance plus imagination at least was used in chapter III to object that metaphorism may collapse or otherwise lead on to an imaginationist view of musical expressiveness as being underlying and more fundamental. Similarly my discussion of imagination, especially O'Shaughnessy's view, in chapter V was used to advance my imaginationism about musical expressiveness in chapter V and particularly in chapter VI. And insofar as all of that is true, this is a work not just in analytic philosophical and musical aesthetics, it is also to some degree a work that intersects with the philosophies of mind, psychology, and language in a way that also bears on the disciplines of music and psychology.

In the Introduction to this work, I mentioned the true story of my improvising on my Kashmiri hammer-dulcimer, the *santoor*, in January 1998 when I was living in suburban Washington, DC as a graduate student and about a year away from finishing doctoral work under Jerrold Levinson's supervision. Malcolm Budd had urged me a little while before that (and at a time when I was tempted by an arousalist-projectivist sort of view) to focus on the very experience of hearing music as expressive, and had suggested that the solution to the problem of musical expressiveness must be very simple. I have done just that, and I have urged getting away from words, descriptions, the literal-metaphorical distinction, and instead regarding the experience as primary. Back then, improvising on my *santoor*, I had this very strong feeling that the music *itself* was sad, happy, etc., that I was somehow imaginatively projecting these mental states and other things on to the music. And I had all the testosterone-fueled certainty of a young man that I had solved the problem. Today, I am older if not wiser, and not so sure. But I still think animation is central to hearing musical expressiveness: we imaginatively project life and mental states on to the music in hearing it as sad, etcetera. The music is not really sad, but is only imagined and imaginatively heard to be so.

Confucius is supposed to have said: I am not concerned that I am not known; I seek to be worthy to be known. (In a similar vein perhaps, Cato the Younger is supposed to have said: I had rather men should ask why my statue is not set up than ask why it is.) Regardless of who, if indeed anyone, publishes or reads or honors our work, we should all seek likewise to be *worthy* to be read; this work is an attempt in that direction.

Notes

Introduction

1. What makes music an abstract art form if it consists of sets or sequences of sounds, given that sounds (and musical performances) are physical? The answer may lie in the fact that music is a (primarily) non-representational art (Walton 1988; Kivy 1991), and its content may be more general than that of the representational arts in that purely instrumental music usually expresses or is about, say, the *notion* of struggle or return in general (as a universal) rather than a specific (or particular) struggle or return. Also, the *products* or works of music are abstract, multiply instantiable entities, unlike paintings and carved sculpture, say, the works of which are physically based and singularly instantiated (Wollheim 1980; Trivedi 2008).

2. Tobyn De Marco suggests that my view of musical expressiveness is like the great classical pianist Glenn Gould's musical idealism, according to which, very roughly, music is mainly a phenomenon that exists and takes place in our minds. While I can grant some similarity here, unlike Gould, I do not believe that music itself exists (only) in our minds though I do believe it is created by us and can also be destroyed by us or otherwise cease to exist (Trivedi 2008).

Chapter I

1. Compare Greenspan 1988: 3-14. The cognitive-affective view I favor is similar to the theories advanced earlier by Robert Solomon, Patricia Greenspan, and Ronald de Sousa, amongst others writers; for a review of de Sousa 2011, see Trivedi 2012.

2. Desires will probably constitute some emotions, like love and sometimes anger, but not all of them. Moreover, emotions may often be *caused* by (actual or imminent or possible) satisfaction, or frustration, of desires, but desires need not be *constituents* of these emotions. Desires and their satisfaction (or frustration) may often be *necessary* for some emotions, but this does not show that desires must be

constituents of these emotions. In maintaining this, I will later distinguish between emotions and desires, and also argue against Oakley 1992: 6–37.

3. Oakley also rightly points out that we may have affects without really noticing (or feeling, as he puts it) that we have these.

4. Aesthetic experiences may also involve psychological affects of pain, despite the overall aesthetic pleasure felt. This may happen when, for instance, we listen to sad music, like the funeral march from Beethoven's *Eroica* Symphony. See Jerrold Levinson, "Music and Negative Emotion" in Levinson 1990, 306–35.

5. Compare the causal-evaluative account of the emotions in Lyons 1980, esp. chapters 2 through 4, and also in Nussbaum 2001.

6. This, for instance, seems to be the account of emotions found in Oakley and perhaps also in Sherman 1994.

7. It should be noted that though beliefs and desires *usually* fit the world unidirectionally, there is a sense in which they may fit the world bidirectionally. Apart from true beliefs fitting the world, *some* beliefs (e.g., beliefs about the future such as "It will rain tomorrow" and beliefs involving ought such as "Apartheid ought to be abolished") may involve the idea that the world comes to fit them. And apart from desires being such that the world comes to fit them, *some* desires (e.g., appropriate desires such as the desire to save for a rainy day) may be such that they fit the world in being suitable or befitting.

8. It is not clear, contrary to Oakley's (and perhaps also Aristotle's) view, that every instance of anger involves a desire for revenge. For instance, I may be angry with myself for having done something extremely careless and foolish recently, but it is not clear that such anger involves a desire for revenge against myself or my past self. Similarly, A may be angry with his very beloved brother for having recklessly wrecked A's new car, say, without this involving a desire on A's part to exact revenge upon, or otherwise retaliate against, his brother. Moreover, such anger may last for a significant period of time, differentiating it thus from mere irritation or annoyance. It may be urged, against me, that such an emotion is not one of anger but merely one of deep-rooted disappointment, for it does not involve a desire for revenge. But it is not clear that this response works, for it begs the question, making the issue merely verbal.

9. And thus it may be true to say that satisfaction of the desire, and having the desire in the first place, are *necessary* for having the emotion of happiness in this case. But that does not show that the desire *constitutes* the very emotion of happiness involved here. An analogy may make this point clearer. Hunger (i.e., the appetitive desire for food) and its satisfaction may sometimes be necessary for having the objectless "emotion" (or mood, as I will argue presently) of contentment after having had a hearty meal, but it would be absurd to claim that hunger is constitutive of (i.e., that it is an element of, or a component of) contentment. Moreover, the satisfaction of hunger may sometimes *cause* such contentment, but

it would be absurd to claim that hunger is constitutive of this contentment; for in general, causes need not be constitutive of their effects.

10. That beliefs alone do not suffice for emotions, without the addition of affects at least, can also be shown by the fact that one can assent to the requisite belief without having the emotion in question (see Oakley 1992, 28-31). Another problem with excluding affects from an account of the emotions may be, as Oakley points out, that some emotions, e.g., certain kinds of admiration and envy, can only be distinguished by affects. Oakley's example is that of my feeling admiration towards a courageous mountaineer, and my being envious of him. Here, the belief involved is the same: that X is a courageous mountaineer and I am not. The desires involved, if any, may also be the same, i.e., the desire to be like X; note here that unlike jealousy, envy need not involve a desire that the person who is envied not have whatever attribute it is we envy him for. The only thing that may distinguish admiration and envy here may be affects, i.e., while admiration involves an affect of pleasure without an affect of pain at my lacking the mountaineer's courage, envy may involve an affect of pain at not having the mountaineer's courage.

11. In making this distinction, I draw upon Searle, who thinks that whilst conscious, we are always in some mood or the other (1992, 140-41).

Chapter II

1. Collingwood claims very roughly that the process of creating "art proper" involves the artist articulating or clarifying in her imagination (and communicating to others) what she is feeling; and Tolstoy claims very roughly that the artist expresses or communicates via her work if she arouses in her audience the same mental states she felt. See Collingwood 1958; and Tolstoy 1898/2011. For criticisms, see, for example, Bouwsma 1954; Hospers 1955; Tormey 1971; Davies 2006b; and Trivedi 2004a. For a careful defense of Collingwood against Tormey, see Robinson 2005; and for another defense of Collingwood, see Ridley 1997.

2. It is clear that music may be expressive of emotions, moods, feelings, or something like these passions, but it is not clear how music can be expressive of thoughts and beliefs, given that music does not normally have intentional objects, nor does it refer to anything, unlike thoughts and beliefs. Moreover, given that emotions also typically have intentional objects, it may seem that music may be expressive not of emotions but rather of something like them, vis-à-vis moods and feelings. This conclusion that music cannot be expressive of emotions can be avoided if one grants that the *idea* of an intentional object might be conveyed musically; see Jerrold Levinson, "Hope in the *Hebrides*," in Levinson 1990, 336–75.

3. Compare Levinson 1996, 101–02, wherein it is charged that Vermazen's view as applied to music is simply "too intellectualized."

4. Levinson 1996. A persona-type view has also been proposed by psychologist Roger Watt at Stirling University who suggests that music creates in our minds "a virtual person" whose character, feelings, and behavior may be inferred from the music; see Sloboda 1998.

5. Similar reservations concerning how often in hearing music as expressive we imagine an indeterminate musical persona expressing its emotion, if we do so at all, have been raised in Stecker 2010; Davies 1997; Budd 1989; and Ridley 1995.

6. Derek Matravers 1998: 184–85 provides an instance of this conflation: "Although belief that [Beethoven's Fifth Symphony] is optimistic is not caused by any single feeling, it is nonetheless controlled by—and dependent on—beliefs caused by feelings aroused by particular passages within the work." Against Matravers, I submit we can recognize optimism without necessarily being aroused to hope, and the belief that the symphony is optimistic does not depend on arousal but on our experience of the music itself and its character.

7. Compare Roger Scruton 1997, 145: ". . . to say that a work of music is associated for me with certain feelings, experiences, memories, etc., is to say nothing about its musical character. Expression, by contrast, belongs to the aesthetic character of a work of art. . . ."

8. Compare Davies 1994, 199; Kivy 2005, 149–50; Matravers 1998, 117. Matravers notes this problem of the reversal of the order of things that arousalism faces, but it is not clear what he has to say in response. However, he also claims (1998, 194): "Failure to understand a work might mean that *its expressive properties—those which have a capacity to arouse feelings* in a qualified observer—would be missed . . ." (emphasis added). Despite all his other claims, this seems to be an unwitting admission that (perceiving) expressiveness causes arousal, and the two are distinct.

9. See, for example, Matravers 1998, 159: "An explanation . . . in which it is explained *why* an emotion is felt, *how* it was aroused, and *against whom* it is directed . . . there is no reason (according to the arousal theory) for thinking such an explanation will be available in the aesthetic case." I suggest that the emotions (if they are that, and not non-intentional moods or feelings, as they might be sometimes) aroused musically could be directed at the music as animated (in the sense I explain in chapter VI) or at the music's persona, and they could be aroused because we empathize or sympathize or identify with the music as animated or with its persona. In offering such an explanation in chapter VI, I believe my view explains more than Matravers's view which does not explain the cause and the object of musical arousal. Matravers (1998, 161) also thinks that music cannot be an appropriate cause of sadness the way death is an appropriate cause of sadness, and that musically aroused feelings are not justified. Against Matravers, I submit that music can be an appropriate cause of sadness, depending on its expressive character, for it is very human and natural to feel sad when we hear sad music, just

as it is very human and natural to feel sad when we see sad people. And, musically aroused feelings can be justified either by appealing to the expressive character of the music, or by appealing to the aroused feelings of competent listeners as a group.

10. Ridley 1995. For different kinds of resemblance-based theories, see Kivy 1989; Davies 1994; and Budd 1995.

11. Compare Scruton 1997, 145: ". . . how can I respond sympathetically to the grief in the *Masonic Funeral Music* if I do not attribute grief to the *music*?" This in turn will lead, I think, to our basic problem of musical expressiveness, to wit, how we can be said to attribute grief to something *inanimate and insentient* such as music.

12. Matravers (1998, 98 and 111), claims expressive artworks are analogous to expressive people, and claims to have provided a unified account of emotions in art and in life. But I would urge that this partial analogy supports a unified account more in accord with my imagination-based view than with his arousalism. I am also puzzled by Matravers's claim (1998, 112 and 120) that it makes no sense to ask when during a performance a musical work expresses grief. While it is true that music does not usually do so at a given instant during a performance, nevertheless often one can say, I think, either that the music expresses grief during bars 15–47 say, the grief being resolved a few bars later, and so on; or one can say that the music expresses grief throughout.

13. This claim in Matravers that it is appropriate to feel sad when we hear sad music is similar to the claim in Ridley, which I discussed and criticized on similar grounds, that our sympathetic mirroring response when we hear music suits the music. On a different point, Matravers (1998, 170 and 181) approvingly quotes Bouwsma's famous claim that "sadness is to the music rather like the redness to the apple, than it is like the burp to the cider"; see Bouwsma 1954. But I would submit that my theory is closer to Bouwsma's claim than is Matravers's arousalism, for just as gulping cider causes the burp, similarly musical sadness (and musical expressiveness in general) *causes* or evokes arousal, if I am right. Moreover, just as redness is a mind-dependent property of the apple, likewise musical sadness (and musical expressiveness in general) is an imagination-dependent and thus broadly mind-dependent property of the music, if I am right. On a related point, I disagree with Matravers (1998, 188): "Part of the analysis of red is the claim that the observer 'experiences x as red'; the analogue in the aesthetic case is that a work 'arouses a feeling' in the observer." I submit that the aesthetic analogue is *not* arousal but rather competent listeners in normal circumstances readily and immediately '*experiencing music (or the artwork) as sad,*' which is different from arousal and need not involve arousal (as Matravers allows) even if the two are often coextensive. On yet another point, I must confess to being baffled by Matravers's claims (1998, 182–83, 225–26) that "cognitivist" notions such as resemblances, imagination, and personae are "*ad hoc*" or "non-explanatory" or "complicated and mysterious" or "invented for convenience."

Chapter III

1. What is the relation between my resemblance-plus-imagination view of musical expressiveness and my similar hunch about metaphors? First, the two views concern different domains (one deals with the realm of sounds and mental states heard in it, while the other deals with words and language) and are thus *independent* of each other. Second, while I admit that metaphors may involve more than resemblance and imagination, which I leave to be explored elsewhere, my view of musical expressiveness involves nothing beyond resemblance and imagination as basic and essential. Third, while I admittedly only have a hunch and not a complete theory about metaphors, my view of musical expressiveness is more developed and closer to completion even if not yet complete.

2. I briefly explore different kinds of imaginings in chapter V; see also Walton 1990, chapter 1.

3. My position on metaphors is continuous with the moderate hypothetical intentionalism about interpretation I advanced in Trivedi 2001b, and develop and defend further in Trivedi 2015.

4. Andrew McGonigal made this suggestion to me in personal conversation.

5. My view in part synthesizes various resemblance-based views of musical expressiveness [e.g., Kivy 1989; Davies 1994; and Budd 1995] with various imagination-based views of musical expressiveness [e.g., Walton 1988; 1994; Levinson 1996; Robinson 2005].

6. I agree with Scruton that a musical work's expressive qualities are *an* important part of its content, but disagree that they are always the most important part; and I am puzzled by Scruton's doubts (1997: 344–46) whether current theories of musical expressiveness could pass his four tests (the "semaphore test," the understanding test, the value test, and the structure test), and submit that many of them (for example, Peter Kivy's resemblance-based theory, Kendall Walton's make-believe-based theory, Jerrold Levinson's persona-based theory), including mine, could easily pass these tests.

7. For more on this, see the later chapters of this book, and also Trivedi 2001a; 2003; 2006.

Chapter IV

1. My own daughters started doing just this as toddlers, especially with regard to simple melodies, even though they did not then know the distinction between literal and metaphorical language or the secondary sense of literal language, nor did they use or grasp figurative language. Indeed, it was only around the age of ten that they first started learning about metaphors, similes, and the like at school.

2. Going beyond non-Western philosophies such as Daoism and Western popular music and musicians such as The Beatles and Frank Sinatra (both of whom Roholt discusses), there are in fact similar ideas also in various non-Western musics such as African and Indian music, where rhythms, complex cross-rhythms, polyrhythms, syncopations, etc., are *felt* and grasped bodily via playing, tapping, dancing, moving, and so on (though I note that Roholt discusses West African and African-American music through the writings of the noted Indian-American musician and theorist Vijay Iyer).

3. A lot of current musical aesthetics, and indeed philosophy, is heavily focused on empirical psychological data, sometimes almost to the total exclusion of philosophy. This might remind one of something the ancient pre-Socratic philosopher Gorgias is supposed to have said: Those who leave philosophy for other studies are like Penelope's suitors who started courting her handmaidens instead. Thanks to my former student Daniel Shayowitz who reminded me of this, which we had come across in our Ancient Philosophy class and revisited later when I supervised his Honors thesis on experimental philosophy.

Chapter V

1. For an excellent overview of philosophical thinking about musical improvisation, see Brown 2011.

2. For critical discussions of Currie and Ravenscroft 2002, see, for example, Nichols 2004; Carruthers 2003; and Todd 2003.

Chapter VI

1. For other critical discussions of Hanslick, see Budd 1985; Davies 1994; and Levinson 1990c.

2. See Kivy 2002, chapter 3. See also my review in Trivedi 2004b.

3. For a fuller statement of the persona view, see Levinson 1996 and also Levinson 2006; see also Robinson 2005.

4. Careful readers will note that I have been making some of these clarificatory distinctions for many years now, and indeed made them earlier in Trivedi 2001a, 416; and also in Trivedi 2011, 230.

5. Budd quotes T. S. Eliot's words (from *Four Quartets*, "The Dry Salvages," V): "music heard so deeply / That it is not heard at all, but you are the music / While the music lasts."

6. Similar claims about the arts and music liberating us are made, of course, in Schopenhauer 1788/1966.

7. Compare Davies 1994, 271 ff. The six rewards canvassed above, and more besides, are also touched upon in Levinson 1990a.

8. See Kivy 2002, and his various other writings.

9. For an account of the emotional rewards (such as catharsis, emotional resilience, etc.) obtained from listening to and being aroused by sad music, see Levinson 1990a and Ridley 1995.

10. In addition to the works by Kivy, Davies, Budd, and Ridley cited earlier, see Boghossian 2002. See also Pratt 1931.

11. Claims about the conventional expressiveness of the minor third and the minor triad are made in Kivy 1989, though he seems to backtrack from these in his more recent Kivy 2002, 44–45, where he suggests these might be sad due to their functions in musical structures, in that they sound restless compared to the major third and the major triad.

12. For elaborations regarding imagining, see Walton 1990, chapter 1; and also my discussion in chapter V above.

References

Arnold, Magda. 1960. *Emotion and Personality*. New York: Columbia University Press.
Balkwill, L. L., and W. F. Thompson. 1999. "A Cross-Cultural Investigation of the Perception of Emotion in Music: Psychophysical and Cultural Clues." *Music Perception*, 17: 43-64.
Balkwill, L. L., W. F. Thompson, and R. Matsunaga. 2004. "Recognition of Emotion in Japanese, Western, and Hindustani Music by Japanese Listeners. *Japanese Psychological Research*, 46: 337-49.
Beardsley, Monroe. 1962. "The Metaphorical Twist." *Philosophy and Phenomenological Research*, 22 (1962): 293-307.
Bergeron, Vincent, and Dominic Lopes. 2009. "Hearing and Seeing Musical Expression." *Philosophy and Phenomenological Research*, 78 (2009): 1-16.
Black, Max. 1955/2004. "Metaphor." Reprinted in *Philosophy of Literature*, edited by John & Lopes.
———. 1993. "More about Metaphor." In *Metaphor and Thought*, edited by Andrew Ortony. Cambridge: Cambridge University Press.
Blackburn, Simon. 1993. *Essays in Quasi-Realism*. Oxford: Oxford University Press.
Blood, A., and R. Zatorre. 2001. "Intensely Pleasurable Responses to Music Correlate with Activity in Brain Regions Implicated in Reward and Emotion." *Proceedings of the National Academy of Sciences USA*, 98: 11818-11823.
Boghossian, Paul. 2002. "On Hearing the Music in the Sound: Scruton on Musical Expression," *Journal of Aesthetics and Art Criticism*, 60 (2002): 49-55.
Bouwsma, O. K. 1954. "The Expression Theory of Art." In *Aesthetics and Language*, edited by William Elton. Oxford: Blackwell.
Bowie, Andrew. 2007. *Music, Philosophy, and Modernity*. New York: Cambridge University Press.
Bowling, D. L., J. Sundararajan, S. Han, and D. Purves. 2012. "Expression of Emotion in Eastern and Western Music Mirrors Vocalization." *PloS ONE* 7(3), e31942. doi: 10.1371/journal.pone.0031942.
Brady, Michael. 2014. *Emotional Insight*. New York: Oxford University Press.

Brattico, E., V. Alluri, B. Bogert, T. Jacobsen, N. Vartiainen, S. Nieminen, and M. Tervaniemi. 2011. "A Functional MRI Study of Happy and Sad Emotions in Music With and Without the Lyrics." *Frontiers in Psychology*, 2: 308.

Brown, Lee. 2011. "Improvisation." In *The Routledge Companion to Philosophy and Music*, edited by Theodore Gracyk and Andrew Kania. New York: Routledge.

Budd, Malcolm. 1985. *Music and the Emotions*. London: Routledge.

———. 1989. "Music and the Communication of Emotion." *Journal of Aesthetics and Art Criticism*, 47 (1989): 129–38.

———. 1995. *Values of Art*. London: Penguin.

———. 2003. "Musical Movement and Aesthetic Metaphors," *British Journal of Aesthetics*, 43 (2003): 209–23.

———. 2005. "Aesthetic Realism and Emotional Qualities of Music." *British Journal of Aesthetics*, 45 (2005): 111–22.

Carroll, Noël. 1999. *Philosophy of Art*. New York: Routledge.

———. 2006. "Film, Emotion, and Genre." In *The Philosophy of Film and Motion Pictures*, edited by Carroll and Jinhee Choi. Malden, MA: Blackwell.

Carruthers, Peter. 2003. Review of Gregory Currie and Ian Ravenscroft's *Recreative Minds*. *Notre Dame Philosophical Reviews*, 2003.11.12.

Cavell, Stanley. 1969/1977. "Music Discomposed." In *Must We Mean What We Say?* Cambridge: Cambridge University Press.

Chen, L., S. Zhou, and J. Bryant. 2007. "Temporal Changes in Mood Repair through Music Consumption." *Media Psychology*, 9: 695–713.

Chuang-Tzu. 1998. *The Inner Chapters*, translated by David Hinton. Washington, DC: Counterpoint.

Cohen, Ted. 2003. "Metaphor." In *The Oxford Handbook of Aesthetics*, edited by Jerrold Levinson. Oxford: Oxford University Press, 2003.

Collingwood, R. G. 1958. *Principles of Art*. Oxford: Oxford University Press.

Cook, Nicholas. 1990. *Music, Imagination, and Culture*. Oxford: Clarendon Press.

Currie, Gregory. 2004. *Arts and Minds*. Oxford: Clarendon Press.

Currie, Gregory, and Ian Ravenscroft. 2002. *Recreative Minds*. Oxford: Clarendon Press.

Dahlhaus, Carl. 1988. *Klassiche und Romantische Musikästhetik*. Laaber: Laaber.

Dalla Bella, S., I. Peretz, L. Rousseau, and N. Gosselin. 2001. "A Developmental Study of the Affective Value of Tempo and Mode in Music." *Cognition*, 80: B1–B10.

Damasio, Antonio. 1994. *Descartes' Error*. New York: Putnam.

Davidson, Donald. 1984. "What Metaphors Mean." In *Inquiries into Truth and Interpretation*. Oxford: Oxford University Press.

Davies, Stephen. 1980. "The Expression of Emotion in Music." Reprinted in Davies 2003, 134–51.

———. 1994. *Musical Meaning and Expression*. Ithaca, NY: Cornell University Press.

———. 1997. "Contra the Hypothetical Persona in Music." In *Emotion and the Arts*, edited by Mette Hjort and Sue Laver. Oxford: Oxford University Press.
———. 2001. "Philosophical Perspectives on Music's Expressiveness." Reprinted in Davies 2003, 169-91.
———. 2003. *Themes in the Philosophy of Music*, Oxford: Oxford University Press.
———. 2006a. "Artistic Expression and the Hard Case of Pure Music." In *Contemporary Debates in Aesthetics and the Philosophy of Art*, edited by Matthew Kieran. Oxford: Blackwell, 179-91.
———. 2006b. *The Philosophy of Art*. Malden, MA: Blackwell.
de Sousa, Ronald. 1987. *The Rationality of Emotion*. Cambridge, MA: MIT Press.
———. 2011. *Emotional Truth*. New York: Oxford University Press.
Egermann, H., and S. McAdams. 2013. "Empathy and Emotional Contagion as a Link between Recognized and Felt Emotions in Music Listening." *Music Perception*, 31: 139-56.
Evans, Gareth, and John McDowell, eds. 1976. *Truth and Meaning*. New York: Oxford University Press.
Evans, P., and E. Schubert. 2008. "Relationships Between Expressed and Felt Emotions in Music." *Musicae Scientiae*, 12: 75-99.
Fernald, A., T. Taeschner, J. Dunn, M. Papousek, B. de Boysson-Bardies, and I. Fukui. 1989. "A Cross-Language Study of Prosodic Modifications in Mothers' and Fathers' Speech to Preverbal Infants." *Journal of Child Language*, 16: 477-501.
Fritz, T., Jentschke, S., Gosselin, N., Sammler, D., Peretz, I., Turner R., and Koelsch, S. 2009. "Universal Recognition of Three Basic Emotions in Music." *Current Biology*, 19: 573-76.
Gagnon, L., and I. Peretz. 2003. "Mode and Tempo: Relative Contributions to 'Happy-Sad' Judgments in Equitone Melodies." *Cognition and Emotion*, 17: 25-40.
Garrido, S., and E. Schubert. 2015. "Moody Melodies: Do They Cheer Us Up? A Study of the Effect of Sad Music on Mood." *Psychology of Music*, 43: 244-61.
Getz, L. M., S. Marks, and M. Roy. 2014. "The Influence of Stress, Optimism, and Music Training on Music Uses and Preferences." *Psychology of Music*, 42: 71-85.
Goldie, Peter. 2002. *The Emotions*. New York: Clarendon Press.
Gomez, P., and B. Danuser. 2004. "Affective and Physiological Responses to Environmental Noises and Music." *International Journal of Psychophysiology*, 53: 91-103.
———. 2007. "Relationships Between Musical Structure and Psychophysiological Measures of Emotion." *Emotion*, 7: 377-87.
Goodman, Nelson. 1976. *Languages of Art*, 2nd ed. Indianapolis, IN: Hackett.
Graham, A. C. 1989. *Disputers of the Tao*. Chicago: Open Court.
Greenspan, Patricia. 1988. *Emotions and Reasons*. New York: Routledge.

Grey, Thomas. 2011. "Hanslick." In *The Routledge Companion to Philosophy and Music*, edited by Theodore Gracyk and Andrew Kania. New York: Routledge.
Griffiths, Paul. 1997. *What Emotions Really Are*. Chicago: University of Chicago Press.
———. 2013. "Current Emotion Research in Philosophy." *Emotion Review*, 5: 215-22.
Hagberg, Garry. 2001. "Metaphor." In *The Routledge Companion to Aesthetics*, edited by Berys Gaut and Dominic Lopes. New York: Routledge.
Hamlyn, D. W. 1994. "Imagination." In *A Companion to Philosophy of Mind*, edited by Samuel Guttenplan. Malden, MA: Blackwell.
Hanslick, Eduard. 1986. *On the Musically Beautiful*. Translated by Geoffrey Payzant. Indianapolis, IN: Hackett.
Harris, Paul. 2000. *The Work of the Imagination*. Malden, MA: Blackwell.
Higgins, Kathleen. 2012. *The Music Between Us: Is Music a Universal Language?* Chicago: University of Chicago Press.
Hospers, John. 1955. "The Concept of Artistic Expression." *Proceedings of the Aristotelian Society* (1954-55): 313-44.
Hunter, P. G., E. G. Schellenberg, and U. Schimmack. 2010. "Feelings and Perceptions of Happiness and Sadness Induced by Music." *Psychology of Aesthetics, Creativity, and the Arts*, 4: 47-56.
Huron, David. 1995. Review of Nicholas Cook's *Music, Imagination, and Culture*. *Music Perception*, 12 (1995): 473-81.
———. 2011. "Why is Sad Music Pleasurable? A Possible Role for Prolactin." *Musicae Scientiae*, 15: 146-58.
Iseminger, Gary. 1999. Review of Scruton 1997. *Journal of Aesthetics and Art Criticism*, 57 (1999): 375.
John, Eileen, and Dominic Lopes, eds. 2004. *Philosophy of Literature*. Oxford: Blackwell.
Juslin, P., and P. Laukka. 2003. "Communication of Emotions in Vocal Expression and Music Performance: Different Channels, Same Code?." *Psychological Bulletin*, 129: 770-814.
Juslin, P., and E. Lindstrom. 2010. "Musical Expression of Emotions." *Music Analysis*, 29: 334-64.
Juslin, P., and S. Isaakson. 2014. "Subjective Criteria for Choice and Aesthetic Judgment of Music." *Research Studies in Music Education*, 36: 179-98.
Kania, Andrew. 2015. "An Imaginative Theory of Musical Space and Movement." *British Journal of Aesthetics*, 55: 157-72.
Kieran, Matthew, and Dominic Lopes, eds. 2003. *Imagination, Philosophy, and the Arts*. New York: Routledge.
Kivy, Peter. 1989. *Sound Sentiment*. Philadelphia: Temple University Press.
———. 1991. *Sound and Semblance*. Ithaca, NY: Cornell University Press.
———. 2002. *Introduction to a Philosophy of Music*. Oxford: Clarendon Press.

———. 2005. *New Essays on Musical Understanding*. Oxford: Oxford University Press.

———. 2006. "Critical Study: Deeper than Reason." *British Journal of Aesthetics*, 46 (2006): 287–311.

Kraut, Robert. 2007. "Emotions in the Music." In *Artworld Metaphysics*. New York: Oxford University Press.

Krumhansl, Carol. 1997. "An Exploratory Study of Musical Emotions and Psychophysiology."*Canadian Journal of Experimental Psychology*, 51 (1997): 336–52.

Kulvicki, John. 2008. "Artifact Expression." In *New Waves in Aesthetics*, edited by Kathleen Stock and Katherine Thomson-Jones. New York: Palgrave Macmillan.

Lakoff, George, and Mark Johnson. 2003. *Metaphors We Live By*. Chicago: University of Chicago Press.

Langer, Susanne. 1942. *Philosophy in a New Key*. Cambridge, MA: Harvard University Press.

Lao-Tzu. 1993. *Tao te Ching*. Translated by Stephen Addis and Stanley Lombardo. Indianapolis, IN: Hackett.

Laukka, P., Eerola, T., Thingujam, N. S., Yamasaki, T., and Beller, G. 2013. "Universal and Culture-Specific Factors in the Recognition and Performance of Musical Affect Expressions." *Emotion*, 13: 434–49.

Laukka, P., and L. Quick. 2013. "Emotional and Motivational Uses of Music in Sports and Exercise." *Psychology of Music*, 41: 198–215.

Lazarus, Richard. 1991. *Emotion and Adaptation*. New York: Oxford University Press.

Levin, Samuel. 1993. "Language, Concepts, and Worlds." In *Metaphor and Thought*, edited by Andrew Ortony. Cambridge: Cambridge University Press.

Levinson, Jerrold. 1990a. "Music and Negative Emotion." In *Music, Art, and Metaphysics*. Ithaca, NY: Cornell University Press.

———. 1990b. "Hope in the Hebrides." In *Music, Art, and Metaphysics*. Ithaca, NY: Cornell University Press.

———. 1990c. *Music, Art, and Metaphysics*. Ithaca, NY: Cornell University Press.

———. 1992. "Musical Composition." In *A Companion to Aesthetics*, edited by David Cooper. Malden, MA: Blackwell.

———. 1996. "Musical Expressiveness." In *The Pleasures of Aesthetics*. Ithaca, NY: Cornell University Press.

———. 2000. Review of Scruton. *Philosophical Review*, 109 (2000): 605–06.

———. 2001. "Who's Afraid of a Paraphrase?" *Theoria*, 67 (2001): 7–23.

———. 2004. "Comments on Nussbaum 2001." *Pacific APA*, 2004.

———. 2006. "Musical Expressiveness as Hearability-as-expression." In *Contemporary Debates in Aesthetics and the Philosophy of Art*, edited by Matthew Kieran. Oxford: Blackwell, 192–204.

———. 2015. *Musical Concerns*. New York: Oxford University Press.

Liljestrom, S., P. Juslin, and D. Vastfjall. 2013. "Experimental Evidence of the Roles of Music Choice, Social Context, and Listener Personality in Emotional Reactions to Music." *Psychology of Music*, 41: 579–99.

Lopes, Dominic. 1997. "Art Media and the Sense Modalities: Tactile Pictures." *Philosophical Quarterly*, 47 (1997): 425–40.

Lyons, William. 1980. *Emotion*. Cambridge: Cambridge University Press.

Madell, Geoffrey. 2002. *Philosophy, Music and Emotion*. Edinburgh: Edinburgh University Press.

Matravers, Derek. 1998. *Art and Emotion*. Oxford: Clarendon Press.

———. 2001. "Art, Expression, and Emotion." In *The Routledge Companion to Aesthetics*, edited by Berys Gaut and Dominic Lopes. New York: Routledge.

———. 2003. "The Experience of Emotion in Music." *Journal of Aesthetics and Art Criticism*, 61 (2003): 355–65.

———. 2006. "Review of Robinson." *Journal of Aesthetics and Art Criticism*, 64 (2006): 283–85.

———. 2011. "Arousal Theories." In *The Routledge Companion to Philosophy and Music*, edited by Theodore Gracyk and Andrew Kania. New York: Routledge, 212–22.

McGinn, Colin. 2004. *Mindsight: Image, Dream, Meaning*. Cambridge, MA: Harvard University Press.

Menon, V., and D. Levitin. 2005. "The Rewards of Music Listening." *Neuroimage*, 28: 175–84.

Moors, Agnes, Phoebe Ellsworth, Klaus Scherer, and Nico Frijda. 2013a. "Appraisal Theories of Emotion: State of the Art and Future Development." *Emotion Review*, 5: 119–24.

Moors, Agnes. 2013b. "On the Causal Role of Appraisal in Emotion." *Emotion Review*, 5: 132–40.

Moran, Richard. 1987. "Seeing and Believing: Metaphor, Image, and Force." *Critical Inquiry*, 16 (1989): 87–112.

Nakata, T., and Sandra Trehub. 2004. "Infants' Response to Maternal Speech and Singing." *Infant Behavior and Development*, 27: 455–64.

New, Christopher. 1999. *Philosophy of Literature*. New York: Routledge.

Nichols, Shaun. 2004. Review of Gregory Currie and Ian Ravenscroft's *Recreative Minds*. *Mind* 113 (2004): 329–34.

Nussbaum, Charles. 2007. *The Musical Representation*. Cambridge, MA: MIT Press.

Nussbaum, Martha. 1994. *The Therapy of Desire*. Princeton, NJ: Princeton University Press.

———. 2001. *Upheavals of Thought*. New York: Cambridge University Press.

Oakley, Justin. 1992. *Morality and the Emotions*. New York: Routledge.

Ortony, Andrew, ed. 1993. *Metaphor and Thought*, 2nd ed. Cambridge. Cambridge University Press.

O'Shaughnessy, Brian. 2002. *Consciousness and the World*. Oxford: Oxford University Press.
Plato, *Republic*. 1920. In *The Dialogues of Plato*, vol. I, translated by. Benjamin Jowett. New York: Random House.
Pratt, Carroll. 1931. *The Meaning of Music*. New York: McGraw-Hill.
Prinz, Jesse. 2004. *Gut Reactions*. New York: Oxford University Press.
Réti, Rudolf. 1961. *The Thematic Process in Music*. New York: Faber.
Ridley, Aaron. 1995. *Music, Value, and the Passions*. Ithaca, NY: Cornell University Press.
———. 1997. "Not Ideal: Collingwood's Expression Theory." *Journal of Aesthetics and Art Criticism* 55 (1997): 263–72.
———. 2004. *The Philosophy of Music*. Edinburgh: Edinburgh University Press.
Robinson, Jenefer. 2005. *Deeper than Reason*. Oxford: Oxford University Press.
———. 2009. Review of Charles Nussbaum, *Notre Dame Philosophical Reviews*, March 2009.
Roholt, Tiger. 2014. *Groove: A Phenomenology of Rhythmic Nuance*. New York: Bloomsbury.
Ryle, Gilbert. 1949. *The Concept of Mind*. London: Hutchinson.
Sartre, Jean-Paul. 1972. *The Psychology of the Imagination*. New York: Routledge.
Schoenberg, Arnold. 1978. *Theory of Harmony*. Los Angeles and Berkeley: University of California Press.
Schopenhauer, Arthur. 1788/1966. *The World as Will and Representation*, translated by E. F. J. Payne. New York: Dover.
Schroeder, Severin. 2013. "Music and Metaphor." *British Journal of Aesthetics*, 53: 1–19.
Scruton, Roger. 1992. "Imagination." In *A Companion to Aesthetics*, edited by David Cooper. Malden, MA: Blackwell.
———. 1997. *The Aesthetics of Music*. Oxford: Oxford University Press.
———. 2004. "Musical Movement: A Reply to Budd." *British Journal of Aesthetics*, 44 (2004): 184–87.
Searle, John. 1992. *The Rediscovery of the Mind*. Cambridge, MA: MIT Press.
———. 1993. "Metaphor." In *Metaphor and Thought*, edited by Andrew Ortony. Cambridge: Cambridge University Press.
Sherman, Nancy. 1994 "Emotions." In *Encyclopedia of Bioethics*, edited by Warren Reich. New York: Macmillan.
Shifriss, R., E. Bodner, and Y. Palgi. 2014. "When You're Down and Troubled." *Psychology of Music*. Advance online publication. doi: 10.1177/0305735614540360.
Sloboda, John. 1998. "Brain Waves to the Heart." *BBC Music Magazine*, November 1998.
Solomon, Robert. 1983. *The Passions*. Notre Dame: University of Notre Dame Press.
———, ed. 2003. *What is an Emotion?* New York: Oxford University Press.

Stacho, S., S. Saarikallio, A. van Zijl, M. Huotilainen, and P. Toiviainen. 2013. "Perception of Emotional Content in Musical Performances by 3–7 Year Old Children." *Musicae Scientiae,* 17: 495–512.

Stecker, Robert. 2010. "Expressiveness in Music and Poetry." In *Aesthetics and the Philosophy of Art,* 2nd ed. Lanham, MD: Rowman and Littlefield.

Stern, Josef. 2000. *Metaphor in Context.* Cambridge, MA: MIT Press.

Stocker, Michael. 1996. *Valuing Emotions.* Cambridge: Cambridge University Press.

Stravinsky, Igor. 1936. *Stravinsky: An Autobiography.* New York: Simon and Schuster.

Swaminathan, Swathi, and E. Glenn Schellenberg. 2015. "Current Emotion Research in Music Psychology." *Emotion Review,* 7: 189–97.

Todd, Cain. 2003. Review of Gregory Currie and Ian Ravenscroft's *Recreative Minds, British Journal of Aesthetics,* 43 (2003): 419–22.

Tolstoy, Leo. 1898/2011. *What is Art?,* translated by Aylmer Maude. Bristol: Bristol Classical Press.

Tormey, Alan. 1971. *The Concept of Expression.* Princeton, NJ: Princeton University Press.

Trehub, Sandra. 2003. "The Developmental Origins of Musicality." *Nature Neuroscience,* 6: 669–73.

Trivedi, Saam. 2001a. "Expressiveness as a Property of the Music Itself." *Journal of Aesthetics and Art Criticism,* 59 (2001): 411–20.

———. 2001b. "An Epistemic Dilemma for Actual Intentionalism." *British Journal of Aesthetics,* 41 (2001): 192–206.

———. 2003. "The Funerary Sadness of Mahler's Music." In *Imagination, Philosophy, and the Arts,* edited by Matthew Kieran and Dominic Lopes. New York: Routledge, 2003, 259–71.

———. 2004a. "Artist-Audience Communication: Tolstoy Reclaimed." *Journal of Aesthetic Education* 38 (2004): 38–52.

———. 2004b. Review of Peter Kivy's *Introduction to a Philosophy of Music* and Geoffrey Madell's *Philosophy, Music, and Emotion. Philosophical Quarterly,* 54 (2004): 199–202.

———. 2006. "Imagination, Music, and the Emotions." *Revue Internationale de Philosophie,* 60 (2006): 415–35.

———. 2008. "Music and Metaphysics." *Metaphilosophy,* 39: 124–43.

———. 2011. "Resemblance Theories." In *The Routledge Companion to Philosophy and Music,* edited by Theodore Gracyk and Andrew Kania. New York: Routledge, 223–32.

———. 2012. Review of Ronald de Sousa's *Emotional Truth. Journal of Aesthetics and Art Criticism,* 70 (2012): 239–41.

———. 2015. "Surplus, Authorial Intentions, and Hypothetical Intentionalism." *College Literature,* 42: 699–724.

Vermazen, Bruce. 1986. "Expression as Expression." *Pacific Philosophical Quarterly,* 67 (1986): 196–224.

Walker, D. P. 1958. *Spiritual and Demonic Magic*. London: The Warburg Institute.
Walton, Kendall. 1988. "What is Abstract about the Art of Music?" *Journal of Aesthetics and Art Criticism*, 46 (1988): 351–64.
———. 1990. *Mimesis as Make-Believe*. Cambridge, MA: Harvard University Press.
———. 1993/2004. "Metaphor and Prop Oriented Make-Believe." Reprinted in *Philosophy of Literature*, edited by John and Lopes. Oxford: Blackwell.
———. 1994. "Listening with Imagination: Is Music Representational?" *Journal of Aesthetics and Art Criticism*, 52 (1994): 47–61.
Williams, Chris. 2003. "Seeing Twice Over." In *Imagination, Philosophy, and the Arts*, edited by Matthew Kieran and Dominic Lopes. New York: Routledge.
Williamson, Timothy. 2007. *The Philosophy of Philosophy*, Malden, MA: Blackwell.
Wilson, Mark. 2006. *Wandering Significance*. New York: Oxford University Press.
Wollheim, Richard. 1980. *Art and Its Objects*, 2nd ed. Cambridge: Cambridge University Press.
———. 1993. "Correspondence, Projective Properties, and Expression in the Arts." In *The Mind and Its Depths*. Cambridge, MA: Harvard University Press.
Young, James. 2014. *Critique of Pure Music*. New York: Oxford University Press.
Zangwill, Nick. 2015. *Music and Aesthetic Reality: Formalism and the Limits of Description*. New York: Routledge.

Index

Abbott, E. A., 158
Adagio for Strings (Barber), 51, 75
Aesthetic Realism, 127–28, 129, 130
analogy theory on metaphors, 64, 65
Anglophone analytic philosophy, 85, 95
animation of sound (music)
    central element of imaginationism, 3, 161, 169
    examples of, 93–94, 135–146
    imagining music and, 135–39, 145, 161
    Kivy and, 145
    See also Beethoven
anti-metaphorist arguments. *See* metaphorism, arguments against
Appelqvist, Hanne, 152
Aristotle
    analogy theory and, 64, 65
    on anger, 172
    on emotions, 28
    on imagination, 98
arousalism theories, 41–47, 167
    overview, 2–3, 4, 31
    simple arousalism, 39–41, 174nn6–9
    See also expression theories; Matravers, Derek; Nussbaum, Charles; Ridley, Aaron
audio-visual theory (Bergeron and Lopes), 143–44

Bach, J. S., 1, 131, 144
Barber, Samuel, 51, 75
Beardsley, Monroe, 4, 55–56
Beethoven
    "Eroica" Symphony, 41, 92, 126, 127, 172
    Ninth Symphony in D minor, Op. 125, 137
    "Pastoral" Symphony, No. 6 in F Major, Op. 68., 2
    "Pathetique" Sonata, Op. 13r, Op. 68, 60
beliefs, emotions and, 16–17, 173n10
Bergeron, Vincent, 143–44
Black, Max, 58, 66–67
blind musicians, 144
Boghossian, Paul, 154–55
Book of Zhuangzi, The, 87–88
Borges, Jorge Luis, 113
Bowie, Andrew, criticisms of, 165–67
Budd, Malcolm
    claims of, 154–55
    criticism of theories, 78, 88
    influential work of, 95
    on musical qualities, 116–17
    as music philosopher, 5, 6, 38, 168
    resemblance-based theories of, 3
    See also resemblance-based theories criticized

Charles, Ray, 144
children
   emotions and, 18
   imaginings of, 99, 104–8, 136, 137, 152
   musical expressiveness and, 86–87, 176n2
cognitive-affective view of emotions, 9–29
   overview, 3–4, 9
   bidirectional fit between concepts and, 13–14, 172n7
   cognitive element of, 12–13
   desires and, 10, 13, 14–15, 171chIn2, 172nn8–9
   emotions and, 9–10, 171chIn1
   intentionality of, 10, 13, 26, 28, 149–150
   physical vs. psychological affects, 11–12, 172n4
   reconciliation with somatic view, 29
   what they are, 10–11, 172n3
   See also Griffiths, Paul; neo-Stoic cognitivist view of emotions; Prinz, Jesse
Collingwood, R. G., 32, 173n1
Coltrane, John, 36, 140
comparison theory on metaphors, 65–66
Confucius, on worthiness, 169
contour-convention view (Kivy). *See* Kivy, Peter
Cook, Nicholas, on musical culture, 118–120
Currie, Gregory (and Ravenscroft)
   arts and, 112–13
   hearing vs. seeing and, 113–14
   propositional imaginings vs. perceptional, 100–104, 111–12, 152–53
   supposing and, 111
   views on imagination, 97, 109–15

Dahlhaus, Carl, 166
Damasio, Antonio, view of, 25
Dao de Jing, 87
Daoism, philosophical, 86–88
Darwin, Charles, 7, 21
Davidson, Donald
   criticisms of, 57–58, 63, 72
   metaphorist view of, 52, 55–56
Davies, Stephen
   claims of, 5, 37, 44, 154–55
   criticism of theories, 77–78, 84–88, 90–91
   on imagining musical expressiveness, 142–43
   influential work of, 95
   musical expressiveness and, 2, 3, 102
   See also resemblance-based theories criticized
daydreaming, 5, 37, 99–100, 133, 159–160
De Marco, Tobyn, 7, 171Intn2
desires, cognitive-affective view of emotions and, 10, 13, 14–15, 171chIn2, 172nn8–9
de Sousa, Ronald, 4, 29, 125

Ekman, Paul, 24
elliptical simile theory on metaphors, 64–65
emotions
   beliefs and, 16–17, 173n10
   feelings and, 10–12
   moods and, 17, 173n11
   musically aroused, 149–150
   Oakley's theory of, 15
   psychological affects and, 12
"Eroica" Symphony (Beethoven), 41, 92, 126, 127, 172
expression theories, 31–49
   overview, 4, 31
   expression vs. expressiveness, defined, 32–33

simple, 31–32, 167
See also arousalism theories;
  Levinson, Jerrold; Matravers,
  Derek; Nussbaum, Charles;
  Ridley, Aaron; Robinson, Jenefer;
  Vermazen, Bruce

Flatland (Abbott)., 158
Formalism (music), objections to,
  124–133, 162, 167
See also Hanslick, Eduard; Kraut,
  Robert; Neo-Formalism; Zangwill,
  Nick
Frege, Gottlob, 76, 85, 96

Gershwin, George, 36, 92
Goehr, Lydia, 153
Goodman, Nelson
  metaphorism and, 3, 4, 51
  as Nominalist, 128
  rejection of theories, 52–55, 72,
    73
grief, 12–13, 19
Griffiths, Paul
  criticisms of theory, 22–23
  integration of approach by, 23–24
  theory of emotions, 10, 21–22
Gut Reactions (Prinz), 24

"Haffner" Symphony (Mozart), 31
Hagberg, Garry, 65
Hanslick, Eduard
  main thesis of, 124
  musical Formalism approach of, 4,
    5, 9, 17
  On the Musically Beautiful, 124
  responses to arguments of, 125–27,
    168
Harris, Paul
  on children's emotional reactions to
    imaginary entities, 105–6
  on children's imaginings, 104–5

  developmental psychologist, 5, 97,
    104
  further claims of, 106–7
  relevance of claims, 107–8
  See also children
Harrison, George, 142

imagination, 97–121
  overview, 5, 97–100
  children and, 104–8
  elusiveness of, 115
  kinds of imaginings, 97–100,
    120–21, 135–142
  mental images and, 98–99, 103–4,
    111, 158
  metaphors and, 62–63, 64, 65
  music and, 115–120
  nature of, 97–100, 120–21
  perceptions and, 100–104, 111–12,
    152–53
  See also Currie, Gregory; Harris,
    Paul; O'Shaughnessy, Brian
imaginationism, 123–163
  overview, 5–6, 123–24
  audio-visual theory (Bergeron and
    Lopes), 143–44
  emotional music examples, 131–32
  kinds of imaginings, 97–100,
    120–21, 135–142
  mental states as imagined in music,
    133–35
  musical arousal, 148–151
  rewards of, 145–48, 178n7
  See also animation of sound (music);
    Bergeron, Vincent; Formalism
    (music) objections to; Hanslick,
    Eduard; imaginationism:
    objections and replies; Kraut,
    Robert; Lopes, Dominic;
    metaphorism, arguments against;
    Neo-Formalism; Zangwill,
    Nick

imaginationism: objections and replies, 151–162
  conventional expressiveness and, 155–56, 178n11
  existence of postulated forms of imagining, 159
  expression and expressiveness conflated, 156–57
  imagining as instance of agency, 160
  inanimate objects and imaginationism, 152
  mental states as imagined in music, 157–59
  music animation as simplistic solution, 161
  music job differs from behavior, 162
  nonpropositional imaginings nonexistent, 159–160
  perception and imaginationism, 100–104, 111–12, 152–53
  perceptual imaginings and, 160
  persona line of objections answered, 161–62
  resemblance and imagination priority, 153–55
  whose mental states music expresses, 155, 162
imaginings, kinds of, 97–100, 120–21, 135–142
improvisation, imagination and, 97
Ineffabilism, 127–29
  See also Zangwill, Nick
intentionality of emotions, 10, 13, 26, 28, 149–150

Kashmiri hammer-dulcimer, 3, 168, 169
Kivy, Peter
  author's response to, 153
  changed position of, 84
  claims of, 154–55
  contour-convention view of, 5, 76–77, 145
  criticism of theories, 82–84, 89–90, 93–94
  influential work of, 95, 131
  musical arousal and, 148–49, 152
  musical expressiveness problem and, 1–2, 3, 171Intn1
  pure vs. impure music and, 43–44
  See also resemblance-based theories criticized
Kraut, Robert, as Neo-Formalist, 5, 124, 131, 132–33, 162

Langer, Susanne, 78
Lazarus, Richard, 26
Levin, Samuel, 63
Levinson, Jerrold
  cognitive-affective view of emotions and, 21
  dedication of book to, 6
  doctoral work under, 1, 168
  persona theory claims, 35–36, 174n4
  persona theory criticisms, 36–38, 49, 174n5
  pure vs. impure music and, 43–44
linguistic philosophy, 96
Logical Positivism, 95–96
Lopes, Dominic, 143–44

make-believe truth, 62, 105–8, 137
mathematical realism, 128
Matravers, Derek
  arousalism theory of, 44–46
  claims of, 44–45, 175nn12–13
  criticisms of theory, 45–46, 48–49
  music philosopher, 2, 3, 4, 31
McGinn, Colin, 103
mental images, 98–99, 103–4, 111, 158

metaphorism, arguments against
  anti-metaphorist position, 71–72, 167
  general considerations, 53, 72
  hearing music as automatic, 60–61
  imagined musical sadness and, 70–71
  music as *imagined*, 55
  possible paraphrases and, 59–61, 72
  questioning of *metaphorical reference*, 54–55
  rejection of theories of Goodman and Scruton, 53–54, 72
  variations of sadness or happiness, 60
  See also Goodman, Nelson; Scruton, Roger
metaphors and metaphorism, 51–73
  overview, 3, 4–5, 51–53
  analogy theory, 64, 65
  Black's theory, 66–67
  comparison theory, 65–66
  elliptical simile theory, 64–65
  paraphraseability and, 4, 52, 55–59, 63, 72
  understanding, 61–64, 72–73, 176n3
  See also Black, Max; Davidson, Donald; "music is sad"
metaphysical realism, 128
moods, emotions and, 17, 173n11
Moors, Agnes, 19
moral realism, 128
Mozart, 31, 133
Museum of Fine Arts (Boston), 152
music, pure, 43–44
musical arousal
  brain imaging and, 151
  how it happens, 148–49
  quasi-emotions and, 150–51
  real-life emotions felt, 149–150

musical culture, defined, 118–120
musical expressiveness
  abstract nature of music and, 143
  alternative formulation of, 2
  audio-visual theory and, 143–44
  children and, 86–87, 176n1
  figurativeness of, 51
  and imagined persona, 36, 174n5
  as philosophical problem, 1–2, 171Ch1n2
  resemblance-plus-imagination view, 53, 176chIIIn1
musical expressiveness theories, 31–48
  overview, 4, 31
"music is sad"
  attribution to music, 45–46, 175nn11–13
  debunked as metaphor, 59–60, 61, 68, 69, 72–73
  figurativeness of, 41–43, 52–53
Mussorgsky, 146

Neo-Formalism, 73, 124, 127, 132
  See also Kraut, Robert; Zangwill, Nick
neo-Stoic cognitivist view of emotions, 17–21
  overview, 17
  claims of Martha Nussbaum, 18
  criticisms of, 18–20
  defense by Nussbaum, 20–21
New, Christopher, 64
Newton, Isaac, 6, 95
Night on a Bald Mountain (Mussorgsky), 146
Ninth Symphony in D minor, Op. 125 (Beethoven), 137
Nussbaum, Charles
  arousalism theory of, 46–47
  criticisms of, 47–48, 49
  music philosopher, 3, 31

Nussbaum, Martha
neo-Stoic cognitivist view of emotions, 9
  See also neo-Stoic cognitivist view of emotions

Oakley, Justin, 15
"Old Man of the Mountain," 152
On the Musically Beautiful (Hanslick), 124
On the Origin of Species (Darwin), 7, 21
Ortony, Andrew, 63
O'Shaughnessy, Brian
  on imagination, 159, 160
  perceptual imaginings and, 97, 100–104, 168

paraphrase, defined, 58
paraphraseability of metaphors, metaphors and metaphorism and, 4, 52, 55–59, 63, 72
"Pastoral" Symphony, No. 6 in F Major, Op. 68. (Beethoven), 2
"Pathetique" Sonata, Op. 13, Op. 68. (Beethoven), 60
Penderecki, Krzystof, 32, 142
perceptual imaginings, 100–104, 111–12, 152–53
persona-based theories, 3, 124
  See also under Levinson, Jerrold; Robinson, Jenefer; Vermazen, Bruce
Prinz, Jesse
  criticism of, 25–28
  Gut Reactions, 24
  reconciliation with cognitivist view, 4, 29
  somatic view of, 9, 24–25
pure music, 43–44

quasi-emotions aroused, 150–51

Ravenscroft, Ian. See Currie, Gregory
realism, types of, 127–28, 129, 130
recreative imagination, 109–13
  See also Currie, Gregory
rejuvenation by music, 145–46
resemblance-based theories criticized, 75–96
  overview, 5, 75–76
  Davies and, 77–78, 84–88, 90–91
  in defense of, 91–94
  expressiveness and, 79–80, 94–95
  Langer and, 78
  See also Budd, Malcolm; Davies, Stephen; Kivy, Peter
Rhapsody in Blue (Gershwin), 36, 92, 140
Richards, I. A., 67
Ridley, Aaron
  arousalism theory of, 41–44, 175nn11
  criticisms of, 49
  philosopher on music, 3, 4, 31, 38
Rite of Spring, The (Stravinsky), 146
Robinson, Jenefer, 4, 31, 38–39
Roholt, Tiger, 87–88, 177chIVn2
Romantic expression theory of Robinson, 38–39
Ryle, Gilbert, 110–11

Schenkerian tonal structures, 118
Schroeder, Severin, 95–96
Scruton, Roger
  as anti-realist (music), 128
  claims on metaphors, 115–16, 117, 118
  imagination and, 98
  metaphorist theories rejected, 52, 67–70, 72–73, 176n5
  See also Budd, Malcolm
"seeing in the mind's eye," 104
simple expression theory, 31–32, 167
Stecker, Robert, 37, 38

Stern, Josef, 4, 58, 63

Threnody for the Victims of Hiroshima (Penderecki), 32, 142
Tolstoy, Leo, 32
Tormey, Alan, 32

Vermazen, Bruce, 4, 31–35
   artistic expression theory of, 32–34
   criticism of, 34–35, 173n3
   See also expression theory, simple

Wagner, Richard, 124
Walton, Kendall, 3, 38, 62, 106
Weber's Clarinet Quintet in B-flat, Op. 34, 154

"While My Guitar Gently Weeps" (Harrison), 142
Wittgenstein, Ludwig, 61, 96, 110, 165
Wollheim, Richard, 3
Wonder, Stevie, 144

Young, James, 94–95, 177chIVn3

Zangwill, Nick
   as Ineffabilist, 128–29
   instrumental music and, 132
   as Neo-Formalist, 5, 73, 124, 162
   response to claims of, 129–131
Zatorre, Robert, 24
Zhuangzi (Zhuang Zhou), 87–88

www.ingramcontent.com/pod-product-compliance
Ingram Content Group UK Ltd.
Pitfield, Milton Keynes, MK11 3LW, UK
UKHW042009140426
5217IPUK00015B/1063